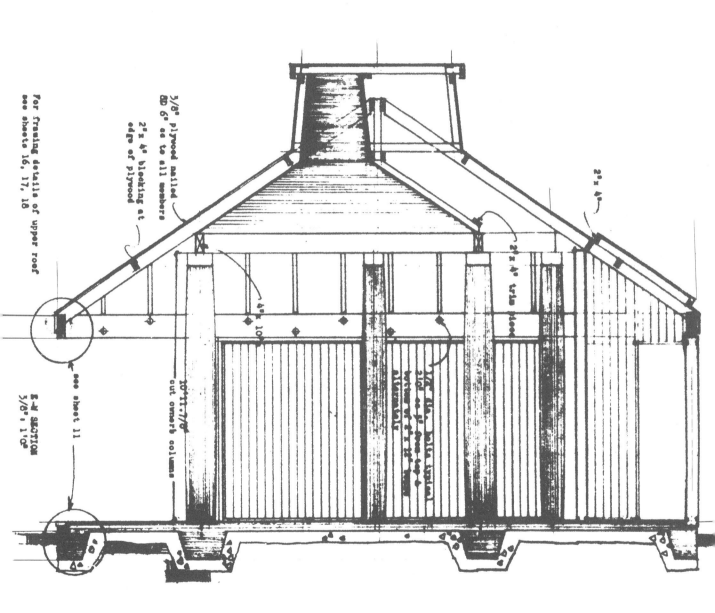

AN ARCHITECTURAL LIFE

Memoirs & Memories of Charles W. Moore

AN ARCHITECTURAL LIFE

MEMOIRS & MEMORIES OF Charles W. Moore

written and edited by KEVIN P. KEIM

A Bulfinch Press Book / Little, Brown and Company

Boston · New York · Toronto · London

FIRST EDITION

The author is grateful for permission to include the following previously copyrighted material:

All text, letters, and illustrations by Charles W. Moore are owned and reprinted by permission of the Estate of Charles W. Moore.

An earlier version of Moore's Principles appeared in "The Work of Charles W. Moore," in *A + U*. Copyright © 1978. Reprinted by permission of Toshio Nakamura.

Letter by Joseph Stein. Copyright © by Joseph Stein. Reprinted by permission of the author.

Letter by O'Neil Ford. Copyright © by O'Neil Ford. Reprinted by permission of Wandita Ford.

Letter by Hugh Hardy. Copyright © by Hugh Hardy. Reprinted by permission of the author.

An earlier version of Richard Peters's essay appeared in *Global Architecture*. Copyright © by Richard Peters. Reprinted by permission of the author.

Excerpt from *Architectural Record*, March 1970. Copyright © by the McGraw-Hill Companies. Reprinted by permission of the publisher.

Remembrance by Robert Venturi. Copyright © 1996 by Robert Venturi. Reprinted by permission of the author.

Remembrance by Denise Scott Brown. Copyright © 1996 by Denise Scott Brown. Reprinted by permission of the author.

Copyrights in the individual photographs are controlled by the photographers, whose permission is required for further reproduction.

Library of Congress Cataloging-in-Publication Data
Keim, Kevin P.
    An architectural life : memoirs & memories of Charles W. Moore / written and edited
by Kevin P. Keim. — 1st ed.
        p.   cm.
    "A Bulfinch Press book."
    Includes index.
    ISBN 0-8212-2167-1
    1. Moore, Charles Willard, 1925–1993.
2. Architects — United States — Biography.
I. Moore, Charles Willard, 1925–1993.   II. Title.
NA737.M65K45   1996
720'.92 — dc20
[B]   95-39905

Bulfinch Press is an imprint and trademark of Little, Brown and Company (Inc.)
Published simultaneously in Canada by Little, Brown & Company (Canada) Limited

Book design by Christopher Kuntze

PRINTED IN THE UNITED STATES OF AMERICA

Title spread: "Twenty-Five-Year-Olds," Photo by Alice Wingwall, Taken in Honor of the Sea Ranch Condominium's AIA Twenty-Five-Year Award.

This book is dedicated first to the spirit of

CHARLES W. MOORE

It is also to my family, whose support made it all possible. Also to everyone at Moore/Andersson Architects, that special Austin focus of creativity and spirit: Arthur Andersson, Patrick Alexander, Gina André, John Barnes, Susan Benz, Gregory Brooks, Steven Dvorak, Hildegardo and Maria Garcia, Mercedes de la Garza, Nan Kinzler, Clyde Logue, Ignazio Pruzzo, Samantha Randall, Suzanne Rose, Barbara Shepherd, Charles Southall, Sherri Stodghill, Gong Szeto, and Chris Wise.

The provision of an inspiring background is not a misplaced
bit of romanticism; it is the architect's lifework.

CHARLES W. MOORE, University of Michigan, 1946

CONTENTS

Acknowledgments

Charles Moore and I began assembling what we called his architectural memoir in 1992, as a chronicle and record of what he thought were his most important experiences, concerns, and enthusiasms. Charles patiently endured my questions about his life, usually over dinner or in the car on our long drives. On one occasion, I was astonished when Charles recounted with clarity his entire yearlong itinerary, from place to place, of his 1949 European tour, as if he had returned only the day before. As much as the book would be a reminiscence, we also hoped that it could be a book that young people might read as an example of an *inclusive* approach to the creative life. We never intended that this would be the "complete works of Charles W. Moore." Rather it is the story of an architectural journey, a celebration of a life spent looking at, writing about, and making architecture.

Charles's life was architecture. Layers of travels informed his essays, his essays enriched his work, his work infused his teaching, and his teaching led back into his travels. As Hugh Hardy wrote: "Everything mattered." To further emphasize Moore's inclusiveness, I asked several of his friends, collaborators, clients, and students to contribute written testimonies. Lawrence Halprin wrote about Charles and the landscape, Kent Bloomer about Charles and education, Donlyn Lyndon about Moore's fertile legacy of words. William Turnbull, Jr., Mark Simon, Ron Filson, Buzz Yudell, and Arthur Andersson recounted their place-making experiences with Charles. This list by no means represents the extent of Charles's close collaborators in architecture or education. How I would have loved to include many more, but the limits of space combined with the breadth of Charles's life required restraint.

The structure of the book is simple. Each chapter contains a major piece of writing or collections of letters by Charles or an essay by one of his collaborators. I wrote an introduction to each chapter and wove throughout the book brief remembrances of students, clients, and friends. Any materials in brackets are editor's notes or clarifications. The sequence is not chronological. To have assembled the book chronologically would have misrepresented Charles's life as a simple progression of days or years rather than the layers of experiences it was. At the risk of temporal confusion, this book, I hope, expresses these colliding layers.

Certain organizations and individuals deserve special thanks.

First and most important, the Graham Foundation for Advanced Studies in the Fine Arts provided a grant that was an integral part of making this book possible. Their commitment and generosity, guided by Richard Solomon, are truly a foundation for the architectural community.

Moore's archives are as widespread as his friends. Collections of letters, drawings, construction documents, and notes are spread among Princeton, Berkeley, Salt Lake City, Los

Angeles, San Francisco, Ann Arbor, New Haven, Centerbrook, Austin, and Washington, D.C. In this volume I have included as many unpublished images and letters as possible. Several additional archives and libraries have been of particular help: the Smithsonian Archives of American Art, the architectural archives at the University of Pennsylvania, the University of Michigan, the University of Texas School of Architecture (in whose stunning Cass Gilbert Reading Room this book was developed), the Yale University archives, Princeton University School of Architecture, and the University of Utah.

Photographers are an important part of Moore's work and indeed all architects' work. Their vision extends architecture into books, journals, and lecture halls. Jim Alinder, Morley Baer, Regula Campbell, Willard Hanzlik, Timothy Hursley, Alan Karchmer, Jane Lidz, Norman McGrath, Christopher Noll, Tim Street Porter, James Volney Righter, and Alice Wingwall all very generously supported my efforts.

Sarah Jane Freymann at the Stepping Stone Literary Agency was largely responsible, with her knowledge and experience, for making this book happen. In the weeks following Charles's death her advice and encouragement were especially helpful. At Bulfinch Press, Carol Judy Leslie and Brian Hotchkiss welcomed us aboard, and later Karen Dane, the editor, saw this complex book through the process with great verve.

There have been so many people who have given their time to reminisce, patiently receiving my visits and phone calls. They include: Virginia Acland, Arnold Agree, the Alinder family, Edward Allen, Gerald Allen, Harvey Allison, Mary Jane Allison, Simon Atkinson, Wayne Attoe, Jacquelynn Baas, Robert Beckley, Edward Larabee Barnes, Chuck Bassett, Tina Beebe, Wayne Bell, Barry Bergdoll, Richard and Mitra Best, Robert Bliss, Nona Bloomer, Hal Box, Gregory Brooks, Marvin Buchanan, Leland Burns, Malcolm Campbell, Robert Campbell, Jean Paul Carlhian, Ashley Carpenter, Henry Chauncy, Dennis Clark, Bill Cochran, Walter Costa, Julia Converse, Michael Crosbie, Sylvester Damianos, Mark Denton, Alfredo Devido, Vernon DeMars, Eames Demetrios, Richard and Kirsten Dodge, Dennis Doordan, Felix Drury, Art Dubin, Steve Dumez, John Echlin, Garrett Eckbo, Joseph Esherick, Mary Margaret Farabee, Martin Filler, Lisa Findley, Peter and Susan Frantz, Mercedes de la Garza, Raymond Gindroz, Paul Goldberger, Chuck Graves, Debbie Green, Daniel Gregory, William Grover, Kenneth Hand, Willard Hanzlik, Stephen Harby, Hugh Hardy, Stanley Hensley, Wallace Holm, Lucia Howard, Timothy Hursley, Steven Hurtt, Shinji Isozaki, Steven Izenour, John Jickling, Philip Johnson, E. Fay Jones, Martha Kirkpatrick, Kimberly Kohlhaas, Dan Peter Kopple, Sarah Ksiasek, Betty Kubota, John Kyrk, Ricardo Legorreta, David Lewis, Maynard and Lu Lyndon, Hilary Lewis, Norma Macdonald, Judith di Maio, Mary Martin, Bruno and Rose Miglio, Peter Millard, Bill Miller, Murray Milne, William Mitchell, Alan Morgan, Patrick Morreau, Robert Mugerauer, Dee Mullen, James Mary O'Connor, Connie Osler, Toshio Nakamura, Terezia Nemeth, Cesar Pelli, Mimi Perloff, Richard Peters, Van Meter Petit, Julie Polletta, Nicholas Pyle, David Rhodes, Don Rice, James Ritchie, Colin Rowe, John Ruble, R. Marcella Scaglione, Naomi Schwarz, David Schorr, Emma Scioli, Vincent Scully, Lilla Shook, Kathryn Smith, Thomas Gordon Smith, Herman Spiegel, John Stamper, Barbara Stauffacher Solomon,

Richard Solomon, Robert A. M. Stern, Dick Stringham, Simone Swan, Adele Chatfield Taylor, Charles Taylor, Betty Thompson, Dmitri Vedensky, Robert Venturi, Andy Vernooy, Francis Violich, Margaret Wazuka, the Weingarten family, Catherine Welch, Harriet Welchel, Richard and Susan Whitaker, John Woodbridge, Sally Woodbridge, King Lui Wu, Rodolfo Ybarra, Marilyn Zuber, and Peter Zweig.

AN ARCHITECTURAL LIFE

Memoirs & Memories of Charles W. Moore

Magic, Wonder, and Charm: The Halcyon Years

My years with Charles Moore began in 1990 with a telephone call to his manager in Austin, Barbara Shepherd. Months before graduating from architecture school, I was told by my dean, Thomas Gordon Smith, that Charles was looking for someone to help with research and writing. I flew from the frigid cold of South Bend, Indiana, to the staggering heat of Austin, Texas, where I managed to get a six-minute interview with Charles while I drove him to class in his banana-yellow Mustang convertible. Later that night, during one of his swimming-pool parties at his wondrous Austin house, Charles introduced me to some friends — "Do you know Kevin? He's coming to work for me in May." Suddenly, in a casual turn of phrase, I was drawn into the world of Charles Moore.

The best way to describe Moore's world is through one of his favorite devices, the geode — a spheroid hunk of rock that seems like any other until it is cracked open, and one discovers the sparkling crystals that encrust its interior. Charles thrived on hidden wonder and fantasy bursting from the ordinary: the impregnable fortress walls of the Alhambra enclosing gardens of myrtle, the ordinary wardrobe as the gateway to Narnia, or a walk down a dark, narrow Roman street that suddenly leads to the light-struck Trevi Fountain. But the metaphor can be extended to Moore himself. He was at once soft-spoken, rooted in midwestern good manners, usually dressed unpretentiously in a corduroy or navy blue blazer. But inside was a mind of remarkable richness, astonishing memory, hypercuriosity, and ingenious imagination.

Geode. Photo by
Van Meter Petit.

"Space leaking up and out" was another important Moore image. At Sir John Soane's House or the Roman Pantheon or Le Corbusier's chapel at Ronchamp, the architecture lifts the spirit away, aerially yanking it upward and bouncing it through complexities in the ceilings, into the lofty world of domes, against shimmering rays of light streaming down or through tiny windows into the sky. The rising quality of the buildings Moore sought in his own work, from the Jobson Cabin in 1961 to his University of Oregon Science Center in 1991. Below, where the feet are planted, one inhabits with bodily physical presence, but above, where the space leaks up and out, one inhabits through the magical transport of imagination.

Charles's ability to look — which he did like a lens, intensifying and focusing — carried his imagination into another dimension. On his legendary field trips, Moore led students and friends on visual conquests of the splendors of places, transmitting his way of seeing the world. His was a contagion of enthusiasm. The trips were frequent and often occurred at inconvenient times, when important deadlines for projects were imminent. (On the eve of one excursion in 1987, Moore casually scribbled in a sketchbook under "Jobs to worry about in Europe" nine houses, two civic centers, a pair of churches, seven corporate buildings, and two book manuscripts.) They were not leisurely vacations. These trips were missions of absorption.

In 1992, for instance, Charles, Christopher Livingston (a Texas graduate student), and I drove two thousand miles from Austin to Sea Ranch, California. Along the way we stayed at the historic Gage Hotel in Marathon, Texas; feasted at the Coyote Café in Santa Fe; drove forty miles over a dirt road west of Los Alamos just to see a beautiful valley; revisited Charles's old Utah haunts, Arches National Park and Dead Horse Point; spent a night with the mayor of Moab (who ran a bed-and-breakfast from his basement); careened down Nevada's Route 50, "the Loneliest Road in America," while listening to Cajun zydeco and João Gilberto; snapped photos of Silver City, a stage-set western town; and stopped, as always, at the Nut Tree, the restaurant contentedly stuck in the sixties (which Charles celebrated in "You Have to Pay for the Public Life"), for split-pea soup and club sandwiches. Finally, we crossed the Golden Gate and wound our way up the coastal highway to the Sea

Jobson Cabin, Charles Moore with Peter Hopkinson, 1961.

Ranch condominium, a building that celebrates the act of arrival.

Unit #9 was for many decades the salon of Charles Moore, where he "escaped" to work on buildings and books. Unlike the stiff salons of Paris, however, this was more like architectural camp. Rolls of tracing paper, models, blueprints, slides, and manuscripts were always scattered about. The constant entourage of associates and students, the steady streams of visitors, and the unexpected carloads of students making the pilgrimage were always welcomed. The phone and fax continuously rang with urgent requests for attention to projects. Work took place during the day, punctuated by sacred routines of walks along the cliffs, lunch at Naomi's Food Company, naps on the window seats, and trips to the swimming pool and sauna. The sun setting over the Pacific horizon signaled dinner, usually involving many people, either at the Gualala Hotel or at other houses along the

University of Oregon Science Complex Atrium, Moore Ruble Yudell, 1989. Photo by Timothy Hursley.

coast — dark evenings filled with laughter, talk of places, and strains of *Der Rosenkavalier* or Elisabeth Welch or Chavela Vargas, the legendary Mexican singer.

To have witnessed the decades of place-making ideas that resonated within that redwood chamber would have been virtually to chart Moore's creative life.

Ever since he was a boy under the spell of his mother, Charles had seen with his own eyes what architecture could be. He understood the power of engaging through architecture the full range of human emotion, whether it be joy or seriousness, simplicity or extravagance. He learned to love places.

Students and architects, particularly ones of my generation, often lose sight of the role Moore played in the radical break from the claustrophobic orthodoxy that strangled architecture for most of our century. Moore's early heroes were Alvar Aalto, Le Corbusier, and Frank Lloyd Wright. Later he admired R. M. Schindler's work and the architecture of the San Francisco Bay Region. However, by the 1950s he was deeply dissatisfied with the faded intensity of the International Style and its homogenizing, arbitrary, and often destructive spread over the surface of the globe.

As one of the most significant reactionary architects of the twentieth century, Moore opposed dogmatic rules and ideology. He admired vulnerability. Perhaps he identified with Francesco Borromini, the underdog of seventeenth-century Rome, and, like Louis Kahn, Moore's willingness to test new ideas often caused him to miss the intended target, but the excitement of the search was what counted. He also criticized the modern mania for originality. The urge always to invent something new, he believed, most often resulted in architecture alien to human experience. He celebrated T. S. Eliot's "Immature poets imitate; mature poets steal" and applauded Cole Porter, who, when once asked what inspired his latest musical, answered, "A phone call from the producer."

If history were a beehive, most twentieth-century architects would stay far away, fearing the sting of nostalgia, but Moore willfully plunged his hands in, scooping out the rich honey of associations. But he was not blindly committed to living a fantasy of some impossible past world. Instead, he reveled in the present and the popular culture of his own time, and then enriched the present with wonders of the past. Moore could absorb influences from anything and was interested in any way that humanity expressed itself — Henry James, kung-fu theater, Piranesi, Saturday morning cartoons, Federico Fellini, Paul Klee, feng-shui, Balinese villages, drugstore science fiction, Chinese painting, modern chaos theory, or the villas of Palladio. He was as intrigued with dilapidated tin-roofed Guatemalan gas stations as the marble splendors of Rome. But Charles didn't collect all of these images merely to be eclectic. Moore's gift was seeing magic everywhere, and then using his Berol 314 pencil to spin hay into gold.

That kind of magical transformation left Moore dissatisfied with the rational. Rational was too limiting. His take on life was always slightly off center, and he could, through a design "flick of the wrist," transform ordinary materials into magical events. Cesar Pelli saw it as "pulling rabbits out of his hat." Ordinary jacks rested on top of classical columns too short to reach their beam in his New Haven house, a hardware store lawn sprinkler became a fountain at the Santa Barbara Faculty Club, and standard mailboxes substituted for lockers in the Sea Ranch Swim Club. It's no wonder that one of Charles's unfulfilled tongue-in-cheek dreams was to build a cathedral entirely out of galvanized corrugated sheet metal for Port Darwin, Australia. In his buildings, axes are seldom direct. Instead they swerve to teasingly catch the edge of some hidden wonder ahead. Moore's roofs are rarely constructions of Georgian symmetry, but fiendishly clever lopsided collisions of gables, hips, sheds, dormers, and peaks. Deeply influenced by Japanese architecture, he had an ongoing enthusiasm for spatial layering, plan layering, figural layering, and decorative layering. And the windows! There weren't to be boring strips or rational grids, but giant walls of glass mingling with overlapping rhythms of pilasters or tiny windows lurking in attic gables.

It was all a tango of the sublime and whimsical, Schubert performed by an orchestra of bagpipes, accordions, and bongos. Moore loved the clammy handshake between high and low art, sweet 'n' sour, "immaculate collisions," old and new, the familiar and surprising,

Columns and Jacks in Moore's New Haven House Kitchen, 1966. Photo by John Hill.

yin-yang, and shotgun marriages between the common and the fancy. Raymond Gindroz compared Moore to Gracie Allen, who could explain the absolutely absurd through the real, and the absolutely real through the absurd. When Moore was in Europe in 1950, he compared the interior of St. Peter's Basilica to the Empire Room of the Palmer House in Chicago, and once in a review of a Sir John Soane biography, Moore quipped that the author and subject were "maddeningly mismatched, as though the definitive biography of Groucho Marx had been written by St. Ignatius Loyola." People often misinterpreted such humor for a lack of seriousness. But wit was only one layer of his full persona, it was only a means to expose the futility of dullness. Charles's crusade was earnest. He wanted to open up and change, to transform the grim seriousness of concrete-plate-glass-boxed-asphalted-curtain-walled-fluorescent-Lally-columned worlds into rich new wonders.

How did he do this? Charles captured his time, which is perhaps the mark of the greatest of artists. He always took advantage. His focus was sharp. He constantly kept on the move and never settled into a comfortable position. "He lived forty years at warp speed," Arthur Andersson once said. And Charles had the very rare ability to live every minute to the fullest, to grasp life gently but wring out its essence, taking care to soak up all of the escaping drops and splashes.

Perhaps his memory allowed him to easily subvert the ravages of time; so that he could willfully reestablish dusty friendships, suddenly reenergize thoughts or intellectual interests that he hadn't thought about in years that suddenly became relevant, or recall, over nasty design snags, some obscure architectural jewel, a stair in Ireland perhaps, that would both brilliantly and poetically solve the problem at hand. He could easily dedicate his attention and lock his focus onto problems, calmly absorbing needed information, unraveling tangles that others had been trying to untangle for weeks. Some of his favorite verbs — spark, plunge, leap, pinch, flash, pierce — all require focused bursts of energy. All of this infused his extraordinary skill as a designer. He was quick but not hasty, natural but out of the ordinary, intensely focused but simultaneously wide-angled.

This dedication made Moore extraordinarily prolific. He was proudest of teaching, which he did at Utah, Princeton, Berkeley, Yale, UCLA, and Texas. Moore coauthored twelve books and wrote scores of articles and essays. Each time he moved to a new university position, Moore established an architectural studio.

The busied production created by these studios required a web of associations. First Moore worked for short periods of time as a draftsman, designer, and collaborator with Roger Bailey, Mario Corbett, Joseph Allen Stein, Hervey Parke Clark, Stephen Macdonald, Wallace Holm, and Lawrence Halprin. Moore's own offices generally began as Charles W. Moore Associates and were filled with energetic young architects and students. In Berkeley, Charles founded MLTW in 1962 with Donlyn Lyndon, William Turnbull, Jr., and Richard Whitaker. When Lyndon and Whitaker moved on, the firm evolved into MLTW/Moore-Turnbull. In 1965, Moore left Berkeley for Yale, where he established an East Coast outpost of MLTW/Moore-Turnbull. However, when Moore and Turnbull established their own practices, the New Haven office reverted to Charles W. Moore Associates. The office

Moore Designing.

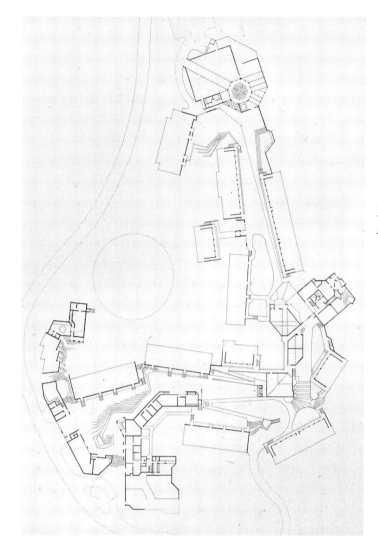

Kresge College Plan,
MLTW/Moore-Turnbull.

moved from New Haven to Centerbrook, Connecticut, and William Grover and Robert Harper became partners — the firm was called Moore Grover Harper. Eventually, several other architects became partners, and the firm adopted Centerbrook as its new name. Next, Moore left the East Coast for Los Angeles. There, he became a major influence at Urban Innovations Group, the teaching office of the UCLA School of Architecture. Simultaneously, he set up an independent studio with John Ruble and Buzz Yudell. It became Moore Ruble Yudell. Finally, in 1984 Moore relocated to Austin, Texas, established Charles W. Moore, Architect, and in partnership with Arthur Andersson it matured into Moore/Andersson Architects.

Centerbrook, Moore Ruble Yudell, and Moore/Andersson still thrive.

Moore's studios were often cramped, housed in basements, spaces adjoining pinball arcades, bicycle shops, or old mill factories, and some even rising from drafting tables

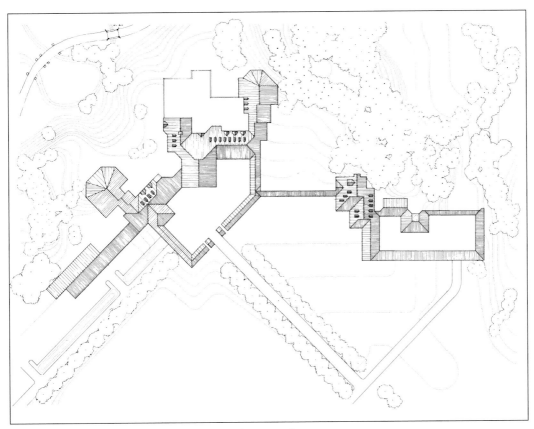

TRINOVA Corporation Roof Plan, Moore/Andersson Architects.

squeezed into Moore's bedroom or living room. They weren't hushed and padded corporate architectural offices and were never formulaic — Charles never owned a single Barcelona chair — and methods were invented as the needs arose. All of his offices teetered with a see-saw gestalt: intense yet buoyantly relaxed, highly productive but in the midst of gloriously mismanaged chaos (when Moore was in town, great pandemonium), immensely enjoyable but frustrating, swamped with too much work yet often poised under threatening financial thunderclouds.

All of the studios were independent. However, his associations always overlapped, and Moore, after beginning another office, continued his collaborations with most of his prior partners, despite ever-expanding alliances with young designers and a host of creative surges with many other architects, engineers, artists, and consultants. One might think that to keep this machine spinning, Moore had to frantically race around frenziedly working. But that was not his manner. He seldom seemed to be in a hurry, *despite always being in a hurry.* Moore was always leaving as he was coming, which often forced young associates to chase him to get input on the many projects at hand. Modern airlines also helped him leapfrog vast distances with Olympian endurance. It was Moore's national architectural franchise, not unified by a catchy logo, but by a spirit of creativity. Marilyn Zuber, one of Moore's assistants, once wrote to him that we "think you should have a big central office — we all do I guess — we just haven't quite figured out how to get it. Ah well — one day." That, perhaps, would have been too easy and boring, and it never happened.

Collaboration was the oil in Moore's machine. He enthusiastically embraced the reality that making buildings is never a solitary feat, but a collaborative venture that must involve, if it is to be successful, the energy and dreams of clients, users, inhabitants, architects, builders, and "even bankers." With so many people involved, however, things seldom ran smoothly. Moore's temper and impatience sometimes flared intensely. He did a lot of things that appeared mindlessly irrational. His criticism could be piercing. And, in turn, everyone who worked with Moore had to learn patience, as mentors often seem to be tormentors. Budgets often plunged into the red, toes were inadvertently stepped on, nerves became frazzled, and extraordinary amounts of work were expected to be finished in desperately little time. But it was all worth it, because out of the mad cacophony of interests, great buildings were made.

One of the pervasive twentieth-century images of the architect is as the "fountainhead" of beauty and truth manifested by Ayn Rand's granite-hewing, handsome Howard Roark. These architects work alone against hostile forces arrayed in opposition to their alleged superior aesthetic virtue. While Moore's inclusiveness deflated the myth of the "hero" architect, it made him a hero of a different sort. Despite his influence and fame, Charles never limited himself to an exclusive architecture clique or peer group; he was as comfortable with students struggling to discover their own paths as he was with the Aga Khan or G.I. buddies or celebrated architects.

This perhaps led to paradoxes. Surrounded constantly by people, loved by so many, there was in Charles's center a loneliness. Though he had countless friends, and was constantly expanding his circle, he had, most think, very few intimate relationships. His fear of being forgotten, many believe, drove his exhausting schedule. His unquenchable thirst for a strong sense of place contrasted his insatiable cravings to be somewhere else. He tempered his subtle but strong ego with self-deprecation. He was a complex man, and those who knew him throughout his life, either as "Chuck," "Charlie," or "Charles," knew him in their own special way, but many felt that they didn't know him entirely. There was always a shade of mystery, another layer to be revealed.

So often, people have asked me, "Are you going to write about Charles's personal life?" which betrays a fundamental misunderstanding. Moore's personal life was public, and his public life was personal. There was little distinction. Like no one else, Charles dedicated his life *entirely* to architecture. Virtually all who were a part of Moore's life, aside from his family and childhood friends, were in some way connected to architecture. Dona Guimares, whom Charles met at the University of Michigan, remained a lifelong friend, confidante, and companion. Though they never married and Charles never had his own children, he was a family man. He was steadfastly devoted to his mother, and he remained especially close to his sister Mimi and her husband and sons, often traveling vast distances (once from the Central African Republic) to make it home for the holidays.

Another misconception about Moore (and indeed about most architects) was his wealth.

Proposed Liberty Entrance, Beverly Hills Civic Center, Moore with the Urban Innovations Group.

His family's money seems to have dwindled by the time Charles graduated from college, and he and his mother often pooled their resources to keep afloat. Profit was never in Moore's focus, and so he was often struggling to sustain his widespread activities. (As early as 1957, while a graduate student at Princeton, Moore wrote, "I grow money-mad, as the bills mount on both coasts.") Partners winced at Charles's casual approach to office finances. His generosity was legendary and was linked to his famous inability to say no, whether it had to do with allowing another student into a crowded class (or helping a student with tuition), suddenly embarking on an adventure to Mexico, feasting on extravagant dinners (which he always paid for), designing museums pro bono, having another martini, or agreeing to lecture in remote schools.

Moore's inclusiveness always extended through his front door, making his own homes vicarious public forums. People were always around. Students who needed a place to live often served as caretakers, cooks, organizational assistants, chauffeurs, and guards against burglars during Moore's frequent absences. Once, in the early sixties, Charles tried to woo clients by cooking them dinner at his Orinda house. It was a culinary disaster; the clients fled to another architect. Charles gave up cooking. But his parties were famous: with great quantities of (catered) food, a lot of laughing, music, singing, and dancing. (Besides martinis, Moore's favorite drink was his own "Governor of Chihuahua." In a large goblet, with a wedge of lemon and ice, mix two parts rum, one part dry vermouth, and one part sweet vermouth.) The parties often featured Moore's memory feats, such as reciting in reverse order the American Secretaries of State; at a legendary one in Santa Monica, Tina Beebe remembered the guests' amazed shock when Charles joined the Brazilian band and sang along word for word — in Portuguese.

Moore could draw out the best in people. Countless lives have been uplifted through his architecture, writing, and, most of all, his teaching. He unhesitatingly advanced others and loved to see people succeed, especially students. Over and over, people have said, "He changed my life." In the often vindictive, back-stabbing world of architecture, filled with overbearing egos, where people are driven to absurdities by fame, Charles remained a gentleman — accessible, soft spoken, supportive, and charming.

Above all, however, was his peerless, undying love for place. The going never stopped, and plans were always drawn out on the calendars for upcoming trips. On December 16, 1993, for instance, we hoped to embark on another road trip from Austin to Sea Ranch.

But that trip Charles would not make. When his assistant, Sherri Stodghill, arrived early on the morning of our departure, she discovered that Charles had died of heart failure very suddenly in his own bed, within the brief span of twenty minutes, without any indication of struggle.

It was a gray and overcast morning. Reservations at the Gage Hotel were canceled; we unloaded the car. In the coming weeks there would be five memorial services across the country where many people would speak eloquently about the man who had changed so much and so many lives. It seemed impossible, in those sullen days, that one with such potent presence for so many had ceased to exist. He absorbed as much as possible out of life, because, for Charles Moore, life was magic. When it was time to go, he vanished as quickly and unceremoniously as if he were simply leaving on another trip, and his spirit suddenly leaked up and out.

Charles W. Moore in 1992.

CHAPTER ONE

Foundations

Charles E. Moore, Charles's Father.

Although Charles Willard Moore was born on Halloween, the eve of Dia de los Muertos, in 1925 in the small town of Benton Harbor, Michigan, and grew up in the even smaller town of Battle Creek, his life was unusually extended even when he was a child.

Charles was the son of Charles Ephraim and Kathryn ("Katie") Moore, and the brother of one younger sister, Mimi. (Through his father's first marriage, Charles had one stepsister, Lilla, who grew up in Arizona.) His mother was short and often wore a hat and gloves. She was outgoing, vivacious, colorful, and endearing. Paradoxically, Charles's genius isolated him socially, while his mother expanded his world, both geographically and intellectually, beyond the monotonous conventions of the American Midwest. She taught Charles to absorb ideas and to see the world in a way that built the foundations for his architecture and love of place.

His father was an imposing bon vivant (known as "big boy" to the children), whom Charles grew to physically resemble. His father had inherited interests in several newspapers in Michigan and Indiana, but had little interest in them, so he dabbled in an assortment of ventures: he co-owned the first automobile dealership in Battle Creek, ran two farms, managed the Willard estates, and dipped into real estate development and built, for instance, two houses on "Hiawatha Hill" bordering Goguac Lake. One of the houses, a simple, unadorned, white clapboard structure, was Charles's home for most of his childhood.

The house next door belonged to the Brewers, relatives of the Moores, whose granddaughter Martha was only two months younger than Charles (Martha Kirkpatrick today, as she will be referred to throughout the text). For many years, the Moores and Brewers were the sole residents of Hiawatha Heights, and the knoll was the private domain of the three children.

Charles was an acutely shy boy, and throughout his childhood, Martha and Mimi were his only playmates. Surprisingly, he had few toys, so the three would concoct stories, plays, and private rituals in which Charles was often a sultan, Martha his female adviser, and Mimi the Chinese servant. "Chuck's imagination," Martha remembered, "his curiosity, and his capacity to learn were infinite from the beginning." They all loved riding horses on the nearby farms and swimming and sailing; in their canoe, they explored Ward's Island in Goguac Lake, catching snapping turtles and frogs; and they spent time in their chemistry lab concocting fake blood. Evenings, the radio vibrated with Buck Rogers, Flash Gordon, and the Lone Ranger. Charles was a voracious reader as well. In the summer, the children held a mock classroom, where Charles decided to teach himself Greek so he could read Homer in the original. Recess was dedicated to dancing, usually tangos.

The magical times in Charles's childhood, however, were spent beyond Michigan. Kathryn Moore and her husband were socially active, and their financial independence allowed them to escape the bleak winters and spend several months every year in Florida, California, Mexico, or the Caribbean. The trips profoundly influenced Charles. First, he was allowed to plan the itineraries, and in their Packard the family would embark from Battle Creek exploring cities, towns, and the countryside along their way west or south. (At age two, it was said, Charles knew the names of every make of car on the highway.) His father's social connections (he was an acquaintance of W. C. Fields, for instance) exposed Charles to experiences that provided vivid tales: bouts with malaria in Mexico, swank Florida hotels, and being visited personally in the hospital by the Little Rascals — every one — in Los Angeles.

Charles delighted in the exotic: western ghost towns, wooden sidewalks in Arizona, and the Corn Palace in Mitchell, South Dakota. But most of all, Charles loved Los Angeles of the 1930s. The thrill of Hollywood and Grauman's Chinese Theater in the heyday of movie magic, the undeveloped hills and beaches, Pasadena, Route 66, and Catalina Island were all phantasmagorical wonders.

The trips also fostered in Charles an independence in education. Kathryn Moore, a former schoolteacher, was intent on developing Charles's unique intellectual capacities. She willingly permitted absences from school for months at a time, leaving Charles for the most part to be self-taught. When the time for another year's trip would arrive, Charles would announce to his Battle Creek teachers that he was leaving and "would they please assemble his assignments" — often several months' worth. Invariably, Charles would return to Michigan in the spring, after having taught himself the lessons, considerably more advanced than his classmates. The teachers would simply promote Charles to the next grade. However, the economic hardships of the thirties as well as Charles's admittance to high school curtailed the cross-country trips. Charles and his cousin Martha attended separate high schools, and they spent less time together, Martha ex-

Childhood Home, Battle Creek, Michigan.

panding her circle of friends, Charles remaining withdrawn in his own private world.

In high school Charles shunned most activities, but he was the editor of the newspaper, *The Lakeview Crystal,* and the following appeared in his column in 1942, an early indication of his mature thinking and writing:

Corn Palace, Mitchell, South Dakota.

> Of course we hate the dictators of the countries we are fighting. We hate everything they stand for, and we are going to do our best to beat the people who take their orders from the dictators. But this healthy American spirit of fighting energy is, in some places, giving way to a senseless and destructive hatred of the learning and culture of the Japanese, German, and Italian peoples. This hatred disunites our country and throws an unjust burden on the millions of loyal citizens descended from these nationalities. We are making our lives more barren, too, if we ignore these cultures. There is no reason to discard the fine things given to us by such men as Schubert and Mendelssohn, merely because we are fighting their descendants. We are fighting this war so the force of intelligence can live. Let's not discard intelligence in the process.

A classmate remembered:

> Charles was known as "Chuck" to his friends, a nickname he seemed to accept willingly. He was greatly admired by all of the students and one comment was, 'When Chuck was there and they graded on class average, no one else got an A.' He was described as quiet and unassuming, blending with all groups despite his apparent brilliant mind. He coached other students with problems in math or chemistry when asked. Charles was tall and slender with sandy light-brown hair. He did not participate in sports or social activities, rather being somewhat independent but never aloof. When Charles was in Junior High School he played "Blue Beard" in the school play; it was remembered that he had a long blue crepe-paper beard that provoked a lot of laughter, including his own. He enjoyed humor and often had a small smile. One classmate remembers that he had a chemistry lab in the walk-out basement of his lake-front home near the school, and he often spent his free time there. In those days he was a "girl hater," finding them boring and troublesome. He told his fourth-grade class that he had stayed with W. C. Fields at his home when he was in California, and they were very impressed.

Charles's capacity for focused learning, aided by an absolutely startling photographic memory and insatiable curiosity, was not unprecedented in his families' history. Moore often spoke of his Willard ("of willful disposition") ancestors, one of America's oldest lineages which extends back ten generations to Major Simon Willard, who was born in 1604 in Horsmonden, County Kent, sailed to Charlestown, Massachusetts, in 1634, and a year later co-established the colony at Concord, the first in the Massachusetts interior.

Little is known of the next five generations.

Sixth-generation Allen Willard was born in 1794 in Vermont, studied for two years at Dartmouth, and in 1836 took his wife, Eliza, and two sons west. After a month-long journey via the Erie Canal, a team of oxen pulled the pioneers onto Battle Creek, where Willard eventually finished a Greek Revival house in 1863. (In the stair hall hung portraits of Allen and Eliza, which were ultimately passed on to Charles and always had honored positions in his own houses.)

Sharp minds and portentous memories, uncannily like Charles's, were emphasized over and over in Willard histories, down through the generations. Allen Willard was "characterized by an independent way of thinking and by an ardent love of literature, particularly the classics in which he kept up his reading in Greek and Latin languages to his latest year." His copies of the New Testament and U.S. Constitution were literally black with use by the time of his death.

Allen Willard's first son, Charles, had a keen mind: "Though not college bred, Mr. Willard possessed the broad understanding and culture that result from thorough study of the best in literature and current affairs. He was a deep thinker, well read in the world's history, and his retentive memory stored up information that the ordinary man seldom retains"; and later, "His memory was almost an unfailing storehouse, while his faculty of fixing dates was remarkable. This, combined with a good command of language, made the hours pass pleasantly in his company."

Allen's second son, George, read the Bible by the age of seven, mastered *Adams's Arithmetic* in a month when he was eight, and could extract a cube root at will. His father taught him the Greek and Latin he had learned at Dartmouth, and by the time he was sixteen, George was a schoolteacher. Ordained a minister in 1848, George joined the Episcopalian antislavery effort, but ultimately stopped ministering because of the congregation's conservatism. In 1866, he served in the Michigan legislature and was also a regent of the University of Michigan. In 1872, he was elected to the House of Representatives during the Republican presidency of Ulysses S. Grant and served on the committee that nominated the war hero to a second term.

The congressman's daughter, Lilla Willard, married Ephraim William Moore, the grandfather of Charles, the architect.

Throughout his life, Moore discounted his father as a role model; he remembered him being loud, distant, and likely an alcoholic. His father's fleeting paternal interest, however, was replaced by the attention of his grandfather. Ephraim Moore was a dapper newspaper editor, a respected member of the community, for a time its representative in the Michigan legislature, and later the mayor of Battle Creek. He was devoted to learning, loved to travel, and appreciated architecture, which he wrote columns about in the *Benton Harbor Daily Palladium*. "Havana," he reported on March 8, 1910, "is a city of palaces, a city of streets and plazas, of colonnades and towers, of churches and of monasteries, and here are reproduced the customs of Spain, so that a visit to Cuba is almost like a trip to Spain itself." E. W. Moore passed away when Charles was only thirteen years old.

College-Age Moore.

In September 1942, at age sixteen, Charles enrolled in the University of Michigan School of Architecture. Martha joined him at the university as a premedical student a year later, and they reinvigorated their friendship. Soon they met Dona Guimares, who waited tables in the student union, and the three became tight friends. Together, they spent lunch hours listening to classical music and opera in an Ann Arbor record shop. Dona ultimately became a successful fashion, culture, and home-design editor in New York, and their friendship lasted until her death in 1989.

Charles loved the academic world and had his first feelings that he would someday become a teacher. Classmates recall his "quiet aura of confidence." Harvey Allison, a friend, remembered when Charles (his college nickname was "Efoo" Moore) once had to take an economics course. He attended only one or two of the classes during the semester and at the end cracked the book, memorized its contents, and made one of the highest grades.

The attack on Pearl Harbor had emptied the classrooms and studios, and since he was ineligible for military service, Charles found himself in a class of only five or six students who flourished under the intimate attention of the faculty. The humiliation of not being in uniform made his first years at Michigan difficult, since the campus was a training ground and most young men were proudly enlisted. Moore's difficulties were compounded by the sudden death of his father on November 27, 1942.

However, Charles met Roger Bailey, a professor of architecture who would have a profound impact on his life, not only as his first architectural mentor but also as a father figure. Bailey was born in Bradford, Pennsylvania, in 1897 and first studied architecture at Cornell in 1915. After graduating, he apprenticed with John Russell Pope and Hugh Ferriss and in 1922 won the Paris Prize, allowing him to study at the Ecole des Beaux Arts for three years, where he became an accomplished watercolorist. Bailey was working in New York City when the stock market crash threw architects out of work, but he was just then offered a position at the University of Michigan.

Michigan's architecture school, like most in the United States, had discarded the eclectic historicism of the Beaux Arts, and the school during Charles's years was dedicated, under Dean Emil Lorch (whose daughter Betty was Roger Bailey's wife) to a fairly technical approach to design, with a focus on construction technology and specifications. Bailey also

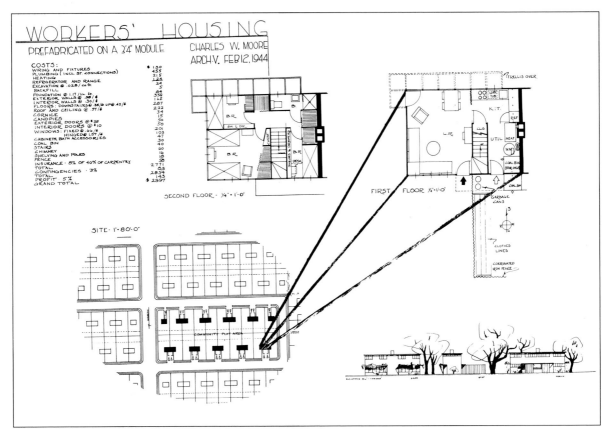

Workers' Housing, Charles W. Moore, Student Project, University of Michigan, 1944.

began a nonprofit teaching office of the school to expose students to professional work, similar to medical students working in hospitals.

Of the surviving projects from Charles's undergraduate course were drawings for "Workers' Housing" in addition to his senior thesis *Living in Men's College Dormitories,* which was influenced greatly by Alvar Aalto and dedicated "to Le Corbusier . . . whose work has shown what can be done." Both the housing and dormitory projects revealed Charles's fascination with modern design. He even scoffed at historical styles and eclecticism: in the back of the thesis he assertively stamped a red "FAKE" over a collage of photographs of collegiate Gothic dormitories, including the Princeton Graduate College! He celebrated William Wurster's "completely delightful" Stern Hall at the University of California, Le Corbusier's Swiss Dormitory in Paris, and Antonin Raymond's project in Pondicherry, India. The thesis exposed Moore's brilliant writing, even at twenty-one. "Of course," he wrote, "there are outstanding examples of livable, even delightful, dormitory rooms but strangely enough they seem to be either in Eurasia or else built for women. Interest in men's accommodations in the United States is almost exclusively archaeological, with the accent on the Gothic, which Brunelleschi discarded before 1500; the dormitories are furnished with variations on a theme by the Tudors identical to pieces which housewives threw out with a shudder upon the collapse of the Roaring Twenties."

Moore spent a lot of social time with Roger and Betty Bailey. With unanimity, people fondly recalled Bailey's charm, worldliness, kindness, and gentle hand; a student, John Jickling, called him "the epitome of the fun-loving, happy, glamorous architect." Having spent time in Paris and New York with great architects, Bailey was well connected and expanded Charles's cultural horizon. The Baileys never had children of their own, and Roger's longstanding affection for and pride in Charles were evident in a letter he wrote in 1954 in support of Moore's candidacy for graduate studies at Princeton:

> Mr. Moore was the most brilliant student it has been my pleasure to work with during twenty-some years of teaching, at Yale, Cornell, Michigan, and now here. His professional work, after graduation, in the Bay Region area, was of the highest order — indeed, I was surprised he would leave the profession for the educational world, with his talent and capacity for the successful practice of architecture. It has been Moore's intention from the beginning, however, to devote himself to education. Even as a student he had this goal in mind, and now feels that a further degree will be of importance to him.
>
> Mr. Moore's personal qualifications are of the best, fine family and all the nice manners and social graces that one would expect. I suspect he was what is known as a precocious child; certainly during his undergraduate years his intellect seemed to be two jumps ahead of his years. He possesses a photographic memory — an inquisitive mind, a contagious enthusiasm, and some sort of enviable mental stepladder that enable him to keep his sights raised high. He views the goings-on in the creative world through an extremely wide-angled lens, though perhaps his notions of history sometimes lack proper centering. I felt at times he had only one tiptoe on the ground, which indicated, perhaps, a lack of the academic discipline, which he now seeks.
>
> The great need in architectural education, it seems to me, is for men who are not so much concerned with techniques of building, and design, but who might be classed as evaluators, and examine with and for students the architectural trends and productions in terms of qualities and worth. Some professional sight raising is in order, and I can think of no better candidate than Moore, who understands this challenge. Should you accept him, I will be most interested in knowing how his program will be decided.
>
> It is difficult to write in support of one whom I have known for so long and so intimately and with such pride. One gets biased. I am sure, however, that the best things I would know how to say of anyone I know, who might ask my support, I would say for Charles Moore. This obviously is going "all out" and that is what I mean it to do.

Though their influence was very important, neither Ephraim Moore nor Bailey influenced Charles as fundamentally as his mother. Clearly, Charles and his sister, Mimi, were the center of Kathryn Moore's life. She constantly urged Charles to do his best, to make a differ-

Kathryn Moore, Charles's Mother, Departing on a Family Trip.

ence, and in turn, he strove to fulfill her expectations and make her happy. They were close confidants and exchanged frequent letters, often several times a week. Her letters generally covered the events of her days and friends, were punctuated with forties and fifties colloquialisms and spellings ("nope," "thru," "betcha," "sorta"), and were often filled with her vivid descriptions of places. The level of their architectural dialogue was astounding.

In one extraordinary letter, dating from 1957, Kathryn Moore summed up the important qualities of Charles's childhood: the influence of his grandfather (tellingly his father is not mentioned), Charles's passion for travel, and the love of place that she so continuously nurtured in "Chuck":

Chuck, My Darling:

Your Wednesday letter received Sunday eve, and was I ever happy to receive it and to know your Fellowship was officially announced. Chuck, it is just wonderful! I am so happy for you. I KNOW what it means and not just from the $2,200.00 standpoint. Where ever you go you give the best of yourself, and that is such a wonderful characteristic. I see so many of Grandpa's influences in you, and I am mighty proud of it. You couldn't have had a better guide.

Your Charleston trip sounded most strenuous, but knowing you wouldn't do it otherwise. Weren't you fortunate to find such a pleasant room? Could just picture where you were. Remember when we were all there together? Can close my eyes and see the beautiful old city, with its fascinating wrought-iron grills and the gardens, the lovely old gnarled trees, and flowers in profusion. When we were there the magnolias had finished their bloom, too, but everywhere were great tins of flowers and shrubs. You know I am so grateful for all the trips we have had, because now thru your eyes all the lovely places pass in review.

Charleston, South Carolina.

On October 12, 1958, Kathryn Moore passed away in Pebble Beach, California.

In the following essay, Moore recounts his childhood and his first feelings about being an architect.

One of my favorite stories from my childhood concerns my great-grandfather who was a farmer in Michigan. Like many who bravely ventured westward from the established East (naming their new towns New London, Athens, or Toledo to connect with remembered places), my great-grandfather lived in a beautiful Greek Revival farmhouse. But he was also eager to express his connections to the Old World in a more personal way, so he kept his farm records in Latin and his personal diaries in Greek, languages that had been passed down from my great-great-grandfather who had managed to learn them while he studied at Dartmouth for two years. When my great-grandfather became a regent at the University of Michigan, he introduced coeducation, for the first time in an American state university, by duping his fellow regents, who were not receptive to such liberal notions, with a resolution in Latin that was so cryptic yet high-sounding for the non-Latin speakers, it passed without objection. When they realized their mistake, they were too embarrassed to admit they didn't know Latin, and the resolution stood.

My grandfather Moore was quite wonderful and had a lot of influence in the town since he was a publisher of a string of newspapers in Michigan, and then the mayor, and until he died when I was thirteen years old I wanted to be a newspaper editor or publisher like him. For some years early in my childhood we lived with

Ephraim and Lilla Moore, Charles's Grandparents.

him in his house in Benton Harbor, and he taught me to read when I was about three. When I was a little older he would take me around to various newspapers belonging to friends of his, and he helped me to print my own newspaper when I was eleven.

Eventually we moved away, and my father built two cottages and then a house on the lake in Battle Creek, which was very ordinary and I guess typical of what people were building in those times, modest and unassuming. But after my grandfather died my parents decided to build a room on our little house for me, and when the man came with plans, I thought they were just fascinating. I began to make my own plans for houses, inventing uses and people who might live in them and what they would want, and I guess that's when I decided to be an architect.

When high school was over, I went off to the architecture school at the University of

Michigan in Ann Arbor, where I met Roger Bailey. The program, like most others in the country, was at one time Beaux Arts, but by the time I got there it had changed and was ordinary and sort of technical, with only a few courses in architectural history, taught by Frederick C. O'Dell, and Jean Hebrard was a design professor with an impressive heritage of Parisian architect ancestors. I also had a lot of free time to take other courses, which included ones in Greek literature and poetry. Most of them, though, were in architecture, which I didn't have any trouble in since I was a good student. There weren't many of us, since most were fighting the war, so Roger let us work in a little office that he set up, which was called Roger Bailey & Associates. There were some small houses to work on, nothing ever substantial, but it was good experience and helped me to understand how buildings were made and drawings finished and so forth. He also had work for us making drawings that other architects hired him to finish, so that was good for learning too.

Almost every year of my childhood there was a long automobile trip with my parents and Mimi, from Michigan to Florida or California and back months later, when it was no longer winter in the north. My teachers would give me my lessons, which I would work on during the trips (which sometimes lasted months), and then return with them completed, and most of the time my schoolmates in Michigan were behind.

Long before the trips were to begin, I would figure out the combinations and numbers of ways that we could reach our destination over highway routes through any number of towns, stopping to see the sights with stays at hotels along the way. I found it all terribly exciting that we could go to so many places and see so much, and the thrill of visiting places I had read about, such as Civil War battlefields, was edifying.

Depending on who won the toss of the coin, we spent winters in Florida or California. When my mother won we went to California, when my father won we'd go to Florida, where his father also spent winters. My father won more often than my mother did, so California was always more mysterious and by most accounts far more beautiful than Florida. The winters when I was one and two and five and not again until I was thirteen and fourteen and whatnot were spent in Hollywood or Pasadena, and then we would return to Michigan when April came. California always seemed like heaven and Michigan the opposite — because that's where the cold reality was.

Los Angeles was, when I was five, a very different city from what it is now. There were more people from Iowa and fewer from around the globe. The sounds in the streets were a little less exotic, it seemed, to a midwesterner. But they were strange enough, and the sunshine was a little cleaner, and the brown stuff hadn't penetrated quite so effectively as it has by now. The architectural changes that have come in the half century since then have, I think, mostly been ones of scale, and it seems to me most of the changes have made it harder to appreciate the place. Perhaps they had a little too prematurely seen the future, and so after World War II they tore down so much of our world to make way for the revolutionary world of

Charles in His Battle Creek Study. Watercolor Attributed to Mimi Weingarten.

skyscrapers in the park that most architects were dreaming about. I suppose things may seem less mysterious and wonderful as they get closer to one's own time, but what upset me was the lack of sensitivity that allowed so many new buildings in Los Angeles to become identical to ones in Omaha or New York or elsewhere. There used to be things that couldn't have been anywhere but Los Angeles, such as the architecture of the thirties and early forties, which was, in most cases, quite small and often, to its advantage, marvelously tacky. It was magic, and it left me a heavy California fan since I was a child. My mother and sister moved there when I was twenty, and my sister went to U.S.C., and my mother lived there the rest of her life. So California, more than Michigan, has been my home.

San Francisco from Moore's Boarding House, 1948.

Radio Station, Mario Corbett, 1948.

CHAPTER TWO

Beginnings

"Wonderful" was Charles Moore's highest compliment, and that's how he described San Francisco in the late 1940s. World War II was over; the city was filled with palpable hope. No city in America had been built in the midst of such diverse natural features, and in the streets thrived a public life with all the charm of Europe. Most of the high-rise development had not yet occurred, so the city's dramatic hills (Moore lived in boarding houses on Nob Hill) were still easily identifiable as the dominant features of the city. This human scale counterpointed the awesome wonders of the Golden Gate, the vast expanse of bay, redwood still growing along the ridges, and the hills of Marin.

The next six years would be an intense period, when Moore would gain experiences around the world, marking his beginnings as an educator and architect.

After graduating from the University of Michigan in 1947, Moore went to San Francisco with dreams of becoming a Bay Region architect. He was aware of the roots and traditions of California architecture rising from a Spanish colonial past of missions and adobes; how the ideas of Louis Sullivan and Frank Lloyd Wright gradually migrated west and mingled with the decorative traditions of Japan and Spain. Important early practitioners were Bernard Maybeck, Julia Morgan, Willis Polk, John Galen Howard, and Charles and Henry Greene. A second generation followed, led most importantly by William Wurster, as well as Gardner Dailey, John Dinwiddie, Mario Corbett, John Funk, and Joseph Esherick. There were important exchanges between north and south: Los Angeles, freer and less restrained than San Francisco, tended to be more modern, more influenced by the German and Viennese schools by way of Richard Neutra and R. M. Schindler, while San Francisco remained dedicated to the more traditional arts and crafts use of material. Both regions, however, stressed the integration of indoors and outdoors in the idyllic California climate.

Moore's first job in California was with Mario Corbett, a sophisticated architect and talented designer known for simple, austere, redwood-finished houses. Corbett built several of these houses on Wolfback Ridge in Sausalito, in addition to a radio station that was unabashedly modern: large expanses of plate glass and concrete floors perched on I-beam stilts high over the San Francisco Bay. Moore described Corbett's office as tiny — only three or four young designers. Corbett seldom pursued new work, and since his income fluctuated, so did his employees' salaries. When Corbett was hospitalized, Moore and the others were left to run the office (a coworker, Walter Costa, said it was a little like *Lord of the Flies*), and when the money dwindled, Moore was compelled to find work elsewhere.

Joseph Allen Stein hired Moore next. Born in 1912, Stein had a remarkable education and career: He studied at the University of Illinois, at the Ecole des Beaux Arts at Fontainebleau, and at Cranbrook Academy under Eliel Saarinen and Carl Milles. He then apprenticed under Ely Jacques Kahn and Richard Neutra. Moore had great respect for Stein and found working for him to be "wonderful because he was interested in ideas." Stein regarded architecture as a means of addressing social problems, having witnessed the squalid, inhuman living conditions of the California migrants in the thirties. Stein was also strongly committed to landscape and, along with Garrett Eckbo, Burton Cairns, Vernon DeMars, and Francis Violich, was a key figure in "Telesis," a progressive group of Bay Region architects, landscape architects, urban planners, and industrial designers with roots in the Farm Security Administration. They believed that their work as designers of the human realm should be collaborative and reflect a sensitivity for the broader "environmental" realm. In Stein's office, Moore worked on the McCarthy Townhouse, which featured free-flowing space arranged on one level, floating planes for walls, and large plate-glass windows looking out into a garden designed by Eckbo. Stein, however, was growing discontent with the political situation in America and the tremors of red scare persecutions. Eventually, he went to Mexico, spent time in Israel, and finally settled in India where he became one of its most prominent architects.

In 1995, Stein wrote from India:

> I was grieved to hear of Charles's death. He was an integral part of a very happy and constructive period of my life and practice when our office was in San Francisco directly across from Frank Lloyd Wright's delightful Gump's Shop on Maiden Lane. The office consisted of only four of us, my wife, Margaret, who did the accounts, color consultancy, etc.; Roy Maru, a talented young designer and draftsman subsequently partner in a leading San Francisco architectural firm; Charles; and myself. I think it was Charles's first job, and we were warm friends and very young. Also, it was a period, just after the Second World War, when hopes were high. . . . My memory of our association is of happy years — the terrible war was won — but there was the shadow of the Atomic Bomb and the looming war in Korea. We young architects in the Bay Region were, along with planners and landscape architects, involved in a seminal project, "Telesis," and had much to do with the fact that the development of the burgeoning Bay Region was not worse than it is. The reason being partly that the members of Telesis subsequently occupied significant positions in the official planning organizations, University, etc. Charles, of course, went on to play a major part in designing Sea Ranch, which was highly expressive of the Bay Region Style, and I consider one of the model expressions of an organic, regional style in architecture. . . .

After Stein left America, Moore was again out of a job, but soon found work with Hervey Parke Clark, an affluent architect who practiced with John Beuttler. Clark was the quintessential gentleman architect who generally conformed to popular trends. With social connections fostered at the Pacific Union Club and his Woodside residence, he attracted wealthy clients and built many houses for San Francisco's elite. Clark immediately recognized Charles's potential, and instead of using him as a draftsman (a typical job for young graduates), he allowed Charles to work as a designer. Moore worked on the early design phase of the home economics building for the University of California at Davis, a thoroughly modern, rationalist building, with stark institutional efficiency.

Moore cleared another career hurdle in 1949 when he passed the California architectural licensing exam (2 of 110 candidates succeeded), and at twenty-four, eleven years after those workmen built the addition in Battle Creek, Moore was an architect.

San Francisco was a forward-looking architectural scene, and "the city was to its young architects," said architect Mary Martin, "what Paris had been to Beaux Arts students. And we all felt here's somebody special. Charles was very young, very intense, and still looking for a real direction." Not only did Moore spend important time learning the practicalities of construction, but he was influenced by the Bay tradition of designing modest houses with palpable human scale and strong connections to site. Even more important, Moore recognized California's unique dilemma in balancing traditional craft and innovation. In 1958, Moore wrote a brief introduction to a lecture on the Bay Region school. The essay struck at the roots of Moore's struggle to define a point of departure from both pure traditionalism and high modernism. Although the piece was specifically about California architecture, it addressed the broader issue of the balance between innovation and tradition. It is a key document.

Along the highways on the West Coast are billboards advertising a kind of beer, which announce, "It's lucky when you live in California." For over half a century this has been quite literally true, especially for architects. There have been magnificent sites, plentiful good wood, a benign climate, quite a lot of money, and a way of life which is perhaps more comfortably informal than any way of life that has ever existed before anywhere. On top of this has been a native tradition of putting together pieces of wood to make buildings which are easy, natural, and highly decorative. The building tradition is so easy, and so attractive, that for this half century, while it has scarcely changed at all, it has been thought excitingly "contemporary" by the rest of the world. It was "contemporary" in 1908, and the same thing is good "contemporary" design in 1958. But the architect in California working in the local idiom has two new problems to cope with. There is on the one hand the 1200-year-old Japanese tradition of putting together pieces of wood similar to his own with refinements and excellences which he can scarcely ignore, however different the two cultures are. On the other hand the architect has to face California's explosively expanding population, and the attendant urbanization, the need for buildings in cities, bigger than ever before, made of a new set of materials, and calling for a kind of organization more formal and less picturesque than he can manage in his present idiom. The West Coast architect has behind him a tradition which includes some of the pleasantest houses in the world. But he cannot any more create his buildings on a feeling for that tradition alone. He is faced with choices among other manners and other accomplishments, if he is to do his best with his materials and for his changing environment. Like it or not, he is an eclectic. He is faced with problems which have never existed for him before, and it is incumbent on him to understand them and the influences acting on him, to be able to crystallize their meaning for himself and only then to be able to push them to the back of his mind, to practice "creative forgetfulness" so that he is free to create an architecture which will be the answer to these problems.

Quite unlike Chicago or New York, immigrants, arriving from both directions, made California a place of cultural collision between the oriental and occidental, and blended with the California appetite for "contemporary" living to produce unique architecture. Collision, synthesis, eclecticism, historical absorption, and layering would become central to Moore's work.

Despite his growing professional experience and aspirations for teaching history, Moore still had not been to Europe, an important rite in a young architect's development. In 1949 he won the George Booth Traveling Scholarship, a prize funded by the founding patron of the Cranbrook Academy. Before Moore left, Roger Bailey hired him to teach, upon his return to America, in a new architecture school at the University of Utah. Bailey sent Moore off "to develop a method and program of teaching architectural history in some manner that people of any given era can become alive and real. That [means] covering their cultural, political, religious, and economic conditions and the influence of their culture on the rest of the world, or vice versa."

With a classmate from Michigan, Peter Frantz, Moore embarked from New York City for London. (On the voyage Charles remembered a British waiter who snootily wondered why Americans eat their corn on the cob. "To prove a point," Charles said, "I ate twelve ears.") In addition to photographing and watercoloring, Moore was one of the first to make sixteen-millimeter films documenting urban spaces in an attempt to shatter the static nature of photography and create a sense of "feeling" for the details and spatiality of the places. Despite bureaucratic hassles of filming in occupied countries, he shot color movies of the Château of Chenonceaux, the Alhambra, Piazza San Marco, Trevi Fountain, Acropolis, and monuments in Karnak, Egypt.

According to his extensive letters (again, there was an extraordinary correspondence with his mother), Moore had great escapades touring cosmopolitan capitals and isolated villages, soaking in the visual riches of Roman fountains, Byzantine mosaics, Gothic cathedrals, and Spanish hill towns. (In Spain Charles scheduled a rendezvous with Dona Guimares, and they tooled around the Iberian Peninsula in a rented Citroën that Charles ultimately bought and imported to America.) Some visits were especially providential: in London he discovered Sir John Soane's house, in Marseilles he was struck with Le Corbusier's Unité d'Habitation, and he remembered fondly snow falling in the Alhambra Gardens in Granada. Charles was immersed in the tradition of the eighteenth-century Grand Tour, although updated with Leicas, Cole Porter, Citroëns, Carmen Amaya, martinis, Ingrid Bergman at Rome's American Academy (she was visiting its president), European reconstruction, cold-war spies, and the almighty dollar.

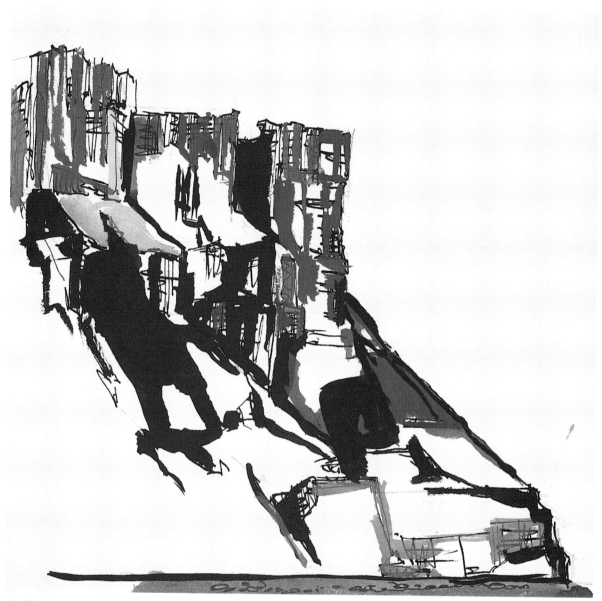

Utah Landscape, Charles Moore, c. 1951.

Each place Charles proclaimed to be more "wonderful" than the last.

When he exhausted his grant, Moore returned to the United States and drove to Salt Lake City in the Citroën, probably the first ever to reach Utah. In September 1950 he began his first semester of a lifetime of teaching. His first yearly salary was $4,725.

Roger Bailey had visited Utah only two years before and was taken with the untapped potential of the West and Salt Lake City. With catching enthusiasm and charm, he convinced the university president to allow him to establish Utah's first architecture school —

the first school, in fact, between Denver and California. He assembled an energetic, young faculty: James Acland, Gordon Heck, Stephen Macdonald, and Moore. The faculty and students shared their first common space in a basement and then moved to an army mess hall, left over from war training, where there was space for drafting (three students to a table), a faculty office (where meetings were held within earshot of the students), and a lecture space in the corner of the room. These were the barest amenities in which to begin a school, but Bailey and Moore found the excitement of inventing a curriculum from scratch a suitable substitute for luxury that, all things considered, was fitting for Utah's make-do, pioneer spirit. Bailey encouraged the young faculty to develop innovative ways of teaching. Late at night, they would all gather at one of their houses to discuss their progress, constantly improvising new directions for the school. Close friendships formed. There were often parties uplifted by Charles's tremendous wit, and weekends were taken over by watercolor excursions to Zion, Bryce, and the Four Corners.

Most of the G.I. Bill students were older than their sage professor: "Chuck" Moore was twenty-six years old and taught both architectural history and design. In his history course (he often taught sitting cross-legged on top of a desk), Moore drew on the arts and music in order to broaden the chronological perspective and to encourage the notion that buildings are not made in vacuums independent of the culture of their times. Moore also stressed connections between the history classes and the studios, urging students to apply lessons from the historical sites to their own design problems. One project, for instance, was based on T. S. Eliot's *Murder in the Cathedral*. "The excitement," according to Moore, "had been in thinking about new ways to educate young architects, and developing a program without having to struggle with an established academic order — starting it all from scratch, as it were."

On the side, Moore worked in a small office that Stephen Macdonald set up and helped with small residential projects. (Norma Macdonald recalled that Moore would come to the office after a long day of teaching, stretch out on the windowsill, and take a nap, which always amazed the young draftsmen in the office.)

Moore's time at Utah allowed him to collect his thoughts about his recent experiences in Europe. Here he began to develop his ideas of architecture as cultural history, the primacy of site, and the perception and scenographic manipulation of space. He tried to express these ideas through early, unpublished book projects; the first was a study of Byzantine mosaics:

> I have recently returned from Europe with some 2000 colored 35 mm. slides of various architectural features. Among the most successful are those treating the Byzantine and Early Christian mosaics at Ravenna, Torcello, and Daphni. In looking over the literature in these fields, I have noticed that good colored illustrations are almost completely lacking, and on this basis, I should like to propose a small but fine book of perhaps fifteen colored plates accompanied by a short, readable essay on Byzantine spatial relationships and the use of mosaics in their architecture which has formed the basis of my presentation of Byzantine architectural history to students at the University of Utah.

Moore also wanted to return to Europe on a Fulbright Scholarship to study either at the American Academy in Rome or the Institute of Classical Studies in Athens. (Charles eventually spent time as a resident at the American Academy in 1975 and 1981.) He planned to do this in conjunction with graduate studies, and in a letter to Joseph Hudnut, the dean of Harvard's Faculty of Design, Moore wrote in 1952:

> In my teaching, I have discovered that many of our students find it difficult to grasp the idea of visual control of open space, and I believe that the material we have to present to them is quite inadequate, although we base it on Camillo Sitte's authoritative book on the subject [*The Art of Building Cities*]. With this in mind, I should like to extend his book, by adding documentation in the form of photographs of works already studied by him, and with an analysis of his theses in terms of twentieth-century space-time theories.

Hudnut passed Moore's letter on to Walter Gropius, but ultimately Moore swerved away from Harvard and the increasingly musty smell of the Cambridge Bauhaus.

Moore's beginnings in Utah had much to do with Bailey's permissive academic spirit and willingness to give young faculty enough breathing space to work out new ideas, as Moore wrote:

> Roger Bailey is one of the great American architectural educators. I knew him as a teacher at the University of Michigan when I was an undergraduate, taught in his department of architecture at Utah for two years and have kept close contact with him since. As a teacher he was inspiring and as a department head provided the most exciting opportunity I have ever experienced for the development of an architectural curriculum, and for the development of his young faculty as well as his students. The development of young teachers and, recently, of graduate students has continued in the years since. His devotion to architecture and to education have been an important stimulus to many of us: I for one count him the most important (and in many ways the most exciting) influence on my career.

Roger Bailey. Courtesy University of Utah Graduate School of Architecture.

Too soon, however, the halcyon days of Utah ended, and plans for graduate school were postponed. In 1952 Moore was drafted for service in Korea. He was commissioned as a

Lieutenant Moore, 1953.

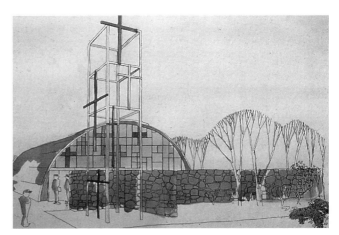

Quonset Hut Chapel, Charles Moore, 1953.

second lieutenant and left Utah for training at Camp Roberts in California. He was then stationed in an engineering group near Seoul. Fortunately, Moore did not face any combat, leaving him to enjoy the isolation, challenge, and independence that the army offered. He helped design grade schools, tuberculosis hospitals, an officers' club for the Eighth Army, and chapels, mostly with industrial, prefabricated parts designed with the simplest plans and sections so as to be easily reproduced on sites throughout Korea. For instance, Moore designed an army chapel using a Quonset hut, replacing one end with stained glass and creating a space frame tower-crucifix-sign reminiscent of the BBPR Memorial in Milan, which he had seen in 1950. Furthermore, he also designed in 1951 a road sign featuring a giant red arrow pointing the way to his battalion, an early hint of supergraphics.

Moore spent leave absorbing Eastern mysticisms, visiting Hong Kong, Korean towns and temples, and important sites in Japan, such as Ryoanji, Katsura, the gardens of Kyoto, and even Wright's doomed Imperial Hotel in Tokyo. Most of it was architectural revelation, since very little had been published on Eastern architecture at that time. Charles was stunned by the craftsmanship of timber structures more than a thousand years old, interiors austere yet highly refined, masterful spatial layering, and the highly tuned sensitivity for water and gardens. In all, Moore's military service was a positive experience (again an example of how he took advantage of any kind of opportunity) that not only compensated for his inability to serve in World War II, but provided the camaraderie that friends say helped him shed his childhood shyness.

When he was discharged, Moore began his graduate studies at Princeton. In order to earn extra money, he marketed a small mail-order catalog of his architectural slides. In 1955, he received the following prescient letter from O'Neil Ford:

Korean Supergraphics, 1953.

Katsura Villa, Japan.

During my recent visit to the University of Arkansas, Mr. Williams showed me many of your European colored slides and your catalog. I would like very much to have this catalog and any new work you have acquired since its printing.

I have through the years made a sizable collection of slides of old houses and buildings in this area (Texas Border, East Texas Classic Revival, Central Texas Pioneer German), and I wonder whether or not you would be interested in seeing sample copies of these with the idea that you might begin a collection of early works in America. We are badly in need of material from the Victorian period and the work from 1800 to 1850. Then too, I feel we might begin to fill the gaps in our education by knowing more about the general period usually represented by Maybeck, Curtis of Kansas City, Willis Polk, Greene brothers, and all the other vigorous designers of that era. I am further interested in the period right after the Civil War, which produced the first cast-iron tall buildings. They are everywhere. Almost every city that was fully developed by 1870 has pertinent examples that go entirely unnoticed by the local architects.

I just think you have a fine opportunity to build yourself a substantial business and do a great work for architectural education.

Forty years later, at the end of his teaching career, Charles Moore was the first professor to hold the O'Neil Ford Centennial Chair in Architecture at the University of Texas at Austin.

The following collection of letters and travel diary excerpts are drawn from Moore's correspondence between 1949 and 1950 from Europe, Egypt, and the Near East. They are illustrated with his original slides and watercolors.

London
Thursday, September 29, 1949

Dear Mother, Aunt Bus, and Aunt Lou,

I got your letters today — it was so wonderful to hear from you. By now you are on the plane for L.A. I was so glad to hear about all the doings in Benton Harbor and Chicago, and glad to know that our things will all be out of the Wyatts and in California, that will save a trip to Michigan when I get back next summer.

The last two days in New York were the most hectic of all. I finally did all the things Roger had asked me to do, got my baggage insurance and all sorts of things and got all packed and ready to run for the boat. We had B. J. Barnes (the girl who worked for Corbusier, and is a friend of the Baileys) over to Dona's for dinner one night. We enjoyed her, and she told us about all sorts of things and places in France. The Frantzes arrived two days before we sailed, and the last night we (they, Peter, Dona, and I) went to see "The Madwoman of Chaillot" the best one in town — it was wonderful — then we did the town, ended up over on the Palisades above Geo. Washington Bridge where there's a great all-glam night club with all the trimmings.

Peter and I had a nice stateroom on the Caronia (a beautiful new ship), with toilet and shower and everything. Met all sorts of interesting people on the way over. British, American, and a Chilean girl from New York, and a lot of fun — we're all going to get together in London this weekend, maybe. I was sick for a couple of days in the middle, when it got rough, but otherwise it was a beautiful crossing, and of course it was exciting to land in Southampton and come up through the country to London — we had trouble about our reservations, but it's all fine now. London is dirty and badly smashed up, still, and poor and grim, and dry (no rain this summer), but of course it's fascinating to see all the things I've always heard about, and all the houses built in quiet little curving streets around squares with beautiful trees make it lots of fun to be around — it's all very quiet, even the cars are little, of course, and quiet, and it's much nicer to be in than New York — after California, New York seemed awfully noisy and dirty and unpleasant this time.

We've seen something every minute, so I can't begin to describe all the things. I love the Christopher Wren city churches, and the shops in Bond Street are fun — the bookstores are wonderful. Yesterday and today have been the West End, Buckingham Palace area, and the area around the Houses of Parliament, then we took a boat down the Thames past the old city of London (very badly smashed) to the Tower and back to Big Ben.

~

Fontainebleau
Monday, October 10, 1949

Dear Mother, Aunt Bus, and Aunt Lou,

. . . There's just nowhere to begin about Paris — I can't imagine that anywhere in the world (not even San Francisco!) could be anywhere near so exciting and charming and delightful and everything else. Mimi and Saul just must come here — she'd love every minute of it. We decided we'd better leave before we just stayed there and never got any farther, but will be back for a little while, and then I think there will be time to really enjoy it in the spring. I didn't have any idea that all of the things I'd always heard about, like the sidewalk cafés and the Champs Elysées and the bookstalls along the Seine could be this wonderful. The only initial disappointment was Notre Dame. We walked down there late one night after the theater, arrived at 2:00 a.m. with just a full moon shining on it, and the darn thing looked like cardboard (but that was just from the front — the back was wonderful, with the flying buttresses). You just couldn't realize that a big city could be so human and so much fun to be in — all this especially after New York (after 2 years in San Francisco, it seemed like a great trap) and London — I'm not even being polite about London, although Peter keeps defending it. The people enjoy being uncomfortable and "bucking up," I think, and that food — ugh — I can't see why they bother to survive — the day in the country at Oxford, though, was *delightful,* and we went to Windsor Castle on the way back. Then another day we went to Kew Gardens — it was sunny and warm (like it was all the time in England) and really beautiful.

There's just no way to tell you in a letter about the French food. We started with Escargots (snails), which were wonderful, and every meal since has been a delight — wine costs less per litre than gasoline.

[Fragment missing] . . . with the devaluation, we got a middle-size Citroën (the bigger body, the 4-cylinder motor) for $20 less than we had paid for the little Simca. Mr. Alfondarr is still in Paris, and showed us how to work everything. It's a wonderful car, nice and roomy, and lots of fun to drive — we've had it since Friday night, and have had a wonderful time scooting around in the wild Parisian traffic (their famous traffic dangers are just nothing compared to L.A. but it's going to take a lot of flying to get around those fancy London intersections in the wrong side of the road).

≈

Chartres
November 10, 1949

Dearest Mother and All:

We intended to spend four days in Paris, ended up finally leaving after eleven. We came on the 60 or 70 kilometers to Chartres. We wanted really to study this cathedral, which is by far the best of all, so we've been here a week. I have taken some movies. It's incredibly beautiful. Yesterday was especially fun. We ran into a professor from the University of Chicago, who was measuring things in the building, so had all the keys, and he spent the day showing us around the high places where people aren't ordinarily allowed to go. I was glad you didn't know where we were when we were climbing up the steep roof in the rain by hanging on to chains, just like pictures of climbing the Alps. Remember all the climbing around in "The Hunchback of Notre Dame"? The building is really as wonderful as Joe Stein and everyone said it would be.

≈

Sevilla

Dearest Mother and All:

. . . The trip through Spain has been very exciting, much too much to tell about. The North is all wild and terribly poor. Almost all the people seem to be really cold and hungry. The country looks like that part of Mexico we saw from Guadalajara over towards San Luis Potosi, completely bare, with mud towns with great towering churches sticking up out of it. We went to Burgos, because the cathedral is supposed to be wonderful. It had so much incredibly bad stuff about it. We were most disappointed. Stopped in Valladolid to see an interesting college, then spent a couple of days in Salamanca (which has all sorts of wonderful buildings with mud huts in bare, open country just a few steps away). All these towns looked wonderful from a distance, like Baghdad floating in the desert. There sure aren't any of the French niceties, though, like wonderful small-town inns with (always) good beds and wonderful food. You get an occasional dish in Spain that's just marvelous, something called paella with a rice base and everything from land and sea thrown in, and eggs à la flamenco. Mimi would love the great plates of "jambs" which are sort-a-like prawns with the shell still on. You peel them one by one and eat hundreds. But other than these and a few other items, the food is uniquely, totally lousy. Just about as bad as you get in some parts of Nebraska, maybe even worse, maybe as bad as in England (no, not that — only the English have that fiendish genius for making good food nauseating).

. . . The trip continued — went from Salamanca to Avila and Segovia which are at the foot of the great high snow-covered Guadarrama (Madrid is on the other side). Both beautiful little towns, built on cliffs and hills with the walls still intact and even Roman ruins. Saw some wonderful gardens — out of ink — at La Granja, near Segovia, then went to Madrid, stayed at a de luxe hotel — the Astoria — had expensive American martinis, and pretended like we were rich Americans

Charles and Dona Guimares Touring in the Citroën Traction-Avant.

for a night and a day — nothing of any special interest in Madrid, except the Prado museum and money — it's just like any of the great rich cities in the world — which seems pretty funny in a country like Spain. We went on to Toledo the next day, which was just the opposite (it was the capital before 1500), tiny and on a bunch of cliffs in the desert but with a fantastically rich set of buildings, paintings (hundreds of El Grecos), everything. It's as though every artistic treasure in the United States were suddenly to turn up in Bisbee. Finally, after a couple of days in Toledo, we came south, over the mountains to Andalucia, where it's warm and sunny (some of the time) and much richer, or so it seems — sort of a California atmosphere to it — only more kinds of palm trees. And the Arabian (Moorish) architecture is so wonderful I can't begin to tell about it yet. A wonderful mosque in Córdoba, and the Alcázar (palace) here is one of the most beautiful buildings I've ever seen, with all its patios and fountains and pools. Then here too there's the world's biggest Gothic cathedral, but the Moorish stuff is so much better that we don't pay much attention. The hotel is wonderful, too, with dozens of patios — it's expensive, for Europe ($1.25 each — we each have a room) but worth it. That de luxe hotel, one of the 3 or 4 best in Spain, actually cost $2 each, but we had great private bathrooms and things.

Next we go around the tip (Cadiz and Gibraltar) to Málaga, then to Granada and Barcelona — Nice by Christmas time.

Rome
Friday, January 27, 1950

Oh Sister Dear:

Now the martinis are drunk and the dinner is eaten and I haven't wandered off to a party for the first time in God knows how long because I have a headache so I will write you — you can imagine what a mess the letter will be on account of the headache, but on the other hand I am at an advantage because I have only just this morning at 3 o'clock finished a long letter to Los Angeles full of nothing but facts, which you will doubtless get a copy of (no doubt my diatribe about the Roman Catholic church carefully removed) so that now I don't have tomes with any facts at all like how many feet to the top of that wonderful Colosseum or how many times I've met Julius Caesar in the Forum on rainy days or how many Coca-Cola signs the neon companies have made. I might mention that Rome is absolutely *the* most wonderful place in the world, and the American Academy is *the* most wonderful place in Rome. We have a continuous set of parties all full of fascinating people — with architects and painters and composers and sculptors and landscape architects and more architects — then there are the archaeologists and people who are very nice in the daytime, but they're not the type for the parties, as who would be but us creative ones? And everyone lives in this great wonderful palace with steam heat and cats here and there, and there is a fine library and all the permanent ones have great studios besides having bedrooms — *huge* studios that are mostly all fixed up (the only things the architects do in theirs is throw cocktail parties, so naturally they're all fixed up for that) — the painters and the sculptors, on the other hand, have painter's and sculptor's type studios. The film situation is loused up, which gives us an excuse to stay, thank God (though I must take a train to Nice this weekend to relieve the film mess — right back, though) but next week we must go on — to Cairo (three of us again maybe the third a fellow here on the Paris Prize — very nice, apparently).

I guess it's all in the other letter about how Early Christian and Romanesque things are wonderful and even some of the Renaissance, including say the Sistine Chapel, but not, for instance, Raphael who is disgusting. But the list of yea's and no's is too long a one, and the countryside is really *sooo* beautiful. Paris the city is of course handsomer, but the country here is so much finer, all in all Rome is the place Rome is the place Rome is the place . . . for me. After a couple of years I'm going to scurry around like mad for a Rome Prize so as to come to this superb place. It's on the Janiculum, the very top, with great views of all Rome. You should do everything, everything, everything, do you hear me everything, to come to this part of the world — how about that consular job? What can you work?

~

Egypt, 1950

"Random Observations, mostly unsubstantiated"

The flight from Rome exciting with the Britishers, us too, aboard running from one side of the plane to the other as Salerno, then the Bay of Naples, Vesuvius, and Capri showed up below, as usual, no more interesting, really, than a map. The mountains higher and with snow toward the Gulf of Laranto, and Aetna quite perfect above the clouds. Dark then, and the Cairo airport warm and Mexico City–smelling, with dead fruit or something — a wait while some customs man tried to prove I was a pilot from Israel, which took long enough for the BEA bus to leave without us, so we rode miles across the desert to Cairo in a free taxi — the sky very big and bright — and the air warm, to a great decaying palace called the Continental Savoy, a move later to a smaller, darker, but rather livelier establishment — with better cuisine — but still that watered-down Anglo-International variety — the loudest horns in the world.

Americans' apartments in the flashier suburbs just like the States, only with Other People in control in the kitchen, "Third Man" music and "Kiss Me Kate" on the phonograph, and canasta.

A drive in a Packard convertible to the place where the camels start the small walk to the Pyramids, and past them to the Sphinx, lots of camel-men grabbing us and putting us on the beasts, which were broad and strangely comfortable, people lit cigarettes and bounced about. The Sphinx, much smaller than one supposes, but finer, too. Though the chief reaction to the pyramids is probably merely wonder that one is *there*. We climbed a little — they're rough, and seem almost vertical from upon their sides. Guides run (!) to the top and back in 8 minutes or so, for a large prize, but it would surely take anyone else a thankless hour. Very impressive from the perch, though, to see the Nile valley end, suddenly, along a winding dusty road, and the desert begin. The Moqattam hills loom large behind Cairo, but the city itself is rather indiscernible from here.

Along some dirt roads to Memphis (of which we saw nothing) and Saqqâra, the stepped pyramid of Zoser, strangely satisfying, that form — with the accompanying temples — the one with the well-known half-Doric columns on the ends of stub walls. Not much in the way of exciting space, but of course exciting anyway, for the tremendous antiquity. All sorts of pits and walls and things that will doubtless make sense on a plan, but are hardly recognizable. A guide to point out a hole where sacred boats were kept. It seems that the inundations came annually to the edge of the cultivated area (the same then as now), and boats must have carried the funeral procession to the mortuary temple on the edge of the desert, where a ramp began toward the other temple and the burial place. Then some distance away (all this vague because of the Arabic proceedings, in which I took no part), the mastaba of Ti, with really exciting painted bas-reliefs on the walls, the color still intact and beautiful. Ti seems to have been a land owner and court official, early in the V dynasty. Almost as impressive as the color and the fine drawing, the very skillful disposition of the assorted-sized figures, animals and all on the wall — the star attraction to date (in contrast to the trip to the King's and Queen's chambers in the great pyramid, which was merely hot and cramped, like going into a rather dinky cave). From Ti's tomb, a very elegant looking bedouin gentleman in flowing robes cleaner than the others', took us to the temple of the Bulls, not far away. This required everyone to have a small hot dripping candle and the accompanying sheepish look, to march in a weaving train through great black empty halls, underground, and to stare at great black sarcophagi in niches, for sacred bulls, all very exotic.

. . . Many movies, for the first time in a long time, good ones, too, like a thrilling little Henry James *The Heiress* that managed to set all sorts of responsive chords going, and, most particularly, a really fine *Le Diable au Corps,* really mature and moving cinema. It makes it seem a real privilege to be, for a while, in such a grown-up hemisphere, and it becomes very easy to feel, with no justification at all, quite completely French.

. . . The Egyptian Museum good for endless numbers of visits, with staggering quantities of magnificent things, exposed among even more staggering quantities of stuff that's just plain dull. Egyptian art is nothing if not repetitive, but items, if they can be viewed singly, are often of such exquisite workmanship and design that a museum showing only a few of them could be a tremendously exciting place.

. . . The Cairo Museum of Arab Art is enough smaller to be more readily assimilatible, and has some really charming things — fountains that are turned on by the guides when we walk in (one of them in the back of this nook), lots of handsome geometrically worked wooden doors, and other fittings for mosques. But most pleasant of all, the minor arts, the ceramics and bronze things for daily use done often with the finest craftsmanship level I've ever seen, but most important, done with a fine human sense of kindness and comedy, combined with real elegance of design. (Most especially, the birds show this, bronze ones and the ones a peculiarly handsome kind of gold and white ceramic that seemed to be very much in evidence.) Lots of lamps from the mosques, supposedly of great beauty, left me cold, but some Persian tiles in the next room with some buildings (the Kaaba in Mecca) shown in effective distorted perspective (like Bethlehem and Jerusalem beside the apse in S. Clemente in Rome, done in mosaic) were magnificent.

The American Express fixed us up with expensive tickets on what is surely the world's dirtiest train, to Luxor. But the arrival there had all the aspects of Torremolinos and Taxco and all the (few) other places with real charm. Bright moon, a warm night, a carriage ride through moon-colored empty streets and a palm grove to a hotel called the Savoy, whose name must be enshrined forever; directly on the Nile bank, with a terrace for tea and palm tree silhouettes and tremendous decaying ceilings. Another Agatha Christie setting, only this one failed to develop the requisite cast, nobody really seems interesting enough to murder. There was, to be sure, Abdul, who helped run a souvenir shop next door, and who had somehow picked up colloquial English in an American Mission School in the Sudan or somewhere.

The only Egyptian I remember who could make his countrymen seem funny, this done with offers to sell us the temple of Luxor, in the manner of the Sphinx vendors (price for Luxor was $200, but he'd trust us for the rest if we only paid $10 now). Or would we like that handsome jug, guaranteed to come from the tomb of Tutankhamen?

The big hotel in Luxor, a not very pleasant place, is, I hope, the only hotel in the world that has an entrance fee (20 P. T., 60¢) for nonguests who enter the lobby.

The University of Chicago maintains its Oriental headquarters a few minutes away from the Savoy, along the river road to Karnak. They are, it was admitted, a product of Rockefeller's megalomania, or desire to avoid taxes, or both, and are fantastically elegant for the handful of Egyptologists therein. Tea in the patio at dusk under the bougainvillea was exceedingly pleasant, with knowing conversation.

∼

Istanbul
Saturday, March 4, 1950

Dearest Mother, Aunt Bus, and Aunt Lou,

Istanbul is a fascinating place. Hebrard, at Michigan, had said that S. F. and Rio and Istanbul were the three most excitingly located cities in the world — and I guess he knew what he was talking about. It looks strangely like San Francisco, but very dirty and decrepit, and burned over, with all sorts of vacant lots. The only wooden city we've seen this side of the Atlantic — of course it's cold here, and has rained, which is difficult after the weather in Egypt and Cyprus — the place is a lot like Cincinnati, too, for some reason. The wooden houses make it look very American, but the hundreds of minarets on the skyline, and all the domes of the mosques, make it most exotic.

Istanbul.

Athens
Thursday, March 9, 1950

Dearest Mother, Aunt Bus, and Aunt Lou,

. . . Not any sightseeing today, except to visit a U. S. destroyer in the harbor —
guests of some ensigns we'd met yesterday — no boats were running on account of
the King & Queen of Greece were inspecting the U. S. ships, so we & the ensigns
hired a little pink & green rowboat and rowed out to the destroyer for lunch, with
everybody standing at the rail (they only do that for heads of state) grinning at us
messing up all the procedure in our rowboat — we had lunch on the ship & came
back late this afternoon, it was lots of fun, but it was certainly a relief to get away
from all those Americans, navy ones at that. . . .

We've seen the Acropolis — just once so far — of course and it's really the
most wonderful group of buildings I've ever seen — really breathtaking. I won't
try to say anything about it until I've seen other ancient Greek things, so I'll have
somewhere to begin. At the moment, words can't describe it.

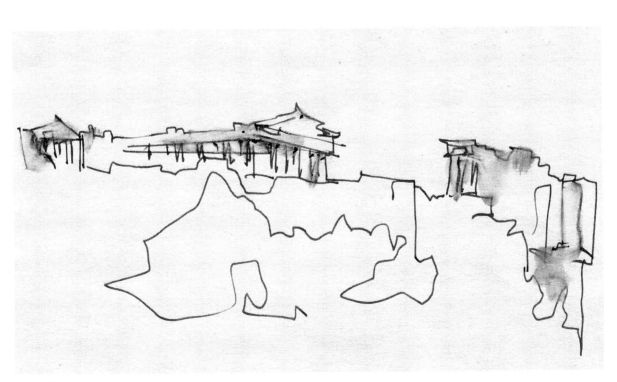

Acropolis.

Easter
Amstag, Switzerland

Dearest Mother, Aunt Bus, and Aunt Lou,

. . . and then, in the afternoon, to Mycenae — which was fun even for us, the same age — but it was one of the few places I've ever been, like the Roman forum, that seems still to have the people in it who were there once. It was a beautiful day, but a little forbidding in those ruins, and you could stand on the floor of what was the palace court and just *see* Clytemnestra and Aegisthus fixing Agamemnon's wagon, and imagine Electra streaming around the ramparts afterwards. There's still enough to make it all seem possible.

. . . then next day went out to the Palace of Minos at Knossos — 15th century B.C. and older, but it looks (it's restored) like a sort of modernistic version of Frank Lloyd Wright — that manages to be beautiful — Spiro (the Rome Prizer) and I decided to name it Taliesin Near East — we took lots of pictures and are going to expose FLW who probably has never even been there, poor man.

Palace of Minos, Knossos.

≈

Venezia
Monday, April 24, 1950

Dearest Mother, Aunt Bus, and Aunt Lou,

. . . then to Vicenza for the night — we saw lots of the Palladio work — some of which was very exciting, the Olympic theater, all very stagey, then some palaces, one of them the town museum, and the famous basilica, then we went out into the country to see the Villa Rotunda that so many people like Thomas Jefferson and the English architects after Inigo Jones had copied — it was all lots of fun — but weird with great bulbous statues that they seem to have bought by the hundreds at some factory in the neighborhood, the whole province is covered with them. Then we came on yesterday afternoon to Venice, put our car in the garage on this side of the causeway and got in a little boat, a motorboat, this one, for the Piazza San Marco, out of a little canal, and into the Grand Canal in the rain, but it was all like magic, it's just like all the pictures, and beautiful, all just seems like a fairy tale.

≈

Reggio Calabria

Dear Mother, Aunt Bus, and Aunt Lou,

. . . We had such a wonderful time in Venice — it doesn't seem real — with no cars or even bicycles to disturb the peace. The weather was perfect, still early enough to do the canals, hadn't started smelling yet. I'm going back for a few days to do a movie of St. Mark's Square, which is the finest open space I've ever seen anywhere. . . . We went out to the Lido with them and saw the famous Josephine Baker.

We drove with the Greenbergs (the N.Y. couple) to Padua, mostly to look at the Giotto chapel, then to Ravenna for a couple of nights and a day or so to see the fourth- and fifth-century mosaics — they were marvelous. By this time it was warm enough to swim in the Adriatic — which we did — we stayed another night in the Republic of San Marino, which was cute, like an operetta, went to Rimini (a church, important but ugly), Urbino (a beautiful Ducal palace), and San Sepulcro (a fine painting by Piero della Francesca — Aldous Huxley thinks it is the greatest in the world, which is silly), Arezzo (church) to Florence — but we only had a day in Florence — because we'd spent so much time in other places, before we had to hurry to Rome via San Gimigniano, where all the towers are.

Milan

Dearest Mother, Aunt Bus, and Aunt Lou,

. . . we all went to call on, and were shown around by, first, some of the important abstract painters there (very un-arty, businessmen kind of people, very nice) and then by the Belgiojoso, Peressutti, and Rogers office, who are of course the most important ones there — they'd been entertained (Belgiojoso, rather, who has just been to the States) by Joe Stein, among others, and by Spaulding in L.A., whom Peter's friend works for when he's there. So they were nice to us, and showed us some of their work, which was quite different from the Swiss things, and done under great hardships, but very, very interesting. . . .

Avignon
Wednesday, July 12, 1950

Dear Baileys,

The money received as we shot through Nice — thank you very much — it came in especially handy after (I shudder) a second camera theft — the new Viennese Leica went too — but still in Austria, so it was immediately replaced, with a new one sporting a wide-angle lens and a most distinguished mien.

The headlines in the local communist press are scaring the hell out of everyone

— which brings up my draft board, whom I just wrote a letter because my permission to be abroad was just about to expire. I asked them, while I was at it, to change my registration to Salt Lake, and told them, in the absence of an address for me, to get in touch with you if they want me to fill out some more of their interminable forms — so don't be surprised at any odd-looking notices coming your way.

Re this ever-delightful trip of mine: in the absence of lots of time, we've evolved what seems like a workable scheme, involving doing all the things we had in mind on the Continent, but skipping England entirely, on the theory that if the world is still worth living in *next* summer, a bicycling trip through England would be a fine thing, and one that involved a minimum of transportation worries and expenses. This new scheme has left us time to see some fascinating stuff — Vienna is the one place where I've ever felt I got what the baroque architects were driving at — on top of which the bookstores and food were marvelous, and disgustingly cheap — all very cinematic, too — we even had dinner with a Counter Intelligence Corps agent — dances and folk things in Kitzbühel, Austria, Alps, covered all the things on my Swiss modern list (except in Basel, which was too far) a couple more Maillart bridges, the most interesting, went to Nice to ship baggage about and get sunburned like a lobster, then came on here — the Provence things for the next few days, then Carcassonne, Albi, Puy de Domes, back to Vézélay, and Paris, then a Normandy Brittany trip and time on the Loire and at Chartres to finish things begun.

I *had* forgotten, in Italy, all the things that food could be. Now we're off to climb a tower and see the Golden Hour of Sunset slurping off the Palace of the Popes (the depraved interior of which we spent some of the afternoon staring at). A very quick bientôt.

〜

These next letters cover Moore's time in Korea.

January 20

Dearest Mother,

. . . The morning after I called you we went, as planned, to Travis Air Force Base, and by noon were on our way, on a Navy Super Constellation — beautiful big ship, but hardly any windows, so didn't see too much — laid over 4 hours in Hawaii, at night, but couldn't leave the terminal, so that was a loss — had lunch the next day on Wake Island. I didn't realize a tropical island could be such a mess — all shot up — white coral rock, shacks, and *hot*, then a couple of hours out from Tokyo a propellor came off and took the engine with it. We went into a dive — everyone put his lifebelts on faster than I'd ever seen — but only got really frightened when the crew panicked (sailors were being stewards on the plane) then everyone turned white and started shaking. I was so full of Dramamine that I didn't care especially what we did, but had a nice time watching the people turn pale. It was all O.K. though; we flew in on the other three motors.

Took a bus across Tokyo to Camp Drake. Tokyo is in many terrible ways a lot like Los Angeles — you can ride for three hours on a bus and never get out of the same sort of thing — like Whittier or El Monte on a tiny scale. And with smog all over everything — and rain. But there are all sorts of wonderful things to see, and I've had some marvelous long walks in neighborhoods away from the main shopping streets. Have seen and photographed (but there was no sun, and not much light) two beautiful large gardens, with lakes — had one exciting dinner in a real Japanese restaurant — where no one spoke English — a beautiful house — we sat on the floor and had sukiyaki cooked at the table by a woman in a beautiful costume. Eastern and Western costumes and houses and everything are all mixed up here. But the really Japanese buildings and costumes are mostly as beautiful as they're supposed to be. All the wood is natural, with a wonderful texture — very carefully fitted together — not at all crude like a Corbett house. Some of the handsomest houses I've seen have been the sets at the Kabuki (a sort of half play, half opera theater that looks like Grauman's Chinese). But the fine things are rare, and there's an awful lot of junk. Great bargains in the shops on things like cameras, mostly German, but nothing local I'd look at twice (except in a couple of shops that sell magnificent antique scrolls). No lacquer that isn't awful. Things may be different in Kyoto, or even here after you find the places.

Seoul
February 2

Dearest Mother,

The trip over wasn't much. I carried top-secret documents — pistol and all — left Camp Zama in the middle of the night, after the heaviest snowfall in Tokyo that anyone could remember — it stopped my trip to Kamakura — and I had to stay in all day at Zama — which was a disappointment, but the drive (30 miles or so) from Zama through little mountain villages in the snow to Tachikama Air Force Base, where I caught the plane, was beautiful. All the handsome details of the houses, which had been hidden in the snow in Tokyo, showed up in the villages, in the moonlight. In the snow with the steep roofs, they looked almost like Switzerland, only better. Didn't see much of Japan through the clouds, but as soon as we left Honshu (Japan) it got clear — and Korea was suddenly bright yellow-brown (Japan, just across the straits, is bright green) with mountains like the jagged ones along the road between El Paso and Las Cruces. Quite cold (not really so cold as advertised, though in the 20s and clear and dry — no worse than Salt Lake — and a great deal more comfortable than Michigan), almost no snow. Stayed in a replacement center at Yeng Dung Po (between Seoul and Inchon) for three days — that was a real dump. All the discomforts that people complain about — the town was horribly squalid — everyone cold and hungry, with brown shacks, dusty roads — everything brown.

≈

Dearest Mother,

I pushed through a 9-day Hong Kong leave in a hurry and am thrilled to have come — flew down from Seoul Sunday night — 9 hours non-stop — a beautiful flight — the smoothest I've ever taken — arrived Monday morning and what a beautiful place! I've always suspected Rio looks like this, but didn't realize Hong Kong did. After Seoul (or even Tokyo) the place looks incredibly prosperous, with elegant British cars whizzing around on smooth (!) streets, smart shops full of exciting stuff, wonderful restaurants — but the really exciting thing is the setting — dozens of Mexico City type skyscrapers perched on high vertical green mountains, with clouds swirling around the top of them, Telegraph Hill is 330 feet high — some of the hills here with apartments on the top are 1600. I rode a funicular to the top last night — to see the lights of Hong Kong and the boats in the harbor, and Kowloon on the other side. It was breathtaking!

≈

17 March

Dear Baileys,

A letter from Helsinki suddenly reminds me that the problem of my resignation is perhaps growing rather urgent.

Letter writing has so far been difficult, mostly on account of the unbelievableness of the whole situation. Who is to think, if I try to describe this marble palace, in a corner of which I'm presently sitting at a Mussolini-type desk, not far from the most interspatial martini-giving palace this side of the American Academy in Rome, who is to think that I haven't finally succumbed to some sort of Oriental anti-logic virus? This all to be taken against the background (kept at a respectful distance) of quite a handsome valley in what is certainly the most woebegone republic anywhere. Eight miles to Seoul, but alas our palace (which was once the technical college for the University of Seoul) is so much pleasanter than anywhere else I know of that going anywhere else gets to be something of a chore. Luckily, some of the best Buddhist buildings & tombs are a comfortable walk away. And Koreans do give rather sensational parties. I have a multiplicity of jobs, the total effect of which is rather shattering, but some of the details are very pleasant. Jobs involve being assistant operations officer for an Engineer Construction Group— the one that does most of the big construction in the Eighth Army are — being Troop Info & Education officer, which is rather a good thing — and unofficial Armed

Japanese Temple.

Forces Assistance to Korea office — which means that another architect-lieutenant and I do all the designing we have time for on the projects for Koreans (they put up the land, labor, & native materials. U.S. furnishes materials not available here — U.S. Army units give technical assistance). We're having a wonderful time with native methods and materials, and our own planning — I've done several churches and a high school so far, lately we've made a small standard church (horrors! mass production — but we think it's handsome) and a standard primary school (with our own brand plywood girders — we even found testing equipment in the basement, and have been running materials tests) the demand has grown to the point where we just hand out prints, like *Better Homes & Gardens*. This week I took on a hospital (200–300 beds + 200-student medical college + 150-student nurses college + 100-bed TB sanitarium — very handsome site) which will have to be done on a few odd evenings and a couple of weekends. Already have another TB sanitarium lined up for which we'll have to use the design we develop for the first project. It all sounds frightening — and the lack of study on these things (except for the very few buildings we have to choose as our standard ones) is maddening — but if we don't design them, they'll go without being designed at all. We're the approving agency, and I haven't yet got to the point where I'll sign my name to a classroom with medieval slits in the walls.

All sorts of intriguing information on hot floors and tile roofs — but the national feeling for design is pretty clumsy — not like the Japanese (all my modern-design-for-Korea is coming out astoundingly late — Fujiwara and I've planned, minute by minute, a week in Kyoto and Nara which will be mine, I hope in June).

No word from Princeton much — but word about acceptance (whether or no) should come in a month or so.

CHAPTER THREE

Princeton and Louis Kahn

Dissatisfaction with the architectural status quo was at the center of Moore's years as a graduate student at Princeton between 1954 and 1958. Architectural education throughout the country was ruled by the uncompromising doctrine of high modernism; Mies van der Rohe and Walter Gropius were seemingly indomitable figures who led the indoctrination. It was a time of sober slogans such as "I Like Ike" and "Less Is More." Growing baby boomers required an unprecedented number of new schools, hospitals, offices, and transportation infrastructures all built in massive "urban renewal" campaigns. The daunting momentum of postwar manufacture supplied architects with new materials, highly uniform and easily assembled, as a glance at period advertisements in architectural magazines reveals: "Grill-O-Metrics 3-Dimensional Aluminum Panels," "Concrete slabs cost less with Milcor Ribform," "Congoleum: NOW . . . color and decoration uniform all through," and "You can count on WARE curtain walls" were only a few of the industrial materials aggressively marketed.

In retrospect, it is clear that Moore was perched on the edge of an era, in one of those rare windows of time in architectural schools, where a convergence of faculty, students, and events sparks a period of inspiration and intensity and innovation.

Princeton in the late 1950s had such a phenomenal period. The university and its Gothic campus were very intentionally modeled to evoke in central New Jersey the cloistered aura of Oxford and Cambridge. Students (women were not admitted) wore jackets and ties to classes and black robes to dinner (Charles delivered Latin grace), and everywhere were affluent young men and eminent scholars.

Several qualities distinguished Princeton's school of architecture from others in America. First, the architecture and art departments not only shared a building but fostered strong academic links; extensive courses in art history for architects were required. Second, Princeton had a wealth of permanent faculty members instead of transitory, semester-long visits by notable architects, a common practice at other schools. Even more important, no single figure ideologically dominated the school the way that Gropius did Harvard or Mies did the Illinois Institute of Technology. Last, Princeton's comparatively small class sizes intensified contact between students and professors.

Jean Labatut (known as "Labbie" to the students), one of the last great Beaux Arts educators, represented the rich tradition of the Grand Prix de Rome. He was known as being a major force in the progressive wing of the Beaux Arts, with an interest in visual expression and perception. He was also renowned for his 1939 World's Fair water and fire spectacles. As director of design, his influence was important, and many regard him as one of the most underappreciated heroes of architectural education. Though Moore used some of his phrases such as "creative forgetfulness," he always maintained that Labatut was not as central a figure for himself as he had been for other Princeton students including, several years prior, Robert Venturi.

In addition to Labatut, the major design professors were Enrico Peressutti, Heath Licklider, and William Shellman, a Savannah gentleman with stunning graphic abilities, who taught drafting, drawing, and watercolor — "what he really did was teach us to see," remembered a student, Dan Peter Kopple. And everyone was keenly aware of Louis Kahn, who came to Princeton from his Philadelphia practice to lecture, and later taught a small design studio. Donald D. Egbert, Earl Baldwin Smith, David Coffin, and George Rowley conducted important seminars in history.

Although Moore arrived at Princeton on the G.I. Bill, he struggled financially. In one letter he wrote that he was "trying to find something to fling at my army of creditors to distract them, while I retreat one step further."

Older than most of the students, Moore carried the considerable experience of the previous six years — a world traveler and weathered architect — and became the central figure of a hugely talented quorum of graduates and undergraduates in both architecture and art, including Richard Peters, Donlyn Lyndon, William Turnbull, Jr., Hugh Hardy, John Woodbridge, Dan Peter Kopple, Felix R. R. Drury, Dale Sprankle, Fred McNulty, and Robert Harris. (Moore even shared an office with a young undergraduate, Frank Stella, of whom Charles once complained that he "was always getting paint on my chair.")

The energized interactions amongst these students generated a remarkable creative atmosphere. For the first years, Moore lived in the graduate student college, but later he had his own apartment near campus, which became the salon for the tight circle of architecture students: "It was total magic," remembered Richard Peters "and every night you gathered in Charles's apartment — it was the place to be." Over sherry (99 cents per gallon) and surrounded by Moore's growing collection of prints, books, and folk toys, the students would discuss late into the night slides from Moore's burgeoning international collection, all of them trying to outdo each other with their enthusiastic descriptions. In these sessions and in late-night ones over pizza and beer at the King's Inn, they began to weave together a shared set of enthusiasms, and Moore, as a leader, was often as engaging as the students' professors.

Hugh Hardy, a classmate of Moore's at Princeton, wrote the following reminiscence, which evokes the spirit that Charles helped to spark:

> I first met Charles Moore forty years ago. In 1954 we were Princeton graduate students, and at that time, both the University and architecture were constrained. Conformity was held in high esteem; there was a right way to do things, the good

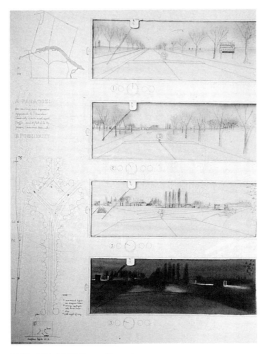
Windshield Wipers Drawing, 1954.

accepted way. Charles did not fit in to all that. No one had seen anything like him. It was not just his size that made him stand out, it was the wry language he used and the way he saw the world. He was not confrontational, but somehow the things he did seemed to be slightly askew from everyone else.

The school of architecture was in transition between the Beaux Arts ideals of Jean Labatut and the pragmatic, architecture-is-business approach of its new dean, Robert McLaughlin. Most of us lived in a gothic monastery, dined in long rows wearing academic gowns (thrown over a wide assortment of other apparel) in imitation of an English university. After his first year of living in Ralph Adam Cram's austere dormitory, Charles moved to the second floor of a house where he assaulted his rooms with color, graphics, and bookcases suspended from coils of perforated metal.

Our class was small, only five, and we were surrounded by rules so that Charles's gentle challenge of conventional wisdom was effective. Not everyone enjoyed this, but for those of us who did, he was the focus of great vitality. Our presentation boards were fixed in size, and on them we were supposed to render projects in tempera with brush, masking tape, and ruling pen, a medium of startling unpredictability. Instead, Charles presented his ideas in limpid, telling watercolors. And for those whose lettering was not up to standard we wrote in ink, using mechanical guides. Charles used pencil with a sure hand. If our assignment was to present a ground-level view of a building, he would put the viewer in an automobile, making the foreground a windshield, dashboard, and steering wheel — through which you saw the building. If an elevation view was called for, he might present his building as part of a great scroll containing its imagined neighbors. Rather than prepare an architectural thesis about buildings, his was about fountains, legitimizing their ephemera as the stuff of serious study.

His irreverence was compelling, and after the initial shock of meeting someone who actually went to architecture school in Michigan, it became obvious he bore uncommon intelligence with grace, leavening it with an uproarious sense of humor. Charles's visual memory was astonishing, having been honed at an early age by numerous cross-country trips with his formidable mother. But this ability was also accompanied by an equally developed capacity to recall names and dates. He also knew all the lyrics of popular songs from the thirties and forties. He even knew their verses! Charles could write clear, eloquent sentences in a first pass, seldom needing to struggle or recompose a confusing first draft. But he never paraded all these gifts, preferring to just quietly advance his own views, without the bombast which so often accompanies alternate ways of thinking and seeing.

Best of all, he was great fun to be with. The questioning never stopped. The looking at things never stopped. We drove all over New Jersey, looking at buildings. I had once seen a great Victorian barn from the train to Philadelphia and asked if he'd like to go find it. In minutes we were off to look, discovering along the way all sorts of visual splendors in places most people would ignore. Perhaps that was Charles's greatest gift, the one that made him such a fine teacher and ultimately a leader in our profession: the gift of making others see. So much of architecture is edited, cropped, and packaged for professional and public consumption. But Charles looked beyond conventional borders and frames to include the steering wheels, telephone poles, parking lots, banalities and flotsam of contemporary culture, as well as a lot from the dustbins of history. He celebrated what more formalist thinkers edited out of architecture, realizing that popular taste often holds a vitality and insight about human nature too valuable to ignore.

And he did love history! We were fortunate at Princeton to have access to instruction in architectural history in ways that were rare for the nineteen fifties. Art and architecture were taught in the same building, and unlike many other architecture schools of the period it was acceptable there to admire work conceived before modernism held sway. Charles did this with joyful, stunning abandon, incorporating ideas and elements borrowed from the past and adapted to totally new settings. His ability to absorb and transform ideas from earlier forms into contemporary expression was clear, if unorthodox, even then.

Architecture was for him a seamless panoply of discovery, not just a single orthodoxy demanding constant proof. That's what made it such fun to explore with him. Everything became interesting, whether the color of a wall, the geometries of a chimney, or the plan of a city. Everything mattered. Architecture was a big subject encompassing all of daily life, not just the stuff of monuments. It's no accident that Charles came to design so many houses, so many dissimilar ways for people to live. He was strongly committed to making places in which people could enjoy the quixotic nature of their own humanity. His rooms nourished all of the senses and encouraged their users to participate in their evolution, even after the architect had finished his work.

As I think about him now I cannot help but realize how shy he was then, how unsure of the appropriate response to the tyrannies and prejudices of Princeton in the fifties. At the same time, I realize how his gentle persistence changed the school and all of us. And now it is clear that in the same way he has done that to our profession, too, making it more responsive to humanistic values, less enamored of buildings made in the image of machines or fortresses. I suspect his sense of humor caused some not to take him seriously, but this response came from misunderstanding his manner, not his seriousness of purpose. Architecture for Charles was to be fully accessible to the public, not just the high priests of our profession. His was an architecture by, for, and of the people. At their best, his buildings expand experience, having an abundance of materials and a richness of imagery. He could make joyous places that seldom appear the same way twice.

Our small group was lucky to have Charles with us, long ago in the fifties. I could never have imagined then all he would accomplish, but it was clear that under his influence architecture would never be the same. He brightened and expanded our limited realm.

Moore's graduate work for his master's and Ph.D. consisted of both history and design. He finished both degrees in three years, an intense time that bespoke his focused approach.

George Rowley, an eminent scholar of Chinese art (at the time the discipline was still veiled in great mystery) was an important influence, particularly because Moore had just returned from the Orient. Rowley's presentations were spellbinding. After introducing at length a particular period, he would suddenly remove, in the dim room, a drape to reveal an exquisite Chinese artifact or rubbing. He stressed the "composition of three" (the pictorial device of layering fore-, middle- and background fields), theories of "chaotically multifarious" landscapes, the simplicity of parts, and the sense of order related to "additive" geometry about which Moore wrote in one of his examinations: "In additive *composition,* the elements, instead of being organized with each other as parts of a whole which is greater than the sum of the parts are simply added one after another, *in space* and in time, to be read as a narrative." The ink-wash technique of drawing a paintbrush across textured paper and responding quickly to the irregularities of its surface to create images also had an impact on Moore's graphic style, and the cascading, tumbling qualities of Chinese landscape scrolls showed up later in Moore's own fantasy drawings.

But there was also a deeper, more fundamental basis for Moore's fascination with the East (what he called in Korea the "Oriental anti-logic virus") that is perhaps described in a passage from Rowley's book, *Principles of Chinese Painting:* "The Chinese way of looking at life was not primarily through religion, or philosophy, or science, but through art. All their other activities seem to have been colored by their artistic sensitivity. Instead of religion, the Chinese preferred the art of living in the world; instead of rationalization, they indulged in poetic and imaginative thinking; and instead of science, they pursued the fantasies of astrology, alchemy, geomancy and fortunetelling."

Just before he passed away in 1956, E. Baldwin Smith taught a seminar "Palace, Temple, City, State," for which Moore wrote his first major Princeton paper on Medinet Habu, the tomb of Ramses III. It was an early study of dwelling symbolism:

"These buildings were, of course, symbols in an even more direct sense, since the walls of stone, where eternity was at stake, were made to serve as the permanent home of the living Horus, the kä of Ramses. The building of a house is often undertaken in our own time, by couples who are anxious to cement a shaky marriage, and who think that the creation of this symbol of security will be efficacious. It is not surprising that Ramses should regard the

Fantasy Layers.

construction of a stone house for his kä as a potent symbol of future security, even though some of its very stones had been erected with the same belief in their everlasting qualities." Moore continued by stressing that Medinet Habu also displayed a dissatisfaction with tradition. "It appears," he wrote, "reasonable to suggest then that Ramses III, late in his reign, found it desirable to substitute a new visual impression for the one which had, until that time, suited the mortuary temples of himself and his predecessors; and innovation replaced a rigid tradition."

Enrico Peressutti in the Yucatan.

The themes of tradition and innovation, context and history, the past and present, would resurface again and again in Moore's Princeton work.

Enrico Peressutti, the dashing architect of the Studio Architetti BBPR, flew between Princeton and Italy while his Torre Velasca "mushroom skyscraper" was under construction in Milan. (According to Peter Frantz, Moore may have briefly met Peressutti in Milan in 1950 when they visited the BBPR office on their European tour.) In his design studio the balance between old and new was a moral and aesthetic dilemma; these very issues Peressutti was struggling with in rebuilding postwar Italian cities, and he carried his concerns directly to Princeton. He championed field trips, and sponsored legendary excursions to the Yucatan, where Moore and others explored the Mayan ruins of Chichén Itzá and Uxmal, engulfed by jungles, in an era when such expeditions were rare, and many of the sites not yet excavated or understood. "Know what a wonderful trip it will be," Moore's mother wrote, "and how anxious you must be to see the ruins and Mexico from the air."

In 1957, Moore was Peressutti's teaching assistant in an architectural studio, where they devised student design projects such as a Jazz Centre for Newport, the rebuilding of a Georgetown block, and the redevelopment of the Chesapeake and Ohio Canal. "Present architecture," Peressutti wrote to Moore in July 1958, "is going through a very important period: the dogma of functionalism being surpassed as an already acquired fact, a wider and more free field of architectonic expression opens in front of us. We are these years, crossing the gate, architecturally speaking, between the recent past and the next future. Through this gate we must lead the students and it is of very great importance that we use in our discussions the right tools well defined and without possible misunderstandings. Because also the students must go through this gate."

During summer academic holidays, Moore returned to Monterey and worked for architect Wallace Holm. Moore designed an unbuilt motel for Cannery Row, "handled delightfully, full of the character of the place" Holm remembered, and also master planned a scheme for the Los Banos High School, also unrealized.

Monterey was also the site of Moore's master's thesis — a proposal to link the city's historic adobes with a pedestrian colonnade, in an attempt to investigate the "relation of the past to the present, and how to make the most of it." He also advocated lowering the major automobile arteries and preserving Monterey's open space with an overscaled Japanese stone garden or "sand plain." Moore's sensitivity and deferential embrace of history was novel for the time, and the project was even featured in the *AIA Journal,* a rare honor, considering it was student work.

Project for Los Banos High School, Monterey, Wallace Holm with Charles W. Moore, 1956.

Moore began the journal essay with an evocative declaration about the emerging relationships between city and history:

> Our relationship to our past is not a simple one. We are not carrying on in our cities an unbroken architectural tradition; but the relics of all the past are available to us as they have never been to a civilization before, and we find ourselves anxious to extract meaning from them, perhaps more anxious than any previous civilization has ever been. Our cities grow quickly obsolete, and are rebuilt. Their buildings do not long retain their usefulness, though sometimes their power over our imagination increases with their age. We cannot seek the comfortable continuity of a medieval village; instead, as Henry James pointed out, "We are divided . . . between liking to feel the past strange and liking to feel it familiar; the difficulty is, for intensity, to catch it at the moment when the scales of the balance hang with the right evenness.

The drawings (Moore sometimes waited until the final night's projects were due to suddenly render his ideas) were accomplished perspectives, the observer framed within the arcade gazing out to the adobes.

When one of the journal's subscribers wrote a critical letter about the project, Moore responded with the following letter:

> I read with interest and enthusiasm your open letter in re Enhancement of Monterey, to Messrs. Watterson, Reed, Labatut, and Moore, and was ready to turn the rascals out until I recalled that I was one of them. I remembered then that my scheme for the "enhancement" of old Monterey was out to protect those very

values that you sound like you're in favor of, the ones that make you like particularly to go to Monterey. My contention, though (and this seems to be the basis for our difference), is that like freedom, which is said to disappear if it is not actively defended, the qualities of a place like Monterey cannot these days remain long unsubmerged without some active help. You take comfort, for instance, in the boats (and I wouldn't change them) that still roll with the groundswell off Fisherman's Wharf. Did you know, though, that not many months ago a bond issue which would have replaced all that with a commercial marina came within a few votes of carrying? You are also optimistic about the pleasures of finding an adobe, unextricated and unenhanced, in the back alleys of a "salty and brawling place like Monterey." I'd like that, too, but there aren't any more. In the absence of any positive plan for hanging on to them, they have gradually disappeared, as Monterey's plaza did, to make way for civic improvements like gas stations, which you didn't mention after your recent visit to salty and brawling Monterey, although there seem to be more of them than of anything else. The place *needs* something. Enhancement, I guess I'd call it.

You don't seem to like my more or less architectural innovations much. I use a big empty space where it exists, and where it seems like it will do the most good to set off some adobes that were built on a wide-open greensward, and you want to have riots in it. The state highway engineers did you one better a few years ago. They wanted to have a freeway there, complete with cloverleaf. And then I made a colonnade for the same reason people have always made colonnades (shelter from the sun and rain, and some sort of architectural unity, otherwise termed camouflaging unfortunate buildings) and you call it a garage. Well, I have you that time. It's too small for your car to fit.

Now I won't apologize for my effort's being a "Master's thesis at heart," since that seems a healthy characteristic for master's theses. And your suggestion that we consider enhancing Manhattan instead of Monterey falls not uncongenially, since another Master's thesis at Princeton has undertaken this past year to do just that, by finding a use for Ellis Island. Apparently it's a word that comes between us: "Enhancement," I gather, makes you see red. Webster stays calm long enough to identify it with advancement, which qualifies generally as a laudable claim. I was brought up, as a matter of fact, to believe that the central task of architects and their architecture is to enhance the whole environment, which often turns out to consist mostly of existing buildings. I grant you that the process is far from automatic; there have to be decisions that advance some things (like adobes) and sink some things out of sight (like Cadillacs, right up to the tail fins). I didn't *bring* the Cadillacs, which are already there. I'm *sinking* them.

It is doubtless captious chauvinism from a northern Californian (but it's irresistible) to wonder whether it isn't a lack of concern for the enhancement of things (satisfying things, which mostly come without tail fins) which has helped cause Los Angeles, with its vast array of first-rate new buildings, to be a city so generally deplored. "Strange," as you point out, "how customs vary . . ."

Monterey Master's Project.

> Yours for adobes on the green, Cadillacs in the ground, and salty brawling riots in the square. And for the groundswell off the wharf, which will come and go without enhancement.

Moore's doctoral dissertation was a far-reaching study of water and architecture, a subject that would occupy his thoughts and lectures for the rest of his life. Again, the idea of absorbing history and using the past to enrich contemporary design was at the heart of his work. From the very opening sentences of the dissertation, Moore stated clearly his discontent with current attitudes, using aridity as a metaphor for the emptiness of his generation's concept of design: "Dissatisfaction is the provocation for every thesis — dissatisfaction, and the hope that the discovery, organization, and possibly creation of ideas might do something to improve the situation. The provocation for this thesis was dissatisfaction with the aridity of much of our own architecture, coupled with the observation that water has just those qualities which arid buildings lack: it invites approach, and it remains captivating for periods of prolonged contact."

He described the outline of his thesis to Carol Selby, a friend who had been the librarian at the University of Utah:

> The thesis is in the throes of confusion and dismay, and I daren't set foot out of Princeton. I went off to the Library of Congress for four days and precipitated a

Proposed Seagram Fountains.

crisis last month. They are right. I should have lots by this time, and instead, practically nothing is put to paper. Even the outline shifts daily. Last week it included a chapter on the nature (physical) of water, a chapter on water symbolism, one long and complicated one on water as symbol of nature in which somehow man's relation to nature, in its power as master of it, or in partnership with it, is tied up with the form of water: still, running, falling, squirting, with hopefully some [?] with the symbolic connotations of it all. Next come, I think, ones about water and geography, climate, sculpture, flowers, rocks. Then more analysis of examples historical and my own — my own being a road from Marble Canyon toward Glen Canyon dam with a design in time through water symbolized on the desert, past all sorts of pools to jets and the dam itself. All this countered by a set of fountains for Park Avenue, the Lever House, Seagram Bldg., St. Bartholomew's Section, which would be great fun if I had less talk and more results. The schedule, which is relatively rigid, demands that I must have a plausible first draft by June, and a final version to present by 1 September, after a summer in Monterey. It must all be over by the start of the fall term, which will be, it seems from here, the millennium, with apartment, hopefully a Volkswagen (no car at all now), and Time. I'm tiring, you may be sure, of this never-ending struggle.

I wish I had a thesis. I'd love to show it to you — maybe in June — I hope. Plans for heading west depend on transportation and things. Are you coming to N.Y. this month? Write me what's going on. Why don't you have the Eames Chair in Detroit — then I can steal it from there if I get nasty enough to do that.

[Charles had loaned Carol his Eames bent plywood chair around 1955. One day, I was with Charles in his Austin house, when a large box arrived via UPS. I opened the box, and in it was the chair. Without missing a beat, Charles glanced at it and said, "Aha, Carol's finally returned my chair." That was in 1992.]

In the Princeton studios, students were assigned to assist other students who were finishing thesis drawings so that all could learn how to cooperatively produce sets of drawings. Felix R. R. Drury, who would later teach with Moore at Yale, was a graduate student who assisted Moore with his water and architecture drawings. The following letter, written from Pebble Beach on July 13, 1957 (where Moore was struggling to finish his dissertation), offers a glimpse into Charles's thought processes behind his design work and the sense of collaboration that Moore brought to the design table.

Alas, the position of my head during those last frenzied hours in Princeton is hardly to be described. As for the large fat envelope, all I can imagine, at this stage, is that I heaped it into the one closet so the moths wouldn't get it. Therefore, first favor: would you unseal the door (the drafting tape has probably already fallen off), beat off the moths I locked inside, and look I think on the floor of the closet — where things are heaped in disarray. The envelope, an 11 x 14 one, I think, contains Labbie's glass slides, rolls of negatives, folded up USGS survey

Proposed Lever Court Fountains.

photostats, zip-a-tone, etc., etc. as well as the vital thesis drawings and photostats, so it should, I hope, be easy to spot in its fatness. If it's not there, then (moan) it just might be stuffed into the top of one of the drawers, at random. I must have been afflicted with some sort of neatness spasm in the apartment — I can't imagine that I would have dropped it casually on campus.

As for St. Bart's. You are, to be sure, quite right. Your sketch of the fountain, reindicated, seems certainly a good idea — the copper plates bare, as you point out, do make the edges work. I messed for hours with the terrace — it's too bare without anything but the lonely bench. Almost everything I tried that seems interesting in itself was much too overpowering for the fountain. I had, for a while, Seagram-like contoured surfaces with straight-lined prows of plants riding above them and merging in places, à la Nicola — too busy — finally tentatively produced the enclosed — the dotted lines represent 2" contours, the solid lines an almost vertical drop — so as to make sort of curved prow shapes that rise above the terrace, hold people precariously around the edges, plants in pockets near the top. Azaleas —

white, when it flowered would suggest foaming water, say the residents of Nippon. What does this do for you? Change anything. I don't really feel I have the right to sit here in California and re-do St. Bartholomew's.

I wish I had found Goodhue's Persian Gardens article. I'll look for it in San Francisco later this month. I looked for it once — obviously not very effectively. Ooooh — another favor: There is a Gordon Cullen article on Immediacy — all very key — on page 237 and thereabouts of some

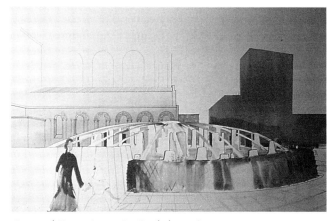

Proposed Fountains at St. Bartholomew's.

Architecture Review — question — which one? (Month-Year-Volume-number) possibly 1952. Would you dig up the date? I have the quotes from the article, from one of Heath's clippings which didn't show the date. I expected all that here — but don't.

I wish I could report more progress than there has been at this end. I've been working steadily enough (with far more sleep, than heretofore) but the results are pathetic — some 15 pages to date — but it's picking up.

Moore's dissertation was controversial with the Ph.D. examiners (Egbert, Coffin, Labatut, Licklider, and McLaughlin) because Moore relied on extensive literary references, from Lao Tse to Edgar Allan Poe to Gaston Bachelard, to trace the symbolism of water. But he also focused on the physical effects of water on buildings, water as expression of nature, and various realms of water in architecture: fountains, canals, pools, and the sea. The design part of the dissertation included fountains and water scenery; on a pedestrian scale Moore designed fountains for the Seagram Building (some quipped "whiskey fountains"), Lever House, and St. Bartholomew's in Manhattan; on a scale geared to cruising automobiles, Moore designed scenarios in which water arced over Highway 89 below the Glen Canyon Dam. Moore completed his dissertation and presented his work to the assembled school in a grand presentation (his mother made the trip from California), for which he played master of ceremonies and orchestrated several hydrologic acts, such as sending streams through specially designed downspouts.

In all of these Princeton projects, Moore was struggling to find expression for a new architectural language — however young, immature, tentative, and full of searching all of the early 1950s boomerang and pork chop shapes and folded-concrete-plate arcades were.

When he was awarded his doctorate, Moore was also made a proctor and then granted a postdoctoral fellowship, so he could stay at Princeton and teach. He continued to work on Camillo Sitte's *The Art of Building Cities* and started yet another project, unsuccessfully planned to be a book, on the history of plaster, with special emphasis on the highly skilled plasterers of Moorish Spain who wrought, with stunning intricacy, geodic interiors.

That extra year at Princeton led to a paramount experience: When Charles volunteered to assist Louis Kahn in a small design studio, Kahn agreed to teach for Princeton students.

Kahn was on his way to becoming one of the most significant architects of the twentieth century. He was a mystic, given to poetics ("Wonder has nothing to do with knowledge"), and based his architecture on pure geometry and a penetrating reverence for materials and light.

Because Kahn rarely could be drawn away from his studios, Moore and the students drove to Philadelphia to present their work. Those who worked in Kahn's office at the time remembered Kahn's generosity in receiving guests and visitors — and his growing acclaim brought many.

Kahn's lessons had a clear and important impact on Moore's work. He pressed the students to validate every detail of their designs. Everything had to have a reason. The purity of form and discipline of geometry were essential, as was Kahn's willingness to draw from historic form and precedent. Several of Kahn's buildings particularly influenced Moore: the American Federation of Labor Medical Building, with its layered "skin and bones" structure; the unbuilt Goldenberg House; and the Trenton Bath House, with its simple cluster of pyramidal roofs. Kahn's structures summoned the power of the aedicula — the four-posted canopy — and the emotional charging of space, which related to a book that was very important for many of the Princeton students, Sir John Summerson's *Heavenly Mansions*.

Trenton Bath House, Louis Kahn, 1957.

In it, Summerson analyzed the aedicula. Besides poetically establishing a place, Summerson also pointed out that the aedicula has been used either to create a dollhouselike miniature world for the imagination, such as the ones that encrust Indian temples, or to do just the opposite — to magnify human presence that might otherwise be dissipated, as the Baldachino does for people within the swallowing void of Michelangelo's dome at St. Peter's. As a manipulator of scale, the aedicula was an important part of Kahn's architecture, and it would become an integral device in Moore's work.

Kahn's inexhaustible dedication to architecture also made deep impressions. Though their expressions would eventually diverge, Kahn and Moore shared an uncommon energy and a childlike curiosity for the world. "It's the fairy tale," Kahn once said, "that is so important. I know if I were to think of changing my profession at this moment I would think of one thing — that I would love to write the new fairy tales."

Many years after Kahn's death, Moore reminisced, "Of course [Kahn] did, in his buildings, make magic and write architectural fairy tales at a time when the world most desperately needed them."

≈

The following is Moore's remembrance of Louis Kahn.

On March 17 in 1974 the world suddenly seemed much older when Louis Kahn died in New York in Pennsylvania Station.

The Yale Art Gallery and the Yale Center for British Art, two buildings flanking Chapel Street, mark the beginning and the end of his career — the architect who for so many of us meant more than any other in our time. As so often happens with architects, that beginning did not come until late. Lou Kahn was already in his fifties when President Griswold asked him to design the Yale Art Gallery. That became, as the critics say, his first "mature work"; it was just 20 years later that death overtook him and stunned the rest of us.

The blow was staggering, not because 73 is so young, but at least partly, I suppose, because we thought he was immortal. He had no connection with death; he didn't even seem to need sleep, and because the loneliness of a great man dying in Pennsylvania Station, ninety miles from home, after a trip from Bombay, and having his very identity mislaid in a series of police blunders, made it shudderingly clear how late in the century it had become. It was suddenly so dark, when the light we all were used to went out.

An obituary described some of us as his "disciples," but I think the term didn't fit. Kahn was never a master in the sense that he required from us some sort of devoted followship. His great strength as a teacher, as he once pointed out, was that he wasn't facile. Things didn't come easily to him. The struggle to understand, and get it right — more difficult but more exhilarating than any architectural struggle I, for one, had ever known — was a struggle which involved him as well as his students. He wasn't, when I knew him best, laying down laws from on high; like the rest of us, he was looking for those laws, and making the search take on a transcendental importance. He said wonderful things along the way that filled our notebooks ("the sun didn't know how wonderful it was until its rays fell on the wall of a room"), but the notes didn't always seem, away from the context of the particular search, to make much communicable sense. Even the buildings, magic as they were and seemed, were not altogether complete and independent of the search. I remember someone asking Kahn how he could justify the elevator tower on his little AFL-CIO Medical Center in Philadelphia as architecture. "That's not architecture," was the reply. (That little building, torn down in 1973, was my favorite work of Kahn's, the clearest and richest expression of skeleton and skin I know of.)

I was profoundly changed by his teaching. I first met him in 1955, in the Princeton Graduate College. He was on a panel about Monumentality (remember that special issue from the fifties?) with Paul Rudolph. I was fresh from some time in Korea, and had never heard of Kahn. I was struck with how small he was, and how badly his face was scarred from a fire when he was a small child in Estonia. And I can't remember anything he said. Paul Rudolph was teaching that term at Princeton, and Kahn had come down from Yale, though he was a Philadelphian. My most vivid image of Kahn at the time (because it was so hard to imagine), was of him as the sidekick of Edward Durell Stone. The two of them, it was said, played violin and piano (for money or dinners?) during the Depression.

In the late fifties, Paul Rudolph went to Yale and Kahn left for the University of Pennsylvania. His office in Philadelphia grew. It was run then by Tim Vreeland, now at UCLA, whom Lou thought was the best American architect. (I think he may have been, as usual, right.)

[Editor's Note: When I contacted Timothy Vreeland about this, he wrote: "Kahn (and Moore) are too generous in their assessment of me. Lou was always very supportive. I went to work for him in 1955, six months after graduating from Yale. The office was small then, eight or nine people at the most. It was not structured at all. No hierarchy. We all did everything. I vividly remember at one point Lou emptying the wastebaskets during a charette because we were all so occupied.

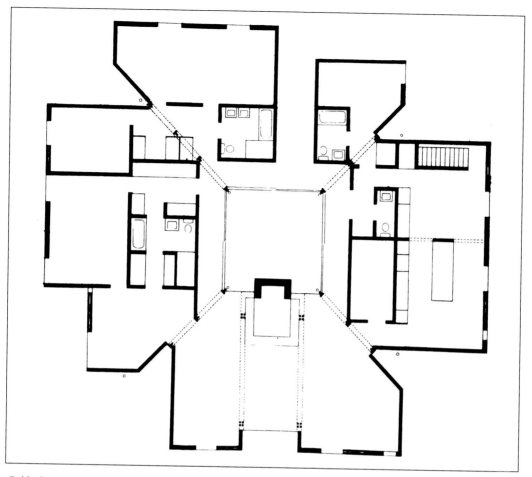

Goldenberg House Project, 1959. Louis I. Kahn Collection, University of Pennsylvania and Pennsylvania Historical and Museum Commission.

As Kahn said, 'There was no one else to do it.' David Wisdom, an older man (the rest of us were in our twenties), was senior draftsman or 'chef d'atelier' as I used to think of him, and he really ran the office if anyone did."]

In the school year 1958–59, when I was teaching at Princeton, Kahn became (on the side, of course) a thesis critic there. I volunteered to help, because every minute with him meant so much to me, so one night a week, four students and I would drive to Philadelphia, meet Lou in his office after dinner, see what was going on, then sit around his desk while he looked at the four theses, and criticized them, and elicited criticisms from us. He talked about his current projects (there was the Jewish Community Center in Trenton, which was never built, and there were the Richards Laboratories at Penn, and later the Salk Center). Those evenings were food for a lifetime, not so much for those aphorisms that were filling our notebooks as for the communicated sense of caring about how the bricks in the Richards Laboratories wanted to sit on each other, for instance, or particularly,

AFL-CIO Medical Center, Louis Kahn, 1950–51.

about the student projects in front of him. Those student projects got the full weight of his concern, not as reflections of himself, but as serious, independent works. His scorn (and it could be very uncomfortable) was reserved for the projects that had been encrusted with the shapes of Kahn's own recent inventions, and his most joyous transports came from the projects where new institutions could find form. His favorite of those theses, I guess, was one done by Robert Church, who became, before his death, Dean of Architecture at the University of Tennessee. Church was designing an athletic center for Stone Mountain, near Atlanta, and Kahn managed to impute an Olympian splendor to the act of suiting up for the events there, or even of parking your car to spectate.

My role after those thesis sessions in Philadelphia had been to expand upon them, back at Princeton with the students. We all read different meanings into them, of course, but every word had had a moment. After that I went to Berkeley, where Kahn would sometimes come to talk, and I found myself again as his interpreter afterwards. That was much harder. The weight of Kahn's thought, and especially his care, was not really compressible into a ninety-minute lecture, and my explanations didn't effect any real reconstitution.

Projects I had seen in his office were built, and some, especially the Salk Center in La Jolla, seemed to possess true magic. And fascinating new commissions came, in India and Pakistan and Venice and across the United States. But the burdens of fame must have brought him closer to despair than even his failing vision (which was repaired). Most of us who had been moved by him speculated about his late works, before they came. Wouldn't they be in some way like the deaf Beethoven's late quartets? Because, thanks in some part to him, we were looking to history for parallels, and for direct inspiration, and for help.

The late works came, but unless I misunderstand, weren't like the Beethoven quartets; they were more confident and complete than Kahn's own earlier works, simpler and clearer, far less tentative, far less full of that searching which lay at the center of my regard for him. There was never, though, not much room for disappointment. Perhaps he had found something at the end of his lifelong quest, and that the preferences of some of the rest of us for the rainbow rather than the pot of gold might be temporary too.

But I don't think it occurred to any of us that he was mortal. He had, like Aalto had, a period of eclipse in student favor during the late sixties, when the rhetoric of search and service underwent sudden change, but the kind of rabbinical sense that he was the grand bearer of a sacred architectural message gave us sustenance because he was there. There was hardly any room left for such grandeur of spirit to arise soon again. And it was even harder, after those dismal lonesome events in Penn Station, to recall that his grandeur was based on deep humility and the honesty of his search, and was transmitted to a great many people, so it did not vanish in the circumstantial act of dying. But Lou Kahn is — must be — a spirit that will live.

Louis Kahn (center) and Enrico Peressutti with Students.

CHAPTER FOUR

MLTW and the Sea Ranch

Moore's first architectural firm, MLTW, was, in its early days, a collaborative venture among four idea-sharing moonlighters.

It began when Moore came to Berkeley from Princeton in September 1959 after William Wilson Wurster, the dean of the school of architecture, invited him to join the faculty, partly on the recommendation of Roger Bailey. Wurster's enthusiasm about drawing Moore away from Princeton was evident in a letter dated November 24, 1958:

> What a brilliant and wonderful record you have. Small wonder that Bob [McLaughlin] regrets anything which will take you from there. I am moved by your willingness to make a decision which will await another one before things are final. I will proceed with as much speed as possible. If you had a portfolio of your work — particularly the executed things — it would be helpful with the committee. Also any reprints of articles. In short, the works.
>
> Please know I realize the richness you are contemplating leaving, and we appreciate the solid ground you represent. At this end we will make no presumptions and will offer you the very best we can do.

When Moore returned to the Bay Area, he began a new series of collaborations with Hervey Parke Clark and even became an associate of Clark's firm. Again, Hervey Clark took advantage of Charles's design skill. An important project, although never built, was a church on the Pacific Union campus in Angwin, California. Charles's hand was absolutely clear, and the project was full of premonitions of his coming work: a broad court surrounding an arcade, a volume shooting up to establish a tower, and broad, crisply edged, angled planes sweeping down to cover the spaces.

Another important project was the addition of a circulation tower to the 1902 Citizens Federal Savings Bank building on an awkward gore corner in San Francisco. It was a vivid opportunity to work with the past and present that Moore struggled with at Princeton, and in the "real world" this kind of sensitivity was absolutely unique. Alan Morgan, another associate, was, with Clark, largely responsible for the design that was built. (Morgan did not develop Moore's first design.) Moore had some involvement with details that expressed a respect for the context, and certain qualities, both in plan and elevation, recall "servant space" ideas of Louis Kahn.

With growing academic responsibilities and a desire to establish an independent reputation, free of Clark's conservatism, Moore chose to break with Clark and Beuttler in July 1962. "More important is my own need to be," he wrote to the partners, "at this point in my career, really intimately involved with some buildings, and responsible, in detail as well as in general, for them."

Thus, Moore was free to devote more time to his own firm.

Donlyn Lyndon and William Turnbull, Jr., also came to the Bay Area from Princeton, and Richard Whitaker, one of Moore's teaching assistants at Berkeley, joined them. Each letter of the firm's name, MLTW, stood for a partner. All had commitments either at the university or in other architecture firms: Moore and Lyndon had full teaching schedules, Turnbull was working for Skidmore, Owings, and Merrill; and Whitaker was finishing his graduate work and raising a young family. From tiny studios and in design sessions at a local diner, MLTW operated on "the midnight oil," led by Moore who, with almost unbelievable energy, was committed to establishing their work.

Aspects of MLTW would become standard qualities of Moore's later architecture firms. First, Moore always filled his offices with students who were given many responsibilities. Marvin Buchanan, Edward Allen, and Richard Dodge were some of Moore's first draftsmen. Second, ideas drove the pencils: there were always strong connections between explorations in the university studios and the ones on the office drafting boards.

Pacific Union Church Project, Clark and Beuttler with Charles W. Moore, 1961.

Whitaker wrote:

> With Charles, teaching was both an optimistic and a subversive act. He had a commitment and belief in the future, while questioning and even overthrowing authority. I suppose you could say his was an act of creating troublemakers. He taught us to suspend disbelief — a studio class with Charles was at least bizarre by any normal standards — and suddenly, just when you thought you were only having fun, you found that you had taken possession of a new set of ideas. You had learned something.

According to Lyndon, Moore was a "pivotal figure" in Berkeley's ascendancy to one of the most important centers of new architectural thought. Together, Moore and Lyndon taught courses in Eastern architecture and design studios. And in 1962, William Wurster and Vernon DeMars appointed Moore chairman of the department.

The years during which Wurster and his wife, the city planner Catherine Bauer (author of the influential *Modern Housing*), were establishing the College of Environmental Design, or CED, were the golden years at Berkeley.

Citizens Federal Savings, Clark and Beuttler with Alan Morgan and Charles W. Moore, 1960–61.

Wurster's approach was antidoctrinaire. He preferred an "organized chaos" of ideas, with the architects, landscape architects, and urban planners all grouped in the CED. There was an extraordinary wealth of talent — Wurster and Bauer; Moore and Lyndon; and Joseph Esherick, Vernon DeMars, Richard Peters, Sim van der Ryn, Ezra Ehrenkrantz, Spiro Kostoff, Norma Evenson, Jack Kent, Patrick Quinn, Francis Violich, Garrett Eckbo, Denise Scott Brown, Horst Rittel, Christopher Alexander, among many others, all of whom represented an array of interests and disciplines from urban theory to building technology, and from mathematics and computers to architectural history. (Once when Peressutti visited, he likened the busy activity in the school to a "nest of ants.")

Wurster was not only the guiding force at Berkeley but was a leading figure in the California architecture scene. He was an unfailing gentleman with a formidable presence, a sense of humor, and a serious commitment to design, sometimes summed up as an "iron whim." He believed in innovation, both in architecture and education, and dismissed stale ideas that were kept alive merely for the sake of tradition. "Gone are the days," Wurster said in his 1969 Gold Medal speech, "that importance is placed on permanence and massiveness. I never will be in the position of an architectural friend of mine who spoke with bitterness that architecture was not permanent anymore. I take exception to his whole emphasis, for there must be great changes, with new things crowding along with rich ideas."

Wurster's California residential design, with its shedlike simplicity and respect for the vernacular, is an important precedent to Moore's and MLTW's early houses. Most important was Wurster's Gregory Farm House, built in 1927, a cleanly detailed, simple group of structures arranged around a court that Wurster derived from local farm structures and, in fact, could be mistaken for such.

The kind of intimate inhabitation that Wurster could evoke surfaced in MLTW's work. When we inhabit, either individually or collectively, we fill a space with personal presence, and make it our own, all having to do with Moore's principle that a house should make its inhabitants feel they are at the center of the world.

In those late night sessions at Princeton, Moore, Lyndon, and Turnbull had begun to develop a common set of imagery, and wanted to test their ideas in actual buildings. "Our work at MLTW was based on two ideas," Moore said, "the second of which was identical to the first." First was the aedicula of Summerson and Kahn, the four-columned canopy that delimited space — a place — by pinpointing a particular, precise, and central spot on the planet. The second idea was the saddlebag: a room, bay, alcove, or window seat attached to a main spine or central space, making an extended place to inhabit with your body or imagination.

Every house that passed through the MLTW studio had either (or sometimes both) saddlebag or aedicular elements. Perhaps the most important was Moore's own house of 1961 in Orinda, California. Though cheap ($5,000) and small (seven hundred square feet), the house caused architectural tremors. In a decisive move of great clarity and wit, Moore boldly broke from the shackles of modernist ideology. It was astoundingly fresh. Modernism's sacred flat roof was swept away and replaced with a pyramidal roof. Even more to the point, the house was a simple pavilion of banal materials, defying the convention that a building had to be monumental in order to be architecture. Salvaged architectural columns supported the roof so the walls could be made of sliding barn doors

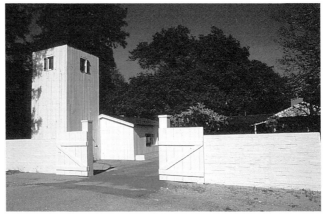

Gregory Farm House, William Wurster, 1926–27. Photo by Daniel Gregory.

that opened the corners, extending the space into the meadow. The bed, bathtub, kitchen, and living room were housed in the same space, sheltered under or around dual aediculas. All of the simple components established subtle layers of space.

Two tiny weekend houses, known as the Jobson House (1961) and the Bonham Cabin (1962), were also breakthroughs. They too were tiny, each fewer than one thousand square feet, and were built with similarly minuscule budgets. Their simple exteriors did not reveal the stunning architectural space that suddenly exploded when you stepped inside. The Jobson House, an aedicula house with saddlebags, was deemed a "redwood tent," since its thin container (golden inside, weathered outside), framed with sturdy beams, evoked powerful feelings of shelter, canopy, and center. The Bonham Cabin was a tiny house with a dramatic wall of glass, hung with "pouches" of space. Since bulky furniture would quickly overcome the limited floor space, Moore incorporated window seats and wide steps, further emphasizing human contact with the architecture. With great notoriety, these three projects established a new "California look" in American design: open space extending into the roof, "exposed" structure, natural materials, outdoor space (with little yardlike landscaping), and a casual elegance.

Pop art and supergraphics were also important developments in Moore's early work and in later work on the East Coast. Artists Barbara Stauffacher Solomon, Mary Ann Rumney, and Tina Beebe collaborated with Moore throughout his career in painting building interiors and developing color schemes. In the first Sea Ranch Swim Club, Stauffacher Solomon originated the painting of bright supergraphic numbers, stripes, dots, and arrows, guiding swimmers to showers and saunas and making a surprising contrast to the unadorned barnlike exteriors. The decoration was meant to be cheap, thin, and easily invented. As the notoriety of the pop art movement increased, Moore commented that "I think the danger in pop art is that if it's taken seriously, it becomes automatically expensive. I think the importance is that the decoration should really be cosmetic — it should be very cheap and able to be redone, changed by the people, and reconsidered by the people who live there." The wild graphics would appear in many of Moore's projects: at Kresge College, Moore and students painted patterns and rainbows; at the Murray House in Cambridge, a lightning bolt zipped across the folded ceiling plane; and the graphics actually were electrified in neon at the Santa Barbara Faculty Club and at Moore's New Haven house.

Photography also played a key role in MLTW's success. Morley Baer, a celebrated architectural photographer, shot many of Moore's early buildings, and his dramatic, striking images were included in many national journals. Whenever Baer was hired to photograph a new house, Moore would accompany him, often carting his own furniture to the site in a pickup truck. He would then empty the client's house and redecorate with carpets, furniture, and Mexican folk art. "Unlike most other architects," Baer recalled, "Charles understood the importance of photography and how spaces photographed. He knew what to do with each residence, what to move in, and how to arrange it to make a great photograph."

Moore's early work, both independent and with MLTW, gained important recognition. Awards came design after design; the Hubbard, Jobson, Orinda, Bonham, Jewell, Lawrence,

Sea Ranch Swim Club I, MLTW/Moore-Turnbull, 1966, Landscape by Lawrence Halprin. Photo by Morley Baer.

Sea Ranch Swim Club I, MLTW/Moore-Turnbull, Supergraphics by Barbara Stauffacher Solomon, 1966. Photo by Morley Baer.

and Johnson Houses all won citations and were published in architectural journals. *Life* magazine also featured the Jobson House in 1965, catapulting Moore to a national audience.

Moore's criticism of high modernism became more unequivocal and eloquent. In the late fifties, Moore began writing book reviews for architectural journals, and as his reputation as an architect suddenly erupted, he was asked to write critical articles aimed at exploring new methods of analyzing places and criticizing the monotonous formalism into which architecture had fallen. Moore's first important article was published in the autumn 1962 issue of J. B. Jackson's *Landscape* magazine. The article, "Toward Making Places," included essays by Moore and Lyndon, as well as Patrick Quinn and Sim van der Ryn, two other Berkeley colleagues. Moore's opening statement revealed the dissatisfaction and questioning that lay beneath MLTW's work:

> Architecture is in a bad way. It is taught as a craft and its best disciples are craftsmen. They learn to respect the nature of materials, to organize surfaces and solids. Sometimes they master the molding of space, and a few can learn to manipulate the magic flow of light (while others learn to manipulate the magic flow of money). Our magazines are filled with handsome photographs of buildings. But, with all this, our environment grows messier, more chaotic, more out of touch with the natural world and inimical to human life. The order of the existing natural world is destroyed, but no order closer to human understanding is introduced to take its place. The chaos shows up alarmingly clearly when numbers of our most distinguished architects are loosed on the same area, from the Berlin Interbau through the Brussels Fair to the Lincoln Center for the Performing Arts, at which the latter a coating of travertine is expected to insure superficial uniformity for a disparate collection of very careful designs.
>
> The more fashionable all this is, the better is the chance that it will be thought "expressive" of something or of somebody's self. In this chaos of self-expression, careful or sloppy, the basic function of architecture has somehow been forgotten: past the provision of merely shelter, past the expressive manipulation of materials or even of space, it is the creation of place, of what Susanne Langer calls an "ethnic domain." This creation of place amounts at first to taking possession of a portion of the earth's surface. Then, architecture being an act, that process of taking possession is abstracted, as life is abstracted by the playwright.

Moore challenged the modernist fetish for highly finished, expensive materials — bronze, steel, marble,

*Murray House, MLTW/Moore-Turnbull, 1973.
Photo by James Volney Righter.*

and concrete for instance — maintaining that materials were secondary to the creation of space.

Moore, Lyndon, Turnbull, and Whitaker wanted to avoid a methodology for design or an esoteric philosophy. Instead, they preferred a lexicon of architectural images accessible to both architects and inhabitants: windows, aediculas, bays, canopies, columns, porches, roofs; stairs, steps, and terraces; walls, and finally, light, including sunlight, skylight, bounced light and thick light. They wanted buildings to be more than pure exercises in abstract ideology that were put-offs and psychological burdens to inhabitants. They wanted their buildings to engage layers of human emotion and experience.

Moore blended principles he had learned in his earlier work in San Francisco with his unique sense of spatiality. He could think in three dimensions, and his spatial wizardry added an entirely new quality to the Bay Region school. The early houses and the condominiums were masterful exercises in spatial surprise: of passing through small openings or porches into spaces that suddenly exploded up — "space leaking up and out." There was also the collision between the use of structure as architectural "expression" (deriving mostly from Japanese post-and-lintel systems) and standardized American stud-wall framing, hidden beneath Sheetrock or wood. They also favored light shining down from mysterious hidden sources, changing throughout the day, a lesson borrowed from German baroque churches. Later Charles designed the Santa Barbara Faculty Club with William Turnbull, Jr.: a plain stucco shell containing a space of stunning complexity and dynamism and electricity that plucked

Santa Barbara Faculty Club.

Giovanni Battista Piranesi, from the Carceri Series.

Santa Barbara Faculty Club, MLTW/Moore-Turnbull, with Donlyn Lyndon, Marvin Buchanan, and Bruce Beebe, 1966–68. Photo by Morley Baer.

Piranesi from across the centuries, transmuting his engraved worlds into drywall, bridges, neon, and flights of stairs.

In projects such as the Coronado condominiums (unbuilt) and the Monte Vista apartments in Monterey, California, MLTW was also developing the idea of the module. As their work matured, they broke down the repetition of modular systems by introducing variations in siting, orientation, and the arrangements of aediculas or saddlebags so that each module would feel distinct and unique and personally inhabitable.

MLTW's most significant commission came in 1962. Castle and Cook, a Hawaiian real estate developer, had purchased a sheep ranch along the rocky coastline three hours north of San Francisco. The company wanted to develop a radically innovative residential community that would be known as "Sea Ranch." Lawrence Halprin, a landscape architect with a considerable reputation for innovative approaches, made exhaustive studies of the local ecology and environment, taking into account the topology, soil, native plants, wind, and climate. He made beautiful drawings and diagrams that stressed the unique, wild qualities of Sea Ranch, forged over the eons, that made it clear that building had to be approached with utmost responsibility. Humans had to tread lightly.

Halprin selected Joseph Esherick and MLTW for the initial phase of Sea Ranch construction; Esherick designed individual houses sunken into the meadow and tucked in a hedgerow. MLTW, in close collaboration with structural engineer Patrick Morreau, designed a cluster of ten condominiums on a site at the very edge of the cliffs.

Louis Kahn's lessons were the most important influences on the design of the condominium. Timothy Vreeland, who worked with Louis Kahn, noted that "not only did Moore thoroughly learn Kahn's lessons, but he was also able to play with them." Moore, Lyndon, Turnbull, and Whitaker established a rule of geometry: everything would be based on squares (unless an overriding human need necessitated its change) or on an explicable form, such as handrail walls following the movement of people ascending stairs.

Over the years, Moore designed many structures at Sea Ranch, with a web of collaborations among architects and artists well versed in the Sea Ranch typology, most importantly William Turnbull, Donlyn Lyndon, and Dmitri Vedensky. The scale of building at Sea Ranch changed, reflecting fluctuating real estate markets, coastal commission restrictions, and shifting personal tastes. Some felt that the original intentions of Sea Ranch were compromised and the clustering principles were abandoned in favor of more lucrative suburban development, with individual lots being haphazardly parceled across the meadows and larger houses intruding on the landscape. Over the years, however, Moore's work at Sea Ranch always followed his original themes.

~

William Turnbull, Jr., wrote:

> Working with Charles Moore was like riding a Freedom Train to the unknown. I boarded the "train" at Princeton Junction; Charles Moore climbed on after his discharge from the Army Corps of Engineers in Korea. His great gift was

Monte Vista Apartments, MLTW, 1963. Photo by Morley Baer.

to include you in his personal journey and make you feel you were critical to its success. How he managed this architectural legerdemain I never figured out, nor probably did many others because it was irrelevant. What was paramount was the joy and delight of discovering new designs together under the umbrella of friendship and a shared love of architecture, geography, and landscape.

Chuck came to Princeton to complete his education with a master's degree and Ph.D. under the G.I. Bill. I remember his first fall in the graduate end of the drafting room, a big awkward man (not a boy like the rest of us), with a head that was round and out of proportion with the rest of his body. And that head produced designs that were different from the rest of us also. His first problem, a church, was not sleek and modern in a Miesian or Bunshaft vocabulary, but downright homey and buildable. Charles did not have to be stylish to be good — interesting fellow — I felt he would bear watching. The Princeton Architecture School was a small place, fifty-five students, give or take, who all shared the same one-hundred-twenty-foot-long studio in McCormick Hall from junior year through their master's thesis. The only separation panels were between the thesis people and the rest of the classes. Lower classes were expected to assist their elders to complete thesis projects which engendered camaraderie and acquaintanceship that went beyond age or class. That is how we got to know Chuck, to work with him, drink with him, go sketching, and discuss important design ideas along the way.

By the time he had finished his master's thesis on Old Monterey, California, he had moved out of the graduate school and was living in a house on 54 University Place. The top floor of this old Victorian featured a sand-box table in the middle of the floor and treasures and toys scattered among piles and piles of papers and drawings. Surveying it all were the two portraits of "the ancestors" who were to follow him from habitation to habitation throughout his life. I didn't realize then, but Chuck always took his family or surrogate family of students and collaborators with him on his lifetime of adventures. Fifty-four University Place became an extension of the drafting room: a meeting place of ideas.

The Charles Moore student was simultaneously the Charles Moore architect-practitioner. When he came to Princeton from Monterey he left behind a number of small houses he had designed for his family and occasional clients. His mother lived in a house he built for himself in Pebble Beach. These small commissions tugged at him in school and in the summers between times. The summer of 1957 he was in residence in Pebble Beach working on his Ph.D. while several of the rest of us were up in San Francisco with summer intern jobs in local architectural firms. Occasional weekends were spent in Monterey, and the Princeton looking, sketching, or talking was just relocated to the central California coast.

In the fall of 1958 I did my first house with Chuck. He was, as usual, up against a deadline to develop drawings for a Monterey potter named Duane Matterson and his family. Probably Chuck had promised it for the summer but it was now fall — October. Chuck invited Donlyn, Bob Harris, and me to help with the project. We spent many coffee breaks in the Green Hall Annex mulling over the design on paper napkins. Ultimately a three-pavilion scheme was designed, but working drawings were by now way overdue. It was decided if we divided the effort between us, we could do the required drawings in a weekend. The weekend we had available was the biggest football weekend of the season, the Yale game. So as the campus partied around us, we sat in the drafting room turning out, with great pleasure and great pride, drawings for this tiny little house. Floor plans fell to me and I drew them like a jeweler. Dimensions were worked out at one-eighth inch. It was only later when I met the carpenter/contractor that I learned to my chagrin that houses may be loved like jewels, but they are built as houses, and a saw cut, itself, is one-eighth of an inch, and field tolerances are plus or minus a half inch. Chuck maintained his good humor and tolerance through the enthusiastic excesses of making our first collaborative adventure.

In retrospect, too, this was one of his great strengths: the ability to reach for excellence without being mired down and incapacitated by perfection. He trusted people to bring to the table the best of their ideas and insights, to throw them into the discussion with enthusiasm, and to not be protective if they transformed themselves into something new and unrecognizable.

After we had moved to California, this joyous collaboration continued, and probably reached its high water mark at the Sea Ranch with the condominium design in November of 1963. Friendships had solidified, so differences in ages were unimportant. Chuck, who had ten years of experience and wisdom on the rest of us, was the acknowledged leader, but we all considered ourselves equal and recognized in each other outstanding design strengths. Collaboration was tuned through little vacation houses: Jobson on the Big Sur Coast where we actually had to paint the interior ourselves to make the budget; Bonham in the Santa Cruz mountains with Warren Fuller; and for Chuck's own house in Orinda we drew up seven schemes before he settled on the pavilion which he then drew himself. (The proceeds from the sale of my '56 Princeton Ford ended up as bricks for this floor.)

The office was a migrating collection of drafting boards. It originated at the dining room table at 69 Panoramic Way in Berkeley which ostensibly was Chuck's apartment. (He had the bedroom.) When I came west in the summer of 1960 I slept in a sleeping bag on the hikia by the porch, and when Donlyn returned from a Fulbright in India to teach at Berkeley in the fall he got the sofa. A one-bedroom rented apartment is indeed too small for live/work space for three large people, so the drafting boards migrated to 1001 Alcatraz Avenue. The space was a low reclaimed basement under a three-story walk-up, a nondescript apartment building painted a dingy gray white. It was below the sidewalk, and the floor had a tendency to flood after a heavy winter rain. The rent was cheap and the projects correspondingly small and the fees smaller. Lots of students drifted in and out helping to build models and make presentation drawings. I can't remember, but I think it was the wet floor that finally beat us — piles of paper, drawings, and models stacked around and under the drafting tables don't take kindly to this kind of microclimate. We moved in 1962 down to the old Southern Pacific depot in South Berkeley at 1001 Heinz Avenue. By then we had formed a partnership, Moore, Lyndon, Turnbull and Whitaker, the names arranged alphabetically after that of the senior member. Sim van der Ryn and Charles Hamf had the back room (accessible through our space), and Bob Chang, AIA, was upstairs with the one bathroom. We had the front room, heavily glazed, that opened up to a porch. The backyard was unmowed grass with several big black acacia trees. Across the street was the abandoned Heinz food-processing plant, and diagonally out the window to the south a weedy vacant lot. Beside us was a mixed collection of blue collar workers' houses, some of which had been transformed into light commercial uses. Not an inspiring address for well-heeled clients, but we were not interested in anything more than any client of any size who would give us a chance to intellectually show the power of our ideas, honed from the teaching of Louis Kahn, Enrico Peressutti, and Jean Labatut, and now transplanted to the California landscape.

The little houses of our practice had now been joined by several commercial jobs, the Fremont Professional Center for Chuck's brother-in-law, Saul Weingarten, and two multifamily housing projects, the Coronado condominiums and the Monte Vista apartments. We had gotten some professional recognition through the *Progressive Architecture* design awards. A year later, when Oceanic Properties was looking for another firm to work at the Sea Ranch in tandem with Joe Esherick, Larry Halprin suggested us. Al Boeke was the vice president in charge of the project and, to his great credit, decided to give us a chance to design the demonstration multifamily housing. On thirty-five acres our task was to show how to preserve the existing landscape while achieving a development density of one unit per acre. This happened in early November 1963. I remember coming back from six months in Washington, D.C., having worked on President Kennedy's Pennsylvania Avenue Project, to be met by Chuck and Don at the airport saying, "We have this tremendous new job and you can't go home. We are spending the night at Chuck's house and going up to look at the site first thing in the morning."

That is how we ended up on the rugged north coast of California on an overgrazed sheep meadow, hard by the breaking surf at the foot of the rocky cliffs. The ground was not flat but shaped into low rocky mounds and swales edged on one side by the ribbon of Highway One and indented on the other by ocean forces seeking the weak points in the rock.

Our initial chore was a master plan, but before we would accomplish this we needed ideas about the units. Because it was vacation housing (fun versus the serious living in city or suburbia), we decided to make them small but spacious like our little single-family vacation houses whose owners had found so attractive. To conserve land they needed to be congregated together like a northern New England farmstead, and the automobiles had to be accommodated as well in the complex. The first schemes were studied on a cardboard contour model. The units were represented by sugar cubes from our office coffee supplies, C&H sugar cubes to be exact, which happened to be made by our client Castle and Cook. We thought that symbolic and the unit size, when scaled, originated the 24-foot module we used in the project. From the model, we made overlay tracings to record the master plan. From the plan, we picked an interesting cluster to develop as a prototype building. The unit interiors were based on the idea of a bed being the genesis of a bedroom. Our bedrooms became giant four-poster beds, two stories high. Once the furniture metaphor was established, the kitchen and bathrooms were stacked one over the other and thought of as giant Victorian wardrobes. The area under the four-poster became a cozy sheltered living space next to the fireplace. It was, as Chuck described it to Boeke and several Castle and Cook directors, like a child's play space under a card table after you throw a sheet over the top.

Perhaps this description was too much for the board or maybe there were corporate financial decisions concerning the project in general. For whatever reason, we were put on hold in January of 1964, which was a little awkward to a small firm's cash-flow position. All our eggs were basically in one basket. I had left Skidmore, Owings, and Merrill to start on the Sea Ranch, and Chuck was also in need of additional income. Larry Halprin came to the rescue, and we worked in his office until later in the spring when the Sea Ranch came back to life.

The demonstration unit site changed to a more dramatic location adjacent to the edge of the ocean and closer to the Esherick General Store. Our conceptual ideas were retained but now the trick was to knit them together with a specific piece of ground that had its own character and opportunities. Our site, a promontory point, was actually a fault block with earthquake cracks running both north and south of us and out to sea. The rock arches and sea caves were the visible manifestations of the forces of nature. The ground itself sloped toward the water and the top of the site was a rocky outcrop, the stub of an old sea stack eroded over the millenniums. All this was covered by very short grazed grass and no trees.

Historically the site at the turn of the century had been the location of a small cluster of buildings servicing a log-loading chute and was called Black Point. Timber cut along the coast was milled and sent down a high line to small coastal schooners and steamers to be carried to San Francisco for construction. In 1907 there was actually a telephone on the premises, but all that was left for us were some old foundations and a beautifully weathered barn.

We took our clue from the simplicity and appropriateness of the barn. Condominium I was formed around two courtyards: one to shelter the inhabitants and one to corral the cars. The units were organized as far as possible to enjoy the views of the white water up and down the coast with less emphasis on looking directly out to sea with the glare of the western sun.

The construction technique of heavy timber framing evolved after much heated discussion, with Chuck's point of view finally carrying the day. Because of budgetary constraints, we were cautious and wanted to stick with the proven

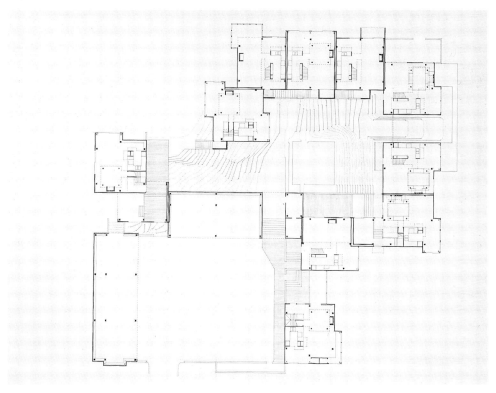

Sea Ranch Plan.

economies of stud and plywood construction. Chuck was convinced that with local timber resources we could build just as economically in heavy timber frame, and he was right. Patrick Morreau engineered the great framework to minimize the number of posts, and the double cantilevering of the corners gave us design opportunities to open up bays for the views. Much of this design work was done around one big drafting table. As long as you made sense you held the pencil, but once your ideas faltered or were intellectually weak, someone else grabbed the pencil and picked up with the design. I think Chuck once described the process of the condominium as four people and one pencil in search of an idea. Along the way we added friends to help us. Ed Allen, with his construction rigor, did many of the working drawings and Marvin Buchanan labored on the detailing.

The drawings were done on big sheets for plans but on 8¹/₂" x 11" paper bound in book form for the details. This was an old Neutra technique and was suggested to us by our young contractor, Matt Sylvia, who had learned his trade working on Neutra buildings. It was also Matt who invented the circular plate connector that was our universal fastener on the job and saved Patrick endless hours of special connection details.

Everyone on the team was a designer or lent their insights to the design.

When we were almost done there was a problem with the elevations. We had elected to cover our single-wall construction with vertical redwood boards which matched the barn and Esherick's store. The problem was the window openings. The windows themselves were nailed on anodized aluminum or fixed sash in wood frames. Chuck did not feel that Don's and my efforts were simple enough or inevitable, so at the last minute he reworked them. We did a beautiful pencil perspective replete with seagulls and surf and sent it off to the board of directors' spring meeting in Honolulu. A telegram came back: "Stop work. It looks like a prison." After the initial shock, we entered into modifications with gusto, adding more bays marking individual units, private courtyards for units seven and eight, and rearranging the tower on unit ten and the parking courtyard. The personalization and idiosyncratic opportunities gave the project additional character. Larry Halprin even imported a redwood stump into the main courtyard. Only one last bump remained in the road. Al Boeke, as the project was nearing completion of the working drawings, felt that ten units filled with four-poster bedrooms might be pushing the marketplace just a little too far. He requested we modify three units to more conventional loft bedrooms. This was done with Chuck saying it didn't matter and the rest of us grousing, but as usual Charles was right.

The building was built by Matt Sylvia and sat on the landscape as a "wooden rock." It was critically acclaimed by the press and brought great delight to its inhabitants. It didn't destroy the landscape but worked in partnership with it, thereby setting a standard of excellence for each of the original partners to try and follow in their own subsequent work.

MLTW broke up in 1965 as the pressures of earning a living took Don Lyndon off to be chairman at the school of architecture at Eugene and Dick Whitaker to

Washington, D.C., and the AIA. Chuck and I stuck it out with his move to Yale and a bicoastal practice until 1970. After that, we continued to work on projects together when they seemed to be of interest to us.

Some of the later projects had the same joy and delight as the early ones. Being fogged in at the airport in Martha's Vineyard, Chuck and I sat cross-legged on the tarmac and conjured up a scheme for the Hines House in Colorado. This had an intensity that carried through the entire design process, and we ended up with Tina Beebe, Chuck, and I painting Southwest Indian designs on the finished dining room walls while Margaret Simon stocked the pantry shelves. However, as time went on, more and more things piled up on Chuck's plate: books, articles, clients, subsidiary offices, with the telephone always a ravenous beast in the background. We could work anywhere and any piece of paper sufficed to record an idea. The happiest times were escaping to the Sea Ranch. Chuck's unit became a chance to focus energy and intellect on a problem. The joy of creating, nurtured and elaborated into fantastic arabesques, was the foundation of the friendships and the soul of this special man.

The Sea Ranch condominium had a stunning impact, both nationally and internationally. The building shifted the focus of an entire generation who were influenced by its implicit respect of the vernacular and the environment, its embrace of the ordinary and common, but also its expansion into a whole new aesthetic. In 1991 it was awarded the AIA Twenty-Five-Year Award in recognition of its lasting impact on design. The citation was as follows:

The American Institute of Architects
is privileged to confer
The Twenty-Five-Year Award
on
Moore, Lyndon, Turnbull, Whitaker

Timeless and enduring, the condominium at Sea Ranch seems to grow naturally from the rocky, windswept coast of northern California, a triumph of innovation and tradition. Echoing the gentle pitch of the surrounding cliffs and the simple geometry of the local farm buildings, the angled roofs tame the wind, at once binding the buildings to the rugged landscape and to the history of the region. Energy efficient, environmentally sensitive, profoundly conscious of the natural drama of its coastal site, they have formed an alliance of architecture and nature that has inspired and captivated a generation of architects.

In the next essay, Moore recounts the experience of designing and making that revolutionary building at Sea Ranch.

The idea of making architecture that actively and energetically appealed to people, a "choreography of the familiar and the surprising," was one of the enthusiasms I shared with Donlyn Lyndon, William Turnbull, and Richard Whitaker back in 1962 when we founded MLTW. Our tiny office, which hailed from a Berkeley

MLTW Twenty-Five Years Later. From Left to Right: Richard Whitaker, Donlyn Lyndon, Charles Moore, and William Turnbull in the Sea Ranch Courtyard, 1991. Photo by Jim Alinder.

basement studio, began, I always like to say, "with one client and four ideas." After completing several houses, we were apparently deemed experienced enough to be approached by a real estate developer to design a ten-unit condominium on a former sheep ranch three hours north of San Francisco.

The Sea Ranch is a ten-mile stretch of rugged coastline where the sea crashes against high cliffs. Seaward of Highway 1, ranchers long ago cleared the meadows (redwoods had once extended to the very edge of the continent) for sheep grazing and planted hedgerows of Monterey cypress perpendicular to coast, making a memorable pattern up the coast. Moving inland, over the wide meadows where the grass was once kept short by the sheep, but is now deep, stands of redwood begin at the top of the grassy hills. This arrangement leaves three types of sites for houses, with an assortment of variations: the edge, where views over the cliffs are uninterrupted; in the meadows, or on the top of the hill; or amongst the redwoods, sometimes with glimpses of the sea through the branches. Along the coast are beautiful old barns that we drew a lot from, along with Fort Ross, the southernmost Russian outpost that was built like barns of timber and wood siding.

There is a freshness, unmatched by anyplace I know of, where the breezes (almost constant) and days sometimes quite foggy or else sunny, and then very dark nights, intensify the feeling of shelter afforded by my houses and others'.

Such compelling beauty made development an awesome proposition. The strip of coast was bought for a planned community of second homes. Al Boeke, who masterminded the development in the early days, hired Lawrence Halprin to study the site and assemble a team, and we were asked at MLTW to design the first condominium. Our concern in designing the condominium was to harmonize with the magnificent landscape, not to dominate it or hide in it, to appear as a congenial partner. In some places, however, there were no hedgerows and something else had to be done to maintain the quality of the landscape, and the qualities which made it worthwhile being there in the first place. Because we could cluster the condominiums in a single mass, we were able to match the scale of building with the heroic scale of the site.

First we decided to make a scheme for some kind of cluster housing that was modeled on a Mediterranean village like Mykonos, close-packed on the greensward by the coast and providing everybody with a chance to huddle out of the wind and away from the view. That, the clients decided, was probably not the best way to lure people to a place a hundred miles from San Francisco.

Next we made models out of sugar cubes to study how close we could put how many units together and still give each residence a view to the sea, preferably either up or down the coast rather than straight out into the glare of the western sun. Coincidentally the model scale of the sugar cubes was twenty-four feet on each side, and that was the module that we finally adopted. What was important to us in the planning was that we expected, even without computer aid, to be able to develop a set of dwellings that were part of a system that was easily repeatable but also could be endowed with individual arrangements. We particularly did not want a blind repetition of anonymous housing units but had, rather, within late-twentieth-century limits of time and money, the opportunity to design especially for individual people's desires and sites.

The structure was made of ten-by-ten Douglas fir columns, and then four-by-ten fir girts, which were applied to the outside of the columns with one girt always resting on another more securely placed one, so that all the way down the hill these pieces had to fall precisely onto one another. Above the top one, then, four-by-four posts held up much more simply the three-inch decking on the roof. This wood-frame structure went up with two-inch fir boarding over it, then building paper, and finally another inch of redwood. Since big timbers were to be found in this area, we believed at the time that our framing system was an economical system. (As it turned out, it was not as economical as expected because floods prevented the delivery of some of the big wood that was to come from the coastal forests to the north, and it had to come from the

Fort Ross.

Sea Ranch Skeleton.

California High Sierra instead.) Because of earthquakes and the required diagonal bracing, the problem of making some bolted connection that was capable of taking all kinds of different angles was a very real one that also threatened to become very expensive.

It was solved, thanks to an idea of the contractor, Matthew Sylvia, by a device which someone called our "Japanese hardware," a big steel plate with holes all around it so spikes could be driven through whichever hole came over the four-by-four diagonal bracing. Since this structure was not all held together like the balloon frame two-by-four stud arrangements of most houses, these ten-by-tens were just barely adequate, according to our engineer, to stand up against the wind on this exposed site. As each twenty-four-foot-by-twenty-four-foot module worked, there were on opposite sides two columns with the girt between making a fairly stable frame. Each of the alternate sides was a single column with a girt balancing on it and resting at its ends on the other girts. The girts could be extended past the twenty-four-foot square to hold up additional bays with particular views of the ocean. Between the twenty-four-foot modules, seizing whatever opportunities availed themselves, we were able to put rooms, porches, and whatever the space allowed.

Unlike the smooth wood of most Japanese buildings, this was not wood that you'd love to run your hands over, since you would get splinters in your fingers if you tried. We saw the condominium as a big heavy barn which is supposed to maintain considerable distance from you even when you are inside it.

Moore's Unit #9 with the Latest Paint Scheme. Photo by Christopher Noll.

Although there were many drawbacks to this way of doing things, one of the good things about having this wooden frame instead of some more rigid prefabricated arrangement was that we could cope with the irregularities of the site and still have a strong, simple form on the landscape.

We played it altogether straight, but were delighted when the unadorned things we made played tricks with people's memories and prompted altogether romantic recollected connections. Some angry passers-by noted a resemblance to the head of an abandoned mine shaft. We noted that too and thought it was great because the very thing we were hoping for was the sense of belonging that weathered wooden buildings (even abandoned mine shafts) in a landscape can manage to convey. Later a friend also delighted us by describing the condominium as a large wooden rock at home on the coast.

Inside, meant to be approached much more closely than the timber structure, were pieces of wooden "furniture," sometimes three stories high, which contained kitchens, stairs, baths, and closets. We made them out of smooth painted wood, much more inviting than the rough framework which stands in contrast to it.

In my own condominium there were a series of paint jobs that I changed over the years. First there were shades of blue followed by a period of uniform gray, and

Sea Ranch Condominium with Barn, MLTW, 1963–65. Photo by Morley Baer.

finally red, white, and black checkers were added in homage to Katsura and Walter
Chatham's house in Seaside. We also added panels brightly painted from India, a
section of an old Spanish ceiling, which we layered on the wall, its cavities fitted
out with toys and abalone shells. The hearth lies under a four-poster aedicula, and
over it there is a bed chamber that achieves visual but not acoustical privacy when
one lets down a great canvas sail with a zipper in it.

Living in my condominium for such a long time has fine-tuned me to the
rhythms of living in northern California, and so has been a significant plus when
designing houses for others seeking the same escape. House commissions at Sea
Ranch have fluctuated, since the California coastal commission believed it important to stop people from making houses for a time, but when it was lifted, I had the
chance to do some others. Clients I am especially fond of, Bruno and Rose Miglio,
commissioned two houses that were made according to two different ideas.

The site for their first house (which they would live in) was on top of the hill,
just short of the forest. We arranged the rooms along a spine that went along the
side of the hill between the adjacent meadows and forest. Then we twisted the axis
so that the rooms incorporated some bends and folds in plan as well as some complex geometries up in the ceiling. All of the rooms, then, offered windows facing
both down across the meadow and to the sea or up the hill into the trees. Barn

doors slide over the windows and across an outdoor space between two of the rooms. We made their second house, based more on the long-useful aedicula principle, but organized the axis diagonally through the space, leading from the entrance to the ocean view.

The Sea Ranch, where I've gone now, for several decades, is a place of recuperation, and has, unlike any other place I know, qualities, having to do with climate, that are both challenging and restorative. It's mindful of the Greek myth of Antaeus, the son of Mother Earth, who often engaged others in wrestling matches, with the catch that the loser would pay with his life. Antaeus had an advantage though: as long as he was in contact with his mother (the ground), his energy was constantly restored, and was unbeatable. When Hercules came along, he realized Antaeus's secret, and lifting him from the earth, was able to squeeze him to death. For years, the Sea Ranch has been my Mother Earth, a place to come away from things, and be recharged.

CHAPTER FIVE

Place Making and Cities

No architect traveled as much as Charles Moore. In the course of a week, he might have flown from Paris to Boston to revise a book manuscript (due in three days), repaired to Connecticut for a design session, flown to Chicago to lecture at a conference, continued on to Los Angeles to work feverishly on a competition, and then embarked with students for a weeklong excursion to Mexico. Jet lag was of little consequence. Moore seemed to live in his own time zone.

His calendars are precious historical relics of his modus operandi, filled with Berol 314 pencil scribbles, mysterious hieroglyphic tangles of flight numbers, reservations, telephone numbers, meeting times, and appointments. He made innumerable sketches for projects on airline cocktail napkins and conducted design conferences in boarding areas. (Wise collaborators offered to chauffeur Moore to or from airports to have his undistracted ear.) Charles's canvas carry-on bags always overflowed with rolled drawings, wads of receipts (if travel occurred near April 15, complex tax returns were usually sorted in the airplane cabin), student papers to be read, and often a Robertson Davies novel poked from his corduroy jacket pocket.

Moore's rootlessness made him always want to be somewhere else; he was an architectural nomadic monk who always longed to escape and who seldom stayed in one place for much longer than two weeks. All of this exhausting travel though was not performed merely to pursue clients or stay in touch with the lecture circuit or inspect building sites. Had he desired, those trips could have been made by others and the lecture schedule curtailed. Charles was addicted to absorption, experiencing as much as possible, learning something new every day, and constantly refreshing his visual memory banks.

He constantly surveyed patterns of human habitation, which he documented in a massive slide collection of world architecture containing nearly ninety thousand images. He could revisit any place, and, no matter how long ago he had been there, he would remember the city's plan, the location of the most important things to see, restaurants, the shop that sold the best carved masks, the hotels, and anything else that offered some visual

Quarry Road House Drawing, 1985.

splendor. Moore would suddenly recall images wildly obscure during design drawings: a staircase in Morocco, a courtyard in Guanajuato, or a chapel in Rome.

A trio of Moore's essays (all published in Yale's *Perspecta*) was an important foundation for his views on cities. The first, "Hadrian's Villa" (1960), was a vivid and witty analysis of the fantasy city of antiquity. Moore compared Hadrian's enthusiasm for travel with John Foster Dulles's and wrote that Hadrian's "undertakings, the avidity of his search for culture, and the gold-plated quality of his success at finding it are nothing short of Texan. And the sheer endlessness of his construction at Tivoli outdistances Versailles (which was, after all, based on a fairly simple idea) and compares with the scale of the twentieth century. The G.M. Technical Center will be equally exhausting to walk among the ruins of, though very probably not nearly so much fun."

The second, "You Have to Pay for the Public Life" (1965), was arguably Moore's most influential written work, one in which he examined California's monumental architecture — in addition to celebrating the Nut Tree restaurant and the Mission Inn. The essay irrevocably changed the way many architects regard place; along with Robert Venturi's *Complexity and Contradiction* and Colin Rowe's and Fred Koetter's *Collage City,* it is one of the most significant architectural writings of postwar America. In it, Moore made his famous tribute to Disneyland:

> More recent years have their monuments as well. Indeed, by almost any conceivable method of evaluation that does not exclude the public, Disneyland must

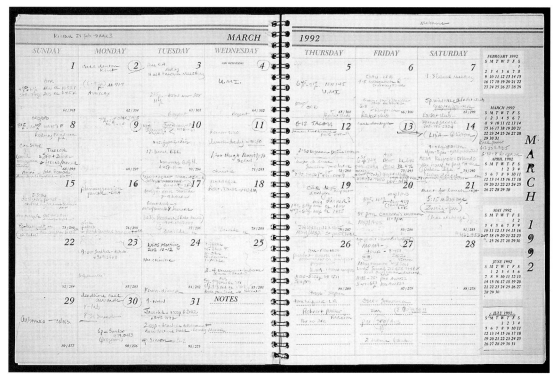

Moore's Calendar.

Moore Photographing.

be regarded as the most important single piece of construction in the West in the past several decades. The assumption inevitably made by people who have not yet been there — that it is some sort of physical extension of Mickey Mouse — is wildly inaccurate. Instead, singlehanded, it is engaged in replacing many of those elements of the public realm which have vanished in the featureless private floating world of southern California, whose only edge is the ocean, and whose center is otherwise undiscoverable (unless by our revolution test it turns out to be on Manhattan Island). Curiously, for a public place, Disneyland is not free. You buy tickets at the gate. But then, Versailles cost someone a great deal of money, too. Now, as then, you have to pay for the public life.

And the third, "Plug It In Ramses, and See If It Lights Up, Because We Aren't Going to Keep It Unless It Works" (1967), was one of the first essays to recognize the emerging electronic aspatial culture by which we are now so entirely surrounded:

> About the time that architects and planners started to bleat about "human scale" as though it had to do, for the first time since Cheops, entirely with man's body and not at all with his mind or ideas, and to rhapsodize about the pleasures of sitting or strolling in the Piazza di San Marco, the heart of Venice and "the finest drawing room in Europe," people were everywhere changing their effective bodies, electronically extending themselves in whole new ways. And while the Piazza San Marco has been repeated on urban renewal sites across the United States (complete with everything but inhabitants), the hierarchy of important places from private to monumental has vanished.

In all of these essays (and in many to follow), Moore celebrated edges and centers, main streets and squares, warning that whenever they are lost in cities and towns, "placeness" dissolves and leaks and spills uncontrollably into the surrounding countryside. He criticized the privatization of the public realm and stressed that public places need to be fostered with time and care and enthusiasm.

Preserving historic buildings was another ideal Moore taught and advocated. When his

Utah colleague James Acland was involved in the struggle to prevent the demolition of Toronto's Richardsonian city hall so it could be replaced with a department store, Moore wrote the following letter, which was published in the *Toronto Globe and Mail* on January 11, 1966:

I was vacationing recently on the north Jamaican coast. One day a guest at the Carib Ocho Rios was pointed out as Philip Givens, the Mayor of Toronto, who, it was said, is presently engaged in an attempt to sell that municipality's old City Hall.

I supposed at first that I was at the mercy of an incipient musical comedy writer ("Mayor sells City Hall!") but finally realized that my informant was serious, and that the strong old building that at once provides a foil for Toronto's brilliant new City Hall, and links it to the city's geography and to its past, is under immediate threat.

Not only that, but by some surreal reversal of public values, its place is to be taken by a perfectly adequate department store, whose institutional grandeur is to be enhanced by its location on Toronto's emerging central square, as well as by a rather special fillip: the old City Hall's tower and the Cenotaph to Canada's war dead are meant to serve as an introduction to the notions, perfume, and yard goods departments.

Pretty clearly, this is grotesque. One can only hope that there is left in Ontario enough sense of Toronto's importance to prevent this tragedy. Only people from Toronto, of course, can actually demonstrate this sense, but if they act, they have the support of a great many of us.

Acland wrote back to Moore that his letter "caused quite a stir," and Moore received the following letter from a Toronto citizen that displayed many of the grassroots feelings that architects, city planners, and politicians ignored in "remaking" our cities:

Thanks a million for writing that letter re old Toronto City Hall in the *G & M,* Jan. 11.

It's a bloody shame that people from outside Canada have to plead to the citizens of Toronto to save an attractive old bldg. (just over 60 yr. old). Our elected members of City Council are a stupid bunch of nincompoops — so drunk with power and their own importance that they no longer have anymore common sense. They have this modern mania to destroy everything that's old; doing their damnedest to copy the Americans (it's only correct that an American like you who has seen so much 'rebuilding' at home should come forward and warn the downtrodden taxpayers of Toronto).

What a craze is sweeping the big cities on this continent! There is no more stability to the life of the people. Everybody is moving; everybody is tearing down and rebuilding. It must be so hard and aggravating to our older citizens and levelheaded new generations who want to stay put — to develop roots in the community.

It is all so sickening.

I detest the new city hall — that monstrosity, an architect's nightmare — that I have yet to see the inside of it. Millions were sunk into that building of the taxpayers' money without the city fathers doing anything to stop it.

Some of the professors at the U of T School of Architecture (Like Prof. Acland) are against the monstrous idea of demolishing the old City Hall; but they just write letters and talk and talk. Why don't they organize a student march of protest to the mayor's office????? Other students invade your deep south in favour of civil rights but will do nothing to save something precious at home.

PLEASE WRITE ANOTHER LETTER SOON — BEFORE THE CLOWNS AT THE NEW CITY HALL WIN OVER THE WILL OF THE PEOPLE. Write and say the matter should be put to vote of the taxpayers at the coming civic elections in Dec.

Because of public outrage and financial oversight, the developers backed away, and the city hall was saved.

Making cities laboratories for architectural investigations was an unchanging component of Moore's university studios. Never fond of giant metropolitan cities like New York City or Chicago, Moore instead took students every semester to more habitable places: Bath, Guanajuato, Santa Barbara, New Orleans, Santa Fe, Newport, San Antonio, Savannah, and Charleston. They were not to be merely visitors. Moore encouraged active participation in the places — as a group they would stay in historic hotels together, have elaborate meals, shop in the markets, and visit the museums and churches. All of these places offered great lessons; Moore taught students that the trick is to look and see and experience.

Jean Paul Carlhian, who often traveled with Charles, recounted some of his experiences:

My fondest memories of Charles are connected with traveling together, for then I had him all to myself.

Lesson #1: Look for something special, preferably unusual, out of the ordinary.

Rome: We first met as Resident Architects at the Academy in Rome as our terms overlapped due to his lack of ability to meet any schedule. So it was Villa Lante, covered with ice. Nicely symmetrical. But here was Charles in a narrow village street taking a picture of a pale-blue wall with a bare bulb.

Lesson #2: Know your classics.

Mantua: Palazzo del Te. Rain. Charles under a ridiculously small umbrella, cameras and all. Pacing back and forth. "What are you doing dancing around like that?" "Learning to read Giulio Romano according to Peter Murray!"

Lesson #3: Learn to see in space.

Sea Ranch: Charles working on a book by the pool. No time for swimming. Then a visit to a client's house in need of a fence to hide the garbage pail. Charles and Dmitri "Consulting." No pencil, no paper, no plan. Charles, waving a hand in space says, "A Di-oop-si-doo here." Then Dmitri says, "Maybe a Oop-si-di-doo there." Then that's it. Consultation is over.

Lesson #4: Learn how to live.

Gualala: But then there was the fresh salmon at the Gualala hotel.

Lesson #5: Draw.

Morocco: Barbara was asked to pack his water colors. On the road of the Kasbahs. Terrace overlooking the desert with the green oasis. Brushes. Water. The wrong pen. Make do.

Lesson #6: Interpret.

Egypt: Two weeks on the Nile. A great deal of napping. Watching the landscape go by with tea and cookies. Trapped again for a sketch. Begin a drawing again, this time with an admiring audience. Start with a few columns, pyramids, and obelisks, soon to become overshadowed by peasant villages.

Lesson #7: Ad lib.

All of these trips led to joint lectures at Tulane. Symmetry without symmetry. Seven hours preparation in isolation. Shoe boxes of slides in complete disarray. Interrupted by a wonderful lunch at Gallatoire's. Two projectors. Subject, "Water." But the projectors wouldn't take the slide carousels. We change into foul-weather gear with water pistols. Water.

Lesson #8: Never cease to experiment.

The American Scene: "I smell a Sullivan bank." I drive. "I know this is near a Frank Lloyd Wright warehouse." Right. Lunch at the restaurant, Bloody Marys with an ounce of vinegar. Why not?

Lesson #9: Enjoy.

Especially in food. Oh, how he loved food! Piazza Navona in Rome, Tartuffos, Corso Ristorante, Monte Biancos.

Lesson #10: Love life.

Kyoto: And then there was Japan, Kyoto. Charles sitting royally cross-legged handling his chopsticks with great dexterity. Eleventh-century beautiful bowls filled with worms. "Look they are alive!"

The exploring never quit. Dona Guimares, Dmitri Vedensky, Charles Jencks, William Mitchell, Wayne Attoe, Peter Frith, and Peter Zweig were also often travel companions on excursions to see English houses or Japanese gardens or the ruins in Machu Picchu, the Himalayas, or the Nile Valley. When Ricardo Legorreta once spoke in San Miguel de Allende about the wonderful jungle garden of follies near Xilitlá, Mexico, there was no question about going, even though it required a grueling drive through remote Mexican mountains. Long flights to Samarkand were booked to meet with the jury for the Aga Khan's Award for

Islamic architecture and to see exotic palaces and tiled mosques. But after forty years of enduring the mind-numbing repetition of the airlines, Charles enjoyed nothing more than loading his Chevrolet Suburban with students and taking to the road, navigating from the passenger seat with a good road map and choosing (probably as he did when he was a child) the back roads away from the interstates, passing through towns seldom visited or investigating some architectural oddity glimpsed through the trees. And always, without fail, stopping someplace wonderful for lunch.

≈

In the following essay, Moore celebrates those civic places, both humble and grand, in which people are made to feel connected and included, because energy was invested in making a public place.

     Placemaking and the state of our cities has been for most of this century at the center of our struggles to define just what it is that we architects are supposed to do, and often, how dismally we have failed to achieve whatever these things are. The manifestoes that promised to make our cities exciting and prosperous and clean turned out to be mostly false, and led instead to the monotone that we now see everywhere. Just how we are to deal with technology and the automobile and the encroaching specter of our electronic society I don't think we've entirely accomplished, so that the distinctions between what should be private and public have been generally neglected.

Charles Moore, Eric Hurner, Dmitri Vedensky, and Dona Guimares in Stafford, England.

Towns and cities have been built throughout history in every culture by groups of people with common aims (they appear from this distance to have been more or less common aims, helped along by isolation), and places in them of religious or civic significance shared the enthusiasms of the inhabitants. Individual dwellings, except for the castles and palaces of rulers, for the most of recorded history composed the coherent backdrop, visually holding the town together. But the places we were meant to remember, the ones that appear on our postcards, were places that usually had a definite function in a religious or civic sense, or else had visual importance in the town, so that the making of places, helped often by pretty locations on a river or in a mountain valley or by the sea (places that had a defensive or some other purpose), was, in an extraordinary number of cases, successful in the terms that we enjoy being in them and looking at them, and often spend our vacations seeking them out.

Nowadays the places where people feel that they belong and are connected to in a physical sense as well as an emotional sense are increasingly rare. This is not helped any by the phenomenon where the outskirts of, say, Phoenix are hardly distinguishable from the outskirts of Boston, apart from some differences in the landscape. The public and the private too have suffered for the fact that the agencies that run our institutions, from elementary schools to commercial centers, regard them as partly exclusive places to be surrounded by parking lots or chain-link fences in ways that certainly do not create any shared public realms that can hold together a community. A public space does not necessarily have to be one where people can gather in a giant group, but rather a place where you, the individual, can go and take possession of, for whatever time you are there, without feeling you are wrestling it away from somebody else or in danger of having it wrestled away from you. The point of it all is, in the terms I have been using, is that the making of places where the public can function, where people as members of the body politic as well as individuals can inhabit, should have some chance of taking over some piece of public space.

At our Kresge College at Santa Cruz, we had a metaphor of a village instead of a village itself since there were not institutions ready to take over the public spaces. Therefore the public space was in a deplorable state: the chairs were upside down with wadded-up paper on the floor, and there was a general lack of sense of ownership of the thing, on the part of anybody or any sets of people. That lack of sense of ownership seemed to be in considerable contrast with the unusually vivid taking over of their individual spaces by students in their rooms.

That problem does not show up very much on college campuses anymore (and things have improved dramatically at Kresge), but it certainly is a taxing one in most middle-size American cities and at every public housing or federally sponsored housing project (ours or anybody else's). Since there doesn't seem to be a sense of ownership of the public spaces (most often people are not even sure what are the public spaces), they tend to be the ones that nobody ever uses and tend to have weeds in them.

The most frightening thing about the twentieth-century city is that the taken for granted but not ever specifically marked out public realm which used to be Main Street, where you could go and have a political parade or collect pennies for the girl scouts or whatever your cause, is now of course defunct in favor of malls and shopping centers where you have to get permission from the owners to conduct your activity. Are there possibilities in which schools and other institutions become more than places that are locked up at four o'clock in the afternoon and shopping centers become more than commercial enterprises, where citizens' groups can have activities?

Some of this falls back to the concerns for the demarcations between the outside world and the inside world and what they specifically do to the public and

Kresge College, MLTW/Moore-Turnbull, with Marvin Buchanan, Robert Calderwood, and Robert Simpson, 1966–74. Photo by Morley Baer.

Columbia, California.

Great Wall of China.

private realms. It doesn't have to be much: there is a
little fence around a graveyard in the Motherlode in
California that establishes the private realm of a few
departed individuals, and marks that privacy with
just about the minimum barrier to hold the world
outside. More considerable wallings, like the Great Wall in China, establishes no
question about the juxtaposition of the public and the private life.

Venice is an interesting place for the really tight juxtaposition of the public
realm and the private one. The houses of Venice are everywhere and just steps
away from the magnificent public arrangements. One can note that they do not
have any cars there, which helps the tight juxtaposition because no parking lots
have to lie between one and the other, and the streets and sidewalks become, of
course, canals and little bridges.

The inhabitation of shared spaces is sufficiently tricky-iffy everywhere in the
world, so that surrogate inhabitors often turn out to be extremely useful. Flowers in
a park in London make it an inhabitable place that gives (I do not think they do it
all by themselves, but they are part of an arrangement) people the courage to lie in
the grass without fear of attack. They are part of a very gentle inhabiting of a shared
public realm whose habitation is carefully agreed on. In Spain, the private gesturing
into the public space that causes inhabitants of dwellings to put flowers on the outside of their windows and decorate the walls and to even have some around the
fountain in a public space, contributes, with private gestures, toward making habitable the public realm.

The Italian scheme that sets marble replicas of people in public spaces as an extension of the notion that people might occupy those spaces is, if you make good
enough statues, a workable notion. In the Piazza della Signoria the presence of
David is especially startling, as you know, but he extends the human act of inhabiting public space, that seems to me altogether to work.

People at Banaras in India inhabit steps and immerse themselves in the sacred

Geraniums in Spain.

Banaras, India.

Ganges and generally bring the place altogether alive. They do it not as a part of any public celebration or coming together since most don't seem to know each other. They sit very much alone and doff their clothes and do their bathing in direct communication with themselves and their religious beliefs and their divinities and not as part of any choreographed joint effort. But it is a place; there is a physical format to there being some kind of community, even though inhabited by separate individuals.

In Mykonos the joint effort of Eastern religious ceremonies and having coffee are seen in approximately the same sense and are regarded as good things to juxtapose in the little spaces in front of the churches. There are places in the world where the recall of public inhabitation is ritualized to a point where it, according to some of us though not to others, works. In the Tivoli Gardens in Copenhagen every device I know of is used to enhance the public inhabiting of a place by individuals one by one, from lights used as surrogate inhabitors, to flowers, to water, and to every kind of diversion that Danish law allows.

The public spaces in American Western towns were obviously regarded as very important, yet the human public spaces against all the wide-open frontier land, free to everybody, had to be marked off by buildings. They did not have quite enough buildings to do it, and so the public gesture was made, building after building, through the thin false front that was made complete, full, and fancy as possible to face the street where the dramas of human life were meant to be going on. The usual imposed building did not have that severe a set of requirements, and so was allowed to be whatever size and shape it needed. In Silverton and Ouray, Colorado, the buildings very directly made an architectural public realm, a stage for whatever human interactions (which of course you have seen enough Western

Mykonos.

movies to know the general nature of) were going to occur.

In the San Ildefonso pueblo in New Mexico, in a climate where the sun is dazzling and for much of the year hostile, the public space is marked more than anything else by shade: a big tree that you can get under, a gallery, and a verandah. Public space is made by the need for the shade cast, and it is made not for people to get together and have a meeting but just as a comfortable place for people to feel free to be a member of the pueblo and is even open for those who are strangers.

In Córdoba, a fountain-well is a place where you come to get water when you do not have it in your house. (Which was the direct inspiration for our laundromat at Kresge College — though not as pretty.) It seems to me an interesting example of a public monument, a space graced by sculptural, architectural attention that is a focus; a place that everybody can use but not in an American sense (a building or a major architectural event), but like that big tree in the pueblo.

At the Santa Barbara County Courthouse, spaces were directly contrived by the architects to be grand, generously public, and then suddenly quite intimate, three feet behind. The Courthouse extends very much the same effects of making the act of entering a building and looking at it, a business of incorporating some kind of available public experience that adds it to the public realm. The lodge at Old Faithful in Yellowstone is so wonderful and it certainly is big and the public goes there and so it is a legitimate spot. It has a curious specialness to it which does not interfere with its making what I take to be a public gesture.

Santa Barbara County Courthouse.

Mendocino City, California.

The main street of Mendocino City, California (which is along and behind the cliffs that go down to the Pacific), lets there be an enfronting of all its buildings, a making public of themselves that really runs to nothing. There is just a little street and then a field which is not a public space particularly, unless you happen to be a tourist with a camera and carefully walk across it, avoiding what the cows have done, to take a picture. But that they are martialled to make a public face for that town is a striking gesture.

There can also be a marvelous merging of the inside and outside that puts individuals into an intensely private society in a very carefully protected private realm at the edge of the public space, the edge of the street. Moorish doors, with their capacity to be in place when they are open as well as when they are closed (unlike our doors which have to be closed or they are flopping around) are an arrangement that just naturally invites penetration. Breaking through the barrier between the private and the superprivate and public makes a memorable gesture. San Miguel de Allende and Guanajuato in Mexico have all kinds of courtyards that are private because they belong to private houses, but they invite at least looking in or some kind of entry, however hesitant. Another incredible thing is in Guimares, in the north of Portugal, a sort of stage-set giant stairway amid a set of little dinky houses that makes a coming together not only of the big and little but of what seems to be a public realm with the very private houses right behind. It makes something very special for that corner of town.

The whole business of having a private world sufficiently available to the public realm so that there is a crossing of it and not a demarcation, certainly contributes to the livability of cities. Charleston, South Carolina, is full of private house gardens which the public is invited to come into. That gesture of coming in is, of course, a

Guanajuato, Mexico.

Guimares, Portugal.

powerful chance for architectural decorating, and the way in which things are made gets to be very important in the attempt to indicate boundaries between the public and the private.

The houses in Charleston work very well. They come right tight to the street and then have their gardens to one side, juxtaposing their individual finery with the public space. The Manigault House has a domical vestibule, and it has a pair of columns, and it has an arch, and it has a triangular pediment — it has everything but a tower. It marks a heroic entry into a private realm behind, and by doing that — by being a kind of in-between realm — it makes an important insistence on the existence of the public realm.

I find it interesting that the way, over and over again, the really important Imperial stuff is announced in Japan (the houses of emperors such as the Imperial Palace in Kyoto) is by making a space that is grand but not individually inhabitable. That is, you can imagine legions of samurai doing something acceptable to the emperor there, but it certainly does not invite human habitation any more than the plaza in front of the Seagram building.

Quite different is the ceiling at the Alhambra, which by way of Russian Easter Eggs, increases the excitement in the space underneath and enhances inhabitability, not only by the owner but by the person wandering through. Flying buttresses at Beauvais are, regardless of what they have to do with human inhabitation of the space, architectural gestures so powerful that they make it public.

The regular forest of columns in the Mosque in Córdoba is one of the most exciting pieces of urban order, because it is as public an order as I have ever seen, especially since it is kind of disorderly. There are walls left over from various buildings and rebuildings that make it not altogether easy to see what the shape of it is. Very delicate statements serve to enhance the importance of a place and make it

Manigault House, Charleston, South Carolina.

Kyoto, Japan.

public. The big Ledoux-like importance of Thomas Jefferson's pavilions at the University of Virginia has a curious function of making it clear that it is a kind of house but not a private place — it is part of the whole institution. And at Chambord the chimneys stand around as silent inhabitors of the rooftop, making it very active, alive, and public within the limits of the court.

Goodhue and Sullivan both made gestures, using in the Nebraska State Capitol and the bank in Grinnell an incredibly rich vein of recollections to make a statement in each of those buildings, a system of ornament to reference the place where it is: the Corn Belt in each case. It is interesting that other civilizations have been a lot freer in their presumptions about what kind of a delicate or private or goofy soul-baring will go in a public place. Medieval gargoyles have very special personalities, and in Tomar, Portugal, the flamboyant use of ropes all carved in stone recalls a set of things that were interesting to people, in the same way that the corn capitals

Córdoba, Spain.

Grinnell, Iowa.

in Goodhue's capitol or the ornament in Sullivan's bank do, with all kinds of crustaceous bar-
nacled stuff they thought was sufficiently
important to carve in stone.

Another building that I am extravagantly in
favor of (again this raises some of the American
problems about contributing to the public realm) is the Quaker meeting house of
the eighteenth century in Sturbridge Village. Inside its mild-mannered colonial
shell is a public space of great surprise: just a frame that is more Japanese than anything else, altogether pure for Quaker meetings, which are altogether pure occur-
rences. Its two-story space in the middle (the building's exterior sets you up to
expect something else altogether) has a U-shaped gallery that gives you the sense of
the joining in the occupation of space.

And then in Cambridge, Le Corbusier's Carpenter Center does as well as any
building on the continent (it does not make a public space outside), of being so extraordinarily alive to what goes on around it, by being cut up the way it is, and
then having that reflective glass so that it both picks up the Fogg and the Faculty
Club and Seward Hall into some kind of crazy dance, and then tells you probably
more than you want to know about the American way — the sort of Tennessee
Valley Authority way — of building bridges and dams and other pieces of concrete.

It seems to me very important that for all things architecture is to be about, that
there be some kind of shared spaces in buildings and cities. I have the impression
that most of the things that we have been doing to get them so far have not
worked out. I guess it could be argued that it is hopeless, that it is a social issue
amenable to manipulation of gestures and locations for celebrations. I do not think
buildings can produce a liberal democratic social order all by themselves, but I do
think that expressive buildings can make a realm in which people, if they have any
predisposition to have any relations with each other, will let them do it.

Long ago, I wrote that Disneyland had replaced in Southern California a public life that gradually had been stripped away. Since then, Disney's magic has been transplanted, on an even greater scale, to central Florida (successful), and even more recently to the outskirts of Paris (unsuccessful). It seems to me that the success of such pleasures as Disneyland and Disneyworld are impressed enough so that people want very much to feel as though they are in some kind of public realm, an indication that there is some place for public life.

Main Street, Disney World.

CHAPTER SIX

Architecture in a Time of Questioning

"Tumultuous at best," "filled with tension," and "anarchy" are only some of the descriptions of Yale and New Haven in the late sixties. The antiwar and civil-rights movements were at their height; Abbie Hoffman and Jerry Rubin were leading demonstrations, Ken Kesey and Wavy Gravy were arriving in the hallucinogenic schoolbus with their tie-dyed entourage. Factions were rioting, the Black Panthers were taking over churches, the trial of Bobby Seale held the attention of the nation, and ROTC buildings across the country were burning to the ground.

It was a time of questioning. Architecture students were often on the front lines of demonstrations; they often were seen as being the most "active" of the activists, since they believed architecture could be a means for social action. Around them they saw the failure of architecture and urban planning — indeed, the Gothic riches of Yale University set within the poverty of New Haven, like an island in a sea, was a daily, jarring example of the widening gulf between the powerful and powerless, rich and poor, educated and uneducated.

Moore arrived in New Haven in 1965, after Kingman Brewster, president of the university, personally recruited him from Berkeley to become chairman of Yale's architecture department.

Moore's predecessor was Paul Rudolph, who had also designed the Yale Art and Architecture building, which aroused both intense praise and derision. Although Boyd Smith served as an interim figurehead, the transition from Rudolph to Moore was a dramatic one.

New Haven in the Late Sixties. Photo by James Volney Righter.

Rudolph had, in the late fifties, arrived to a floundering school (it had been placed on probation by the national accreditation board). As chairman, however, he pulled the program up by its bootstraps, and the next years, according to Jean Paul Carlhian, a professor at the time, were exciting, intense, serious, and idealistic.

Moore's arrival (some likened it to a "California breath of fresh air") brought humor, wit, and new perspectives. He expected that the school would be easily managed because it was considerably smaller than California's College of Environmental Design, and New Haven was quieter than Berkeley, where the free speech movement and the barricades and tear gas were dividing the campus.

But that turned out to be wishful thinking.

Student strikes at Yale between 1965 and 1970 disrupted entire semesters. Many refused to take part in studio projects with questionable moral content, others refused to take classes deemed doctrinaire, while others boycotted the entire academic system. Often, making drawings and models was taboo; instead students were interested in making posters, movies, pamphlets, and newspapers infused with counterculture revolutionary rhetoric. As Moore wrote in "Eleven Agonies and One Euphoria," an article that appeared in the *Michigan Society of Architects Journal:*

> Architects in practice, enjoying until lately an era of unprecedented prosperity, have come in increasing numbers to the schools of architecture, seeking recruits interested in joining them for fun and profit. Increasingly, they have gone away dismayed. They have encountered schools tottering in the grip of undifferentiated agonies, and students either indifferent, utterly hostile to, or planning an instant takeover of the profession. If they went to the most prestigious schools, they will have noticed that "nobody designs anything anymore" and "nobody even makes any drawings," though they might, if they stayed long enough, have been shown some very competent movies or some surprisingly slovenly posters developing a social theme. The visitor will in any case almost certainly be baffled and will in all probability be deeply offended.

Though he did not like the exaggerated behavior and disapproved of the ugliness, drugs, and vandalism of students who were swept up in the revolution, Moore did recognize that some of the basic tenets of their dissatisfaction were genuine: "Schools cannot persist in training people for a vanishing role, and students are already indicating dramatic resistance to any such emasculation. They should be heeded."

Several dissident groups were also vying for attention from within the school. "Group 2" was organized by professors in opposition to Moore's administration. They published outbursts in a student newspaper, *Novum Organum,* and, at one point, even took part in a student demonstration where they burst into a lecture being conducted by Professor Felix Drury, carried him from the classroom, and threw him into the street, returning to the shocked students declaring, "the course has been liberated." The "Committee of 8," composed of two students from each year, demanded student positions with voting privileges on academic committees, petitioning that "we are dissatisfied with our lack of knowledge of the administration of the Department of Architecture. This has caused considerable mistrust and misunderstanding between faculty and students." When the architecture administration granted them some presence on school committees, Kingman Brewster felt that the school had "abdicated authority." Graduate students demanded representation in decision-making processes and funding policy, and many were critical of the imbalanced role of women and minorities in the profession. Yet another group, the Black Workshop (one of the first and supported by Moore), provided guidance to minorities seeking to become architects and vigorously protested the injustices of segregation and discrimination.

The most serious challenge to the administration's authority occurred when members of the planning faculty, some of whom were committed radicals, sent unauthorized letters of acceptance to twelve prospective students, knowing that there were neither positions nor finances to support them. When the students arrived in New Haven expecting to begin their studies, Brewster, who was shocked by the incident, came close to shutting down the school of architecture. He compromised with a plan to reorganize the school hierarchy.

The only thing left was to have the school burn down. And that occurred at four o'clock in the morning on June 14, 1969, when a mysteri-

Yale's Art and Architecture Building on the Morning After the Blaze. Photo by James Volney Righter.

ous fire began on the second floor of the concrete structure. The flames quickly ignited heaps of papers, drawings, cardboard models, and paint solvents that customarily fill studios. Structures that students had built out of plywood and two-by-fours, sometimes three levels high, added more fuel. Soon the fire was out of control and reached such high temperatures that the windows exploded onto the street. The fire then spread up the exterior of the building and gutted the upper floors.

When the New Haven fire department arrived (described as "the real heroes of that night") they quickly covered the valuable historic library with plastic to prevent water destruction. Water cascading through the structure filled the tray-shaped floors like swimming pools, compounding the crisis with fears of structural collapse.

Moore was out of town when the fire occurred. He returned to New Haven to find the school in shambles — a soggy mess in a foreboding, scorched concrete shell. Speculation mounted: radical students, the Weathermen, Black Panthers, and antiwar activists all were suspected. But to sort out the motives of supposed arsonists was difficult, and, in retrospect, many now believe the fire was likely accidental, caused by overloaded extension cords or an overheated wax melter.

One thing was for certain, however: the fire was a metaphor for those turbulent years at Yale, the gutted building symbolizing the hollowness into which architecture had succumbed.

Extensive repairs had to be made to the ruined interiors, so students arriving for the fall semester attended classes in nearby studios and storefronts. In the *Architectural Record,* the following was reported:

> Yale's graduate courses in architecture are being held in New Haven lofts and storefronts and in the remains of the Art and Architecture Building, much of which was gutted by fire last year. Many of the students like things that way, too, according to Dean Charles W. Moore, Director of Studies in Architecture. . . . Within the restructured building will be a restructured school, the result of a student revolution last spring. At present, student-faculty committees have such responsibilities as admission, rules, and choice of visiting critics; and, although the Yale administration is so far opposed to so much student control, Mr. Moore thinks the reforms are working well. Students have control over all but $1\frac{1}{2}$ years of the $3\frac{1}{2}$ year course of study. "People who come looking for 'how to do it' are really desperately frustrated," says Mr. Moore. Mr. Moore is pleased with the school's new emphasis on social consciousness and student liberty, much of which he helped bring about even before last spring's upheaval . . .

The Yale Mathematics Building Competition was another controversial event mired in emotional chiaroscuro that occurred under Moore's tenure. When the university announced plans in 1969 to build an addition to Leet Oliver Hall to accommodate a growing math program, Moore and Edward Larabee Barnes (then in charge of campus planning) proposed the idea of an open architectural competition.

Together Moore and Barnes sought to avoid a competition that would produce an array of heroic, monumental, and signature buildings. "It had been advocated for some time," Moore wrote, "and with some spirit by Edward L. Barnes, myself, and a number of others who thought that Yale could make an important contribution to architecture by having an open competition for a nonmonumental economical working building. This is, I believe, a rare phenomenon; most competitions and most competition techniques are based on fixing the jurors' eyes with a striking gesture. Here the Mathematics Department's requirements and my codification of them into a program were developed to thwart the striking gesture, to require instead a more delicate resolution of forces, visual and functional; our bias, we hoped, was clear."

Architects throughout the United States were invited to participate. In all, there were 468 entries. A jury convened to examine the work, including architects Edward L. Barnes, Romaldo Giurgola, and Kevin Roche; John Christiansen, a Yale student; Charles Rickart, chairman of the math department; Edward Dunn, director of Yale's building and grounds planning; and Vincent Scully, Yale professor of architectural history.

When a scheme by Robert Venturi was unanimously named the winner, allegations of insider favoritism were leveled, as were questions about the propriety of Venturi's eligibility (he was a visiting member of Yale's faculty), and finally came criticism about the building's ordinariness — why should an "ordinary" building be honored? As Moore wrote:

There is a special twentieth-century pattern for memorable architectural competitions: the winner is conservative yet highly competent; among the runners-up are designers of buildings of revolutionary importance for modern architecture (in the Chicago Tribune Tower competition these included Eliel Saarinen and Walter Gropius; in the League of Nations competition, Le Corbusier). This pattern has pleased almost everyone, producing safe buildings for the users and sources of wonder for historians. The Yale Mathematics Building Competition upset this arrangement; the winner was at once the "safe" solution, in the users' terms, and perhaps the most vividly iconoclastic of the entries to the historians. Some of us thought that a splendid confluence; others across the country were noisily put off by what seemed at worst a put-up job, at least an arcane put-on.

Though all of the criticisms and allegations were proven baseless, the controversy continued when Moore published a book, *The Yale Mathematics Building Competition: Architecture for a Time of Questioning,* with Nicholas Pyle. Desiring critical analysis by a figure impartial to the drama of the events, Moore chose Colin Rowe, whose essay was met with passionate opposition and who was ultimately excluded from the publication. Rowe was puzzled by

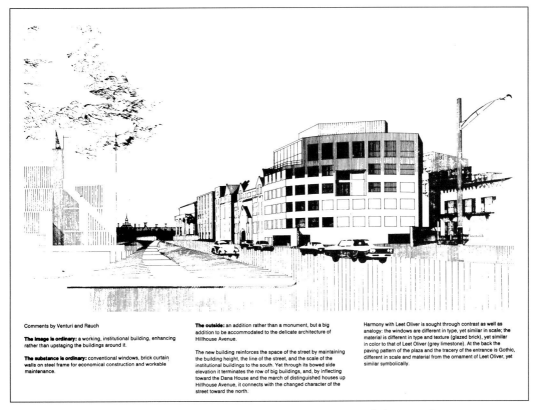

Comments by Venturi and Rauch

The image is ordinary: a working, institutional building, enhancing rather than upstaging the buildings around it.

The substance is ordinary: conventional windows, brick curtain walls on steel frame for economical construction and workable maintenance.

The outside: an addition rather than a monument, but a big addition to be accommodated to the delicate architecture of Hillhouse Avenue.

The new building reinforces the space of the street by maintaining the building height, the line of the street, and the scale of the institutional buildings to the south. Yet through its bowed side elevation it terminates the row of big buildings, and, by inflecting toward the Dana House and the march of distinguished houses up Hillhouse Avenue, it connects with the changed character of the street toward the north.

Harmony with Leet Oliver is sought through contrast as well as analogy: the windows are different in type, yet similar in scale; the material is different in type and texture (glazed brick), yet similar in color to that of Leet Oliver (grey limestone). At the back the paving pattern of the plaza and the tracery of the entrance is Gothic, different in scale and material from the ornament of Leet Oliver, yet similar symbolically.

Yale Mathematics Building Competition Winner, © Venturi, Scott Brown and Associates, Inc., *1969; drawing by W. G. Clark (the firm at the time was Venturi and Rauch, Architects).*

the controversy since he regarded his own review as "tolerably sympathetic — if anything critical of the program rather than the architects."

In the end, after all of the heartache, the building was not built because funding was never realized.

Moore hated confrontations and the ongoing challenges were wearisome. He never boasted any talent for management, and problems often accumulated only to be dealt with too late, after returning from travels. Managing the bureaucracy got in the way of teaching. Moore's first years at Yale, before the swelling of the revolution, were his golden years of teaching, a time when the ideas that would become his lasting contributions to architectural education blossomed.

So often, architecture schools were constrained by a Beaux Arts or Bauhaus formalism with obligatory ideological positions. Charles changed all of that. Like Bailey and Wurster, Moore sought to attract people with wide varieties of ideas, believing that pluralism would enhance the creative process. Moore did not believe in imposing his views on students and especially did not believe in advancing any style or dogma or using the cookie-cutter approach to education, in which professors imprint their design agenda on impressionable students. He did not believe in blocking (or influencing) a student's explorations, nor did he believe in excessive negative criticism. He disavowed the traditional jury system in which each student presented architectural drawings that typically were criticized by professors intent on showcasing their own theoretical or aesthetic positions.

"I saw Charles do many surprising and endearing things," Tim Vreeland, later a colleague at UCLA, remembered, "but the one which struck me most was during a jury, when he got up and presented each student's project, in lieu of the student, to the attending faculty. It was not work that he was particularly familiar with nor was it necessarily very good, but his empathetic understanding of what the student had tried to do prompted him to make the best-possible case for it. I am sure he may have done this many times before, but for me, who had been schooled in the world of tough, stand-on-your-feet East Coast juries, it was an eye-opener and threw in doubt the whole traditional adversarial relationship between teacher and student as a necessary educational method."

Moore's enthusiasm for design and discovery was catching. Student after student recalled the energy and sense of invention and spontaneity that Moore inspired. The young history student Paul Goldberger, for instance, attended Moore's seminar on the Bauhaus. "I remember," Goldberger said, "that class for another reason too. Which is where, in a sense, I began my career. I wrote a paper for that class that somehow struck Charles in some unexpected way, and his reaction led me to believe for the first time that I might have some ideas about architecture worth taking seriously. Not for Charles Moore, the paucity of comments intended to keep students distant from their master, his enthusiasm was all there, and he liked nothing better than to share it with students. That translated for me into a kind of support like none other — the support that gives you the courage to get started."

Exciting "happenings" in the studios were also occurring. Moore's closest collaborator throughout the Yale years was Kent Bloomer, a sculptor and architectural ornamentor; together they taught first year. Since it was a student's first exposure to design, they believed it to be the most important phase in architectural education. Kent Bloomer wrote:

Charles Moore grew up partly in the midwest, partly in the southwest, and after studying at the University of Michigan he completed his formal studies in architecture at Princeton under the departmental leadership of Jean Labatut.

Isabelle Courney, the French-born architectural historian, has focused on the exchange of French and American architectural thought in the twentieth century, which she sees as deeply affecting both cultures. She wrote recently about the circumstances by which the French architect and educator Jean Labatut might be characterized as the last steward of the old Ecole des Beaux Arts, which he attempted to perpetuate or resurrect at Fontainebleau after World War I. Evidently he did not succeed, and so he shut the door and departed for the United States and Princeton in the late thirties.

I mention this because it seems to illuminate one of the forces leading to the juxtaposition of a deeply "American," almost Emersonian, sense of "place-space" with a love of the more fixed, centric, and polychrome architecture of antiquity, a certain "Collision," to use one of Charles's favorite words, of sensibilities. Can you imagine Charles Moore and Jean Labatut meeting each other — the erudite Frenchman and the young American student?

I first encountered Charles Moore about 1964 when I was an instructor at the Carnegie Institute of Technology and Charles came to give his seminal Disneyland lecture. He visited my studio classroom afterward. The wall in that studio included large old sepia photographs of Greek temples and ancient ruins I had collected and mixed together with student projects about polyhedra, catanaries, and modular structures. The atmosphere of the classroom was, in 1964, rather eclectic and even iconoclastic, which revealed my own fascination with artifacts of the Bauhaus (I had studied at M.I.T. and Yale) mingling with ancient classical forms.

Charles subsequently invited me to join the faculty at Yale, and after my return to Connecticut in the summer of 1966, we set out to prepare a first-year syllabus. During the summer's work several of Moore's most fundamental principles became apparent. He held a strong aversion to an individual instructor's tactical withholding of knowledge in order to keep the student's educational development under control. In this respect, he also objected to doses of negative criticism if it was directed at work-in-progress requiring knowledge that the student did not fully grasp as yet. That harsh style of criticism could compel the student to look in a prescribed direction. In the same spirit he did not believe in oversimplifying the requirements of an assignment in order to make the problem graspable and explainable. Multiple and complex agendas were to be included in each assignment. He argued that a studio problem should represent a reasonably complete and probable architectural situation to be addressed holistically, rather than reductively.

In 1966 he clearly felt that many students and faculty were operating under a measure of assumed "canons" and quasi-moral suppositions that were insufficiently tested or argued. He said to me that "inasmuch as the faculty and students talk to each other and criticize works of design in the English language, it was curious that they did not read more books together." He proposed a minicourse called "readings about architecture" to share and incorporate into the crits the thoughts of writers such as Portoghesi, Bachelard, and Summerson. He believed more "verbal" wisdom might address the problem of vulnerability to the imposition of prefabricated beliefs.

Besides reading, and with ever greater determination, Charles Moore valued the actual visitation to sites and the critical nature of field trips. Over the years the dimension of education by travel consumed almost all the other agendas in a Moore studio.

Charles forever insisted that joy and humor were among the most valuable properties of experience and intelligence. He lamented the dull effects of "grim seriousness" as a pervasive attitude in the criticism and consideration of architecture.

And finally, at least as far as this very short list of principles allows, Charles always assigned a great deal of importance to practical technologies. This dimension seems to surprise people who have not taught with him. For example, he initiated the outside building projects at Yale. Once he brought a plumbing fixture salesman into the first-year studio to lecture on the range of available fixtures. He was always devising water machines and bathing contraptions with the students. In one undergraduate class he assigned a fountain to be constructed above a readily available, store-bought child's plastic play pool. He suggested using garden hoses and designing special valves and waterheads. This all took place with the students using the fire escape as a site. Unpredictably, the fountain "backfired" and sent water pouring through the windows of the Religious Studies Department, which occupied the same building. An enraged visiting buddhologist called the police, and Dean Moore was last seen disappearing out the backdoor.

In any case, after that first summer of preparation I still recall our first meeting with the students in which Charles avowed to announce some of his principles. He stood in the carpeted jury pit that Paul Rudolph provided and announced that he did not believe in withholding knowledge. He declared that he would reveal his own strategies as fast as possible and stated, "I have based all of my own work on two principles, the second of which is the same as the first." That extraordinary declaration was in fact reasonable, as he went on to describe the "sameness" that exists between a small building with an aedicula and the small building surrounded with "saddlebags" or sheds. He was announcing his devotion to the concentrically layered plan, or geode, which had been developed in his early work with MLTW.

Later he told me about the "discovery" of the aedicula in Summerson's chapter on the Gothic in *Heavenly Mansions*. He added that he and his colleagues ran into Summerson in London and took the opportunity to thank him for unearthing such a fine organizing principle of design. When Sir John heard that they were actually building aediculas in California he was astounded, as he pointed out that the aedicula had become obsolete by the fifteenth century and was not something to be used today! Fortunately that sort of chronologically or historically determined rationalizing never diverted Charles from looking at all there was to look at in the timeless world of architecture.

Later on in that first day of introduction he said that if all architects had vanished tomorrow they would not be missed immediately by the public-at-large, unlike the outcry that might be expected to follow the disappearance of butchers. He was announcing that architecture was a fragile artifact of culture and that it was not a necessity. He shortly added, however, the notion of the "threshold" theory in which an architect had to earn the license to fly by understanding the bedrock and the needs of the client by providing utility before passing the threshold into a level of desire and the magical properties of architecture.

As the term progressed, it became apparent that Charles Moore's sense of precedent was by no means confined to Europe, and that he represented as well the Mexican and Asian influences in our culture. When he referred to Europe he often said, "Some prefer Rome, some prefer Paris, and some prefer London. I," he said, "prefer Rome." He also preferred Washington, D.C., to New York City.

He dabbled in virtually every medium of design in order to figure out how it might best be taught. At a certain point he even started a small drawing course in which he taught perspective. First he taught one-point perspective and then two-point. When he got to three-point he said, "Well, I will show you how to do this, although it is unlikely many of us will ever get commissions tall enough to require using it!"

After Charles left Yale and went to UCLA, I continued as a visitor to his studios. I arrived one day in Los Angeles and, after a couple of days, he announced we were ready to inspect an important site, which turned out to be Monte Alban in southern Mexico. After Monte Alban we went to Mitla and the gift shops of Oaxaca. We lectured at the University of Benito Juarez with their one projector housed at the old convent of Santa Domingo. We also bought rugs. I returned home a week late.

That kind of direct engagement with places was never unusual in Charles's company. When you visited someplace, like the Mission Inn in California or the Riverwalk in San Antonio, you were not expected to simply stare at it. Feasting in it and sitting upon it were just as important.

When Charles was the O'Neil Ford Professor at the University of Texas he enlisted his small postprofessional studio in the All-Texas Architecture School Competition, which required about five weeks of student time. The problem was to design a museum of American Indian artifacts in Texas. In the meanwhile, he had scheduled a field trip to Indian pueblos, as well as Texan and Mexican sites, which eventually occupied all of the students' time, except for one final weekend. Nevertheless, his small group won three of the top awards for the competition, including first place. That triumph exemplified the productive side of Charles's lack of faith in the dynamics of the drafting room. In fact, I suppose he would probably agree with Marshall McLuhan that the media can direct the nature of the project and the drafting room is too confining and the drafting tables too flat to occupy a major share of the design process.

Charles Moore never demanded that his colleagues or his students do as he did. About twelve years ago I began a course in Architectural Ornament, Design, and Theory at Yale. Charles at first seemed surprised and wondered why I was doing that. Eventually he said I would never get anywhere in my study of ornament unless I showed how ornament and space worked together. Nevertheless, he invited me several times to give lectures and workshops in ornament in Texas. On one occasion I was phoned by his studio afterwards and asked to mail them an "ornament" for use in the World's Fair project they were working on. A year later I asked Charles how it all worked out, and he said they never deployed the ornament or any system of ornament for that matter. Nor, he said, did they use the urban planning systems or color systems that other guests had lectured about and proposed. However, he said the students tried all of the proposed "systems," and it was through a process of critically eliminating those various strategies that they eventually discovered their own best solutions.

Charles Moore was a teacher who believed in the importance of the University. He was, of course, deeply committed to the profession of architecture. He understood, nevertheless, that first of all the university serves to provide education in subjects, languages, and the phenomenon of culture. The professions and the schools are distinctly different institutions, and Charles Moore always reminded us that architecture, after all, is not a property of the profession but rather of the culture-at-large.

Urban designers David Lewis and Ray Gindroz taught as well. Lewis was a champion of involving people in the design of cities, especially those on the lowest economic levels who had been traditionally shut out of planning processes. He advocated enfranchisement. Gindroz also focused on the importance of civic life, and had students design streets within long building corridors as a way of exploring principles that could be used in neighborhoods and downtowns. Denise Scott Brown, Robert Venturi, and Steven Izenour were conducting their studios on Las Vegas and Levittown, which led to their landmark book, *Learning from Las Vegas*. Vincent Scully was teaching students passion for architectural history. And James Stirling, who was designing revolutionary buildings in England, was a visiting studio professor.

One of Moore's great accomplishments at Yale was the founding of the master's in environmental design (MED) program, based on ideas transplanted from Berkeley. Bill Mitchell, who would become a leading educator himself and a coauthor with Moore *(The Poetics of Gardens),* was a student fresh from Australia in the MED program, of which he wrote:

> It wasn't comfortable or reassuring. Like many other recent architecture graduates, I was attracted to the MED Program in the late '60s because Yale under the direction of Charles Moore simply seemed the liveliest, most intellectually exciting place to be — clearly the hot spot for engagement of the issues and debates that were beginning to shake the certainties and platitudes of the architectural world we knew. When we got to New Haven we found ourselves in a community that had

been devastated and divided by some of the most brutal excesses of urban renewal. The Bobby Seale trial rammed raw racial conflict right in our faces. Vietnam and Cambodia brought out massive protests and spawned a menacing police and military presence. The Living Theater successfully invited audience members to remove their clothing and do astonishing things on stage. The Black Workshop became a vivid, challenging presence and staged acrimonious confrontations with university officials. An Oldenberg sculpture inflated itself into a wobbling phallus outside the President's office, then stood there forlornly on its tractor treads through the winter snows. Drugs were everywhere. The building burned.

As far as I can recall — though this may be a bit of an exaggeration — the MED Program had few requirements and no discernible curriculum. But it gave us a license to seek out faculty members who seemed to have something to say and to pursue the investigations and discussions that seemed compelling. Some ended up pounding the Las Vegas strip with Bob Venturi and Denise Scott Brown. Others argued (and argued!) about urban design with Serge Chermayeff. Most of us went to Scully's great theatrical lectures in the Law School auditorium. We showed up when Lou Kahn and Bucky Fuller spoke. We hacked computers. We took courses in forestry, game theory, theater design, polymer chemistry, whatever. We built weird things out of improbable materials. We drew and talked endlessly and drank imprudent quantities of cheap red wine. We each did what we knew we needed to do, and it changed our lives.

Charles Moore was wise enough and courageous enough just to create a space for all this to happen. God knows there must have been pressure to clean it up and get it organized, but he never seemed very much interested in that. He was interested in our intellectual projects though, and from time to time would engage them with the quick, vivid, and learned mind that he so carefully hid behind a hesitantly amiable manner. And he showed us the wit, generosity, and genuine respect for the passions and convictions of others that made his architecture such a wonder.

Most exciting, what Professor Herman Spiegel called "the best thing that ever happened in that school and should have happened in every architecture school," was the Yale Building Program. Not a disciplinarian, Moore could only provide methods or activities that might somehow fit into students' social concerns. Realizing that students wanted to be actively involved in their own education, Moore began a program in which students designed and actually built community structures, some for impoverished Appalachian communities. Despite the phenomenal planning and daunting physical labor (the buildings had to be built in a matter of weeks, usually during inclement weather), the projects were successful and even made the cover of *Progressive Architecture* in 1967. Today the Yale Building Program continues to expose students to practical building experience in projects throughout the country.

∼

The following is Moore's examination of architectural education and recollections of the Yale Building Program:

Of all the memories of Yale, the Building Program is the strongest and for me, the one that I am most proud of. At the time, I thought architecture schools could usefully be grouped into those, on the one hand, whose teachers and administrators believed that mankind already knew how to design and build buildings well enough so that the task was to teach students how to do it too, to start with things the way they were, in the expectation that in time some students may have developed innovations of their own. The other attitude was based on the belief that the buildings that we made and the cities we formed them into were so patently inadequate and such a dubious basis for growth that it was absurd to teach our students in detail and by rote how to do as we do. The Yale Architecture School ran on that latter attitude.

It might be useful, though it is certainly unmannerly, for me to sketch a short and highly prejudiced recent history of architectural education, to describe a land eroded with pitfalls in a search for the developable area which remains. The history of discomfiture, like any modern history of architectural education must start with the Ecole des Beaux Arts, in which students engaged in a series of exercises of great power, charged with the rare capacity to enlist their excitement. The method was to condense a memorable requirement of society into a program which could be responded to with solutions shown as large drawings, beautifully executed on larger pieces of paper; of plans, sections, and elevations of structures, rendered in the subtlety of ink and watercolor wash. Any system, even as it purports to be a solution, was limited by the medium in which it communicates, and the Beaux Arts system, communicating by way of ink and watercolor washes on pieces of flat surface, could only indicate solutions which showed up in that fashion — an era as Buckminster Fuller so often pointed out, when many of the things that mattered the most were turning out to be invisible, going out of sight like the submerged part of an iceberg.

After World War I the Ecole des Beaux Arts process was floundering in irrelevance. At about the time the floundering had become excruciating, revolution developed from the Bauhaus which was concerned with the making of things whose shapes would derive from the processes, hopefully technological, by which they had been made. The Bauhaus architecture, though, was subject, perhaps inevitably, to the same limitations of medium, of drawings in plan, sections, and elevations, and when the dust had cleared the style had changed (as India ink replaced Chinese), but the beaux arts method persisted in most schools, surprisingly unchanged, it was the process then, as irrelevant as ever, by which architecture students drew things that were drawable on large and beautiful plates to hang upon the wall quite independently of the needs of society around them, which seemed more and more untenable to thoughtful teachers and administrators everywhere.

Just after the Second World War many of these teachers launched a fine ship — City Planning — on which many of their hopes and some of the Fine Young Men embarked. The ship sailed slowly and majestically over the horizon and out of sight, quickly to be taken into custody in the land of the Economists and other True Believers. Only somewhat daunted, the same architectural educators more recently have stood upon the same shore to launch another smaller and leakier ship, called Urban Design, on which many of the remaining Fine Young Men have embarked.

Meanwhile, on the shore, made ardent by the urgencies, a pair of religions flourished. The first one, an Apollonian faith, said that there is no God but Technology and the Computer is his prophet. It looks to the quantification of information both human and technical, and the superhuman organization of the quantified bits to bring order out of the senseless confusion which the complexity of the modern world has brought to the still-too-simple building craft. The orthodoxy priesthood of this religion had the faith that organization of information itself is the goal and that building is really an after-the-fact irrelevance best handled by contractors or other menials.

The other religion, a true Dionysian one, was more mysterious, and employed a magic, often Black. Its faith was interaction. In its more conservative form it especially advocated interaction with social scientists who were presumed to be sitting upon the secrets which must be learned in order properly to design the physical environment, and who would, if correctly interacted with, divulge these secrets. In the more radical construct, the Interaction was with the Poor themselves, with people actually in need of the physical facilities which architects can produce; and middlemen had to be chased from the temple. Both these religions, Apollonian and Dionysian were, as so many evangelical religions are, intent on burning. The victim of the torch was, perhaps unsurprisingly, building, which got short shrift from the new high priests.

This then was the politico-religious situation on the shore of our lonely sea, in which the architectural educator found himself in 1968. These two religions had the power to light the imagination; to have ignored them would have been wrong. On the other hand, to have cheered while they burned the books and the buildings would have destroyed, I believe, the very things we were there to promote. The answer, I suspected, was a kind of ecumenism, not so simple, certainly, and not the same thing as the eclecticism of styles which Frank Lloyd Wright and others so ardently decried, but an attempt to use the newfound strength of these faiths while we tried to avoid their more obsessive shortcomings and to turn their power to the cause of building a three-dimensional environment.

In this situation, in 1968, I believed that architecture was only properly teachable in terms of use in response to the people who were to inhabit buildings, their life styles, their concerns, their privacy, and their public realm. To teach architecture simply as the composition of shapes was out of the question. Yet for the designer to be able to operate at all, he had to be able to make things knowingly, to compose shapes and voids, as well as to manipulate programmatic firsts.

We all thought, what better way could there be to achieve any of this but to actually build something with our own hands. Students helped establish a number of criteria from the beginning for the building we would do. First, it had to matter. Whatever it was, it had substantially to change the lives of people who used it. Second, also because of the enthusiasms of students then, any building had to be for poor people. And third, as a practical matter, it had to be of a size that was buildable within the time available to us. We took it that larger problems, ones which were probably not solvable by building alone or on which building might not even make an appreciable dent, as for instance the problems of Harlem, were inappropriate to the first year. Instead the real problems of a small community we might work with, like a rural community in Appalachia, were more appropriate to our capacity and concerns.

Thanks to a liaison with the faculty of the University of Kentucky, especially John Hill, some of the students from the previous first year had come into contact with a very ecumenical priest in Jackson County, a very pretty rural area southeast of Lexington, in which there was one of the lowest per capita income levels in the nation and where the priest, Father Beiding, was seeing to the building of a number of kinds of structures of great local importance. Some of our students, starting with him, went to work with a number of groups nearby and they came, with considerable expertise already developed, to describe to the new first-year class some of the problems and some of the hopes of the people in rural Appalachia.

The students then came into contact with citizens of New Zion, Kentucky, a tiny community in Jackson County, whose need for a community center had been discovered by the Yale students working with Father Beiding. Cars loaded with students started going to New Zion, meeting with the people there, watching astonished, as the residents of the neighboring community walked out of the proceedings, sympathizing with that part of the group which sought to replace the small available site for a community center with a larger and better located site, finally heeding the more conservative voices in the community who demonstrated that that site could not be made available. Meanwhile, the students and the members of the community developed a program starting with all those things which were regarded as desirable, examined them with the people who were to use them, eliminating together some that did not seem either adequately important or adequately achievable to be included, cutting down the program, then adding again to it as the designers allowed, if the demands were strong. For instance, a half basketball court, asked for early, then discarded as impractical, turned out to be possible in the final solution.

The trips to Kentucky began soon after the school year was under way.

Picnic at New Zion, Kentucky.

Back at Yale, there were a series of design programs at the school, where the students developed first a bathing facility, which might be useful in the not-yet-designed community center in New Zion (a community with little indoor plumbing); then designs for the initial ambitious programs, then later designs for small programs, less ambitious but readily buildable, with discussions of alternatives.

Students Constructing New Zion.

The only time the students acted to reject one of the faculty programs was when, in the heat of debate over which site was desirable, we proposed a movable building to be built on the available site, which could be transported later to the more desirable site, if its purchase were to transpire. The students explained to us that such a building would not bear adequate relation to the site (which we, on purpose, had not seen) and was silly anyway, and that was that.

After the students had, in a series of short problems, designed the bathing facility, a big building and a little building, then they grouped in teams of four or five to design buildings. The groups were organized around building systems to which students were attracted: there was a masonry group, a balloon frame group (called the stud and skin group), a heavy timber group, and a sculptured earth group. After the results of their joint activity were assessed by themselves and a faculty jury, they regrouped, this time around strong design ideas which attracted them to one another.

By now, some of the building systems had begun to seem too difficult to pursue, and most of the schemes were based on fairly conservative light wood construction methods charged by the realization that if thirty people were to build a simple wood building in what was initially going to be a space of a week, then the techniques they employed could not be very close to those employed by three or four people building the same building over a period of several months.

Finally, the groups had made their designs, along with a series of individual schemes from a sixth group which had splintered. The faculty for the first year, including myself, Kent Bloomer, who was in charge of the basic design part of the program and worked closely on all of it, Herman Spiegel and Luis Summers, who had been teaching structural engineering to the group, Paul Helmle and Herbert Newman, who had been working with us in the studio, met and picked (in order to avoid French parliamentary problems) three of the designs that seemed to us most worthy of the students' consideration, going so far as to rank them in order of our notion of their excellence. The students picked almost unanimously the design we had ranked number one, the product of a team called Group-Group (which initially had been the Stud and Skin group, but couldn't stand its name).

The work began in earnest, both on the part of the members of the successful group and of others in the class to turn out a set of drawings which would describe how to build the building. Meanwhile, other members of the class organized the logistics in the community, accepting offers of food and lodging. The ladies of the community organized themselves to serve a great buffet at the site each noon during our stay there. Still others in the class set about persuading friends of the school or of their families to donate materials or money. A critical path analysis had shown that it would be necessary for an advanced party of about ten people in the class of thirty to go to Kentucky and build the foundations to give the concrete time to harden before the wooden structure was begun. The building itself had been re-designed in the course of working drawings to remove a three-story tower which had at one stage been on it, but it still contained some 1,800 square feet and seemed a great deal of building to be built in such a brief time.

The advanced party went and in spite of heavy rains, when the whole group arrived a week later, they were ahead of schedule with a hand-dug foundation, footings, block walls, and floor joists, ready to receive the superstructure. The students were beginners and so did not know, when the man at the lumberyard told them that oak, the local wood, was the cheapest thing they could get for siding, that their first thousand nails would bend on the surface of it. They soon gained, however, a vigorous understanding of the capacities of oak. Though complicated by the short time and the large group, the building process was organized altogether by the class. The faculty, still welcomed for their technical expertise and strong backs, were not in any way allowed to organize the operation, which had in fact, overtones of a tolerant version of a Japanese arrangement in which an official Mikadoship elected by the group, while it maintained a useful show of organized authority, made its private peace with an unofficial shogunate, which derived from individual expertise in the group inherited from military careers and summer jobs. The imperial staff and the shogunate worked with extraordinary subtlety and absence of confrontation.

Meanwhile the students who preferred group effort were organized into teams of carpenters to build plywood walls which would then be manhandled into place, while those whose predilection was for individual effort mostly found themselves individually digging a leaching field and attending the dynamiting of a hole in nearby solid rock where a septic tank was to be placed.

The whole group worked for a week, often through driving rains, and when the end of the week came, much was still left to be done. A rear guard of about ten people stayed through most of a second week and finished the closing in, the sheathing, and exterior finishing of the building. There had not been enough plywood to finish the interior, so a group of students went back after school in June and accomplished in two sessions most of the remaining interior finishing.

This then was the process, and I believe it was a success; certainly the excitement of building continued unabated in the group. As an object it was a success, perhaps, for a number of reasons which none of us could really have predicted:

thanks to the scale of its big room and of its openings, it did not look like a house, yet it was, because of its construction and the materials, sympathetic to the simple buildings of the scattered rural community. It was apparently a place fun to be in, where a basketball could be bounced at the same time ladies were sewing without seeming unpleasant for anyone. Because it was simple, because it was built by people that the members of the community liked and enjoyed having among themselves, because it used some of the efforts of the members of the community itself, it was apparently not regarded as an alien intrusion or as something some Martians from Yale left behind, but as a useful facility which was a part of New Zion.

Finished Building!

CHAPTER SEVEN

Habitation and House Making

As his reputation grew, larger and more public commissions occupied the drafting tables, but Moore still preferred designing houses. He understood that making a house was perhaps the most important and lasting expression of an individual's or a family's dreams. Houses express how people want to be in the world.

In 1974 Moore wrote with Gerald Allen and Donlyn Lyndon, *The Place of Houses*. It has become required reading for most architecture students and is a rich resource for those building a house. The book did not contain any secrets or stunning revelations about how to design houses. Instead, the authors sought to demystify house making. They began with a premise that anyone, however limited their budget or experience, could make a house. In it they gave advice like "keep the myth up off the floor," meaning don't make complicated

Church Street South, 1966–69; Jewish Community Center Tower, 1970; and Kevin Roche's Knights of Columbus Tower, New Haven. Photo by James Volney Righter.

plans that get in the way of everyday living; lift the magic into the ceiling where it isn't in the way, so that it fills the space with exciting shapes and plays of light.

An important phase of Charles's career was designing subsidized housing. Marvin Buchanan, who worked in the MLTW and MLTW/Moore-Turnbull offices, said that housing was "fiendishly difficult" because budgets were so thin that even minor changes in design could have an impact on an entire project. Moore didn't think that people should be "condemned to living in squash courts" so he tried to vary the units, break down the box, and draw in natural light. Many of these projects occurred during the Kresge College years and extended the idea of making a "street," arranging the housing units to create protected, inner spaces for neighbors to meet and children play — a place to engage in public life. Until Richard Nixon pulled the rug out from under federally funded housing projects, Moore was able to finish Church Street South and the Jewish Community Tower, both in New Haven, Whitman Village in Huntington, Maplewood

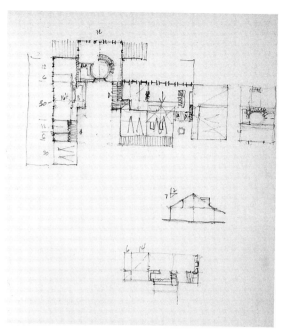

Rudolph House, Robert L. Harper and Charles Moore with James C. Childress, 1981.

Sketches.

Terrace in Middletown, and Orono Housing in Maine. Much later, Moore, with John Ruble and Buzz Yudell, designed the Tegel Harbor Housing in Berlin.

Sketches for houses often began as tiny diagrams on tracing paper, graph paper, or napkins. Moore would roughly block out the plans, often lining them up with building sections and paying careful attention to the space inside and to the shifts in elevation. Alongside these tiny drawings, Moore would scribble calculations for square footages, stair runs, or roof pitches. Collaborators often said that these drawings, when later enlarged, were remarkably accurate.

Moore never regarded designing houses for others as a way to impose philosophies or advance theoretical positions. (In fact, when a critic blasted one of Moore's houses for failing to do just that, Moore shot back, "It's a house, not a hair shirt!") A house had to be the center of the world for its inhabitants, a place to feel centered, secure, and at home. The centering ranged from the Talbert House of the MLTW days, perched precariously on a steep hillside, its saddlebags supported by rickety extensions, to the Rudolph House of Moore Grover Harper — solidly and powerfully set in the landscape, like Stratford Hall.

Moore felt that houses should be filled with the dreams of the clients. And he preferred clients with very specific desires and goals. Some were quite modest, others quite grand. What he disliked were clients who came with carte blanche "design me a house" attitudes. Instead, Moore enjoyed the challenge of knitting very specific requirements together and balancing site, budget, climate, construction, and materials.

Moore listened. He had the ability to convey to others that what they were saying was important. Like an architect-psychologist, he absorbed what they did, where they enjoyed going, what they liked to collect — turning an interaction into a process of self-realization for the clients. Moore would often personally participate in finishing certain details: he helped paint the tower bookshelves in the Halprin House, made the garden in the Miglio House, devised chandeliers from ordinary lightbulbs, and crafted layered cutouts for bare walls. Clients often became his close friends, and many were drawn, of course, into the Charles Moore travels.

~

The following are remembrances of some of Charles's house clients.

Bruno and Rose Miglio, who live in both the United States and Italy, commissioned two Sea Ranch houses, built in 1984 and 1992.

Rose and I met Charles for the first time in 1983 at the legendary Unit #9 of the Sea Ranch Condominium. It was the start of a very important phase of our lives; Charles's wonderful personality brought a new, rich flavour to our perspectives. We had considered for some time building a house at Sea Ranch on a lot we had bought on a whim in 1978. Charles Moore and his friends had created inspiring, new forms of architecture masterfully applied to the Sea Ranch environment. Could we ask him to design our dream retreat there? But what about our minimal budget? Would the famous architect shun us? "You should try," a friend suggested, "after all, everything in America is possible."

Candidly we approached Charles's office at UIG. Our candor was rewarded — Marilyn Zuber, the wonderful manager of the office, encouraged us to come forward to Charles. She told us that Moore enjoyed designing small houses with the challenge of small budgets, and he would love to be involved again at Sea Ranch.

In awe, we headed north, hurriedly collecting in our minds confused ideas of the house we wanted. We arrived at Sea Ranch at 10:00 in the morning. The sanctum sanctorum of Unit #9 was a kaleidoscope of splendid disorder: books, glasses, pencils, drawings, house models, toys, and a pair of ruffled up socks were sparsely everywhere; dominating this chaos was a huge, gentle man, seemingly as embarrassed as we. He waved us in. After a few circumstantial mumbling sounds of mutual recognition and our uncertain search for a direction, Rose and I parked ourselves in front of the spectacular view window and started tentatively to expose our case. Soon, quietly efficient Charles emerged from the chaos

Miglio I House, Charles W. Moore and Urban Innovations Group, with John Echlin and Michael Burch, 1984–86. Photo by Willard Hanzlik.

and guided us with minimal interventions toward complete expressions. We gladly tuned in, formulating our dreams.

Charles was delighted. The house would have barely one thousand square feet of area, a tiny budget, and be built on what he defined as a 'wonderful' lot on a nearby hillside. From that first meeting, the project moved on in pleasant leaps under the constant surveillance of John Echlin and later of Michael Burch, accented by exciting get togethers with Charles whenever he was in town. Arriving from the most distant places on earth and from important architectural endeavors, Charles always found time for our minimal project.

At each meeting wonderful new things happened, Charles's magic would develop ample views of the ocean in front, and of the majestic redwoods in the back for an elegant, slender house, transparent and yet protective and cozy. An S-shaped floor plan, gently stepped in three levels, would hug the hill grade and subtly ensure a dynamic enjoyment of the interior-exterior relationship. A window high on the tower would let the morning sun shine down onto our breakfast table playfully finding its way through the intricacy of the roof truss structure. A walled-in courtyard at the entrance would remind us of familiar Italian scenes. Again and again we would enjoy the creative process of architectural accomplishment, the selection of unconventional, graceful solutions, and the human playfulness that so distinctly characterize the work of Charles Moore.

In 1988 we went to live permanently at Sea Ranch, certainly attracted by the pleasure of living in that house. Whenever Charles was at Sea Ranch he would visit, in a sort of undeclared ritual where food and wine would be appropriately celebrated. Often he would bring his friends, which pleased us immensely. Charles would enjoy the evening, absorbing quietly the sensations from the beautiful environment we had created together.

In 1992, we met Charles in Rome. We dearly preserve in our memories the images of him in Piazza Navona enjoying the music and the water at the Four Rivers Fountain, in Villa Giulia absorbing the mysterious fascination of the Etruscans, and on the Appia Antica painting a lovely watercolor sketch until a sudden April shower chased us away. The frugal, creative glory of Borromini at the church of St. Ivo charmed him for sure, and at the Trevi Fountain, Rose and I quietly watched him slowly pacing around the bowl of the fountain, deep in his own private thoughts and memories, or maybe just entranced by the musical refrain of the cascading water. The punctuation of a refreshing *granita di caffe con panna* was always welcome before we would all plunge into the cavernous interior of the Pantheon. And in the evenings we would slowly roam Trastevere in search of a piazza where old architecture, ambiance, and good food would strike an honorable balance.

Remembering Charles is easy and pleasant. It makes us feel as if he is with us again, with his intelligence and humanity and wit. We are forever grateful for having had the chance of knowing him.

Moore designed a house for Simone Swan on Long Island. Only a few years before Charles's death, he and Simone were collaborating on a design of a museum near Presidio, Texas, where Simone continues an architectural crusade to reinvigorate vernacular adobe traditions.

Charles wanted to see my small apartment, favorite books and art, and asked about my predilections. I later wrote him a long letter, almost a list of what I wanted to *experience* in a house. No physical details. I wrote about the heart of the house being the kitchen, the delight of eating outside, of a place to dance, read, and work, another to see the horizon of Long Island Sound from bath and bed, an outdoor corner in the sun away from the wind, and privacy for my children and friends. Charles met all requirements with brilliance, leaving nothing out, and provided me with a model to fit under the seat of the plane so I could take it to Scotland to show my son. My son didn't like the design, and I, in fear of decisions, also felt deep down that the house was too *New York Times Sunday Magazine.*

Swan House, Moore Grover Harper with Mark Simon, 1975–76.
Photo by Norman McGrath.

Once again I picked up a pen and confided in Charles with ease and trust. His house was perfect, worldly. Experiencing the model had stirred emotions and memories of an African childhood. But I wanted something Zen, of frugal material, austere. Did Charles Moore mind? He was enchanted to meet the challenge once more and produced a different, opposite design. Betty Parsons, seeing this new model, called it an international farmhouse; the artist Gordon Matta-Clark called it Japanese Tudor. It was a snake of a structure (60' x 16'), a shed-roofed motel, just two bedrooms separated by a bath. Charles was tenderly aware that this design would probably frighten me as well; he awaited my reaction with humor and patience. I soon realized that possessing property, owning things, rather than treading lightly on this earth, filled me with doubt and certain moral inhibitions to the point where I consulted a friend, a bishop in the northeast of Brazil. He reassured me that this house would serve as a spiritually protective skin, and a place for healing and conviviality. Everything fell into place.

We moved in nine months later during a glorious September. A Brahman friend blessed it with melted ghee and incense. Friends, visiting from Japan, Lebanon, Haiti, France, or Brazil, would invariably exclaim, "Why, it's just like home!" (I have concluded that white walls and wood beams strike a universal chord.) Alan Lomax, the cultural ecologist, declared with some alarm, "This is a Venus man trap!" During the first years I discovered Charles's secret references in the house, his endearing playfulness: the closet at the head of the stair is a house within a house; the stairs' configuration mimics in small scale ponderous landings from grand Newport houses; and his play of beams high in the living room is mischievously musical.

Kathryn and Randy Smith commissioned Charles to design a house in Los Angeles.

Just after sunset in October 1983, my husband, Randy, and I ascended the steep staircase of Charles Moore's condominium in West Los Angeles carrying cartons of Bum Bum Chicken purchased at Charles's favorite Chinese restaurant. We reached the first landing, occupied by an old wood table that served as desk, dining table, and repository for stacks of mail and rolls of tracing paper. We were following Bill Turnbull, also burdened down with a paper bag of Chinese food, who greeted his old friend, coming to meet us in his pajamas and bathrobe. We were lucky. Charles was groaning with pain, his bad back had canceled his airplane reservations and this impromptu picnic was to be the first design session for our new house.

Charles sank down with a deep sigh into the cushions of the banquette behind the table as the Prawns with Spicy Sauce began filling the house with the fragrance of garlic and ginger. When the conversation turned to our budget and program, Randy carefully outlined our finances and enumerated the number of bedrooms and baths and strongly expressed his desire to have a house filled with light. Knowing our lot was on a steep hill sloping up, I requested a winding staircase that would be the catalyst for a sensational vertical space. Bill seemed to understand immediately and promised, "It'll be magic."

Charles was quiet and I expected him to say, "You need a bigger budget," but instead he gazed at us and asked, "What is your image of this house?" I blurted out, "Mediterranean," partly because Michael Graves knockoffs were popping up all over the place with peach-colored walls and turquoise trim making "Italian villas" undesirable. I knew I was intentionally vague, and Charles stared at me to grasp my meaning. "What is your fantasy of this house?" he asked, not willing to give up. Randy gave me a blank look as if to say, "I hope you can get this one." I was dumbfounded that the conversation was taking this direction even though I had recently reread *A Place of Houses*. I was expecting questions about "the paper trail" and how much trash we accumulated. Looking over at Charles's pile of unopened mail, I wondered if I could tell him about the dream house that existed in my imagination since high school. It was the house that Dick and Nicole Diver, the characters of F. Scott Fitzgerald's *Tender Is the Night*, rented along the French Riviera. Although I had a very powerful image of life in this house, I could not conjure up any specific architectural expression. All I knew was that it was near the beach, elevated with unobstructed views, and the rooms spilled out into the gardens, but I could not crystallize what the house looked like.

I never had to explain any of this to Charles. As soon as I said the house that Dick and Nicole Diver lived in from *Tender Is the Night,* his face lit up and his eyes sparkled. It was obvious that I did not have to say another word. Charles knew exactly what I was talking about. Although he did not make much of a reply, his eyes were eloquent. As Randy summed it up later, the thing about Charles was when you talked, he really listened.

∾

H. Alan Brooks, an architectural historian and friend of Charles's, once said during a visit to Austin that great architects can change peoples' lives with their work. Most often, it is through houses, and in this next essay Charles explores the sources and inspirations for his housemaking ideas, focusing on what it means to inhabit and dwell.

The act of inhabitation, though not celebrated in our time by its own Freud, must be one of the basic human acts, and making places comfortable for people to inhabit (visually, thermally, acoustically, as well as spatially, and conceptually) must be one of the basic human enterprises. Architects, since Imhotep at the very beginning of recorded history, have been in charge of making places, tombs (houses for the dead), temples (houses for the gods), or even residences in which a people's imperial or civic identification might reside, such as the Doge's Palace in Venice or the White House in Washington, D.C. And in the couple of centuries since the Enlightenment, and especially in our own time, it has become commonplace that the chief concern of architects is, or ought to be, providing spaces for people (not just kings) to live and work and play — a place to inhabit some portion of the planet's surface.

Unfortunately, we have not quite learned how to do that. Despite all of our rhetoric, high-sounding manifestoes, questions of style (whether modern or post-modern), that seem to be central to most discussions of contemporary architecture, there is a failure to address our central dilemma, which is, I believe, that in the midst of our skilled composition of increasing numbers of architectural shapes and the availability of just about every means of comfort, our cities and towns grow increasingly hostile and unlivable.

J. B. Jackson listed five benefits that the village granted its inhabitants: security, privacy, sociability, justice, and a place connected to the ancestral dead. These things we seek in the places we make, but since most of us wander far from our ancestors' graves, we are left to rely on the more general gift of memory, which with the other boons, security, privacy, sociability, and justice, we then somehow have to transfigure into the villages of our own time. The village offers validation — everyone has a place. With the city, on the other hand, comes the specter of anomie, the person alone in the world.

It helps too when villages or streets or sections of a city (sometimes even a corner) are loaded with sympathetic people longing for social connections so that they

Smith-Kennon House, William Turnbull Associates with Charles W. Moore, 1989. Photo by Tim Street Porter.

Monterey Adobes.

can function as a village, like Greenwich Village, Castro Street, or a settlement at a tennis village. And even more recently places like Seaside, Florida, have been involved with recreating the kinds of towns whose order and cohesion are supported by familiar things such as picket fences and paint and trees and porches and streets.

Physical places can help us to satisfy our longing for the village. The way we build houses to mark a place, where someone can take possession, is helped when we fashion edges (for security), centers (to support sociability), organization (to make a pattern or order on the landscape, and to imply justice and further privacy), and ornament (to connect us with our past).

I've always felt that the attempts (made mostly in our century) to be innovative and original have achieved just the opposite, since we have so limited the kinds of expression and decoration. I don't have any reservations in saying that the houses I design with the help of friends borrow from various sources or traditions that seem most fitting or appealing to the client.

Throughout our own history, the freestanding house for a single family and groups of houses have been at the center of the American Dream, from the beginning of American settlements in New England or towns in the deep South or homesteads in the West. There has been enough land and enough freedom of movement and a wealth of materials so that the goal of living in and even owning a house with land around it was an attainable one for most of the population. The earliest ones recalled memories of homes in England or Europe (some of them still medieval, when the settlers were first arriving) with canny adaptation to a series of harsh new continental climates: a big central chimney conserved heat in cold New England winters; a central hall encouraged breezes through the house during sultry southern summers. In the Southwest, Spain and the Caribbean provided models for houses built around a patio, or verandahed like the adobes in Monterey, California. In the Mexican provinces of Texas, settlers from Germany and Bohemia invoked their homelands in the cut of a rafter or the framing of a window, while in the Mississippi Valley, the flare of an eave might proclaim origins in France.

Plantation houses in Virginia had to take on the self-sustaining functions and dimensions of a tiny city, often with great architectural elegance, intimating origins in Georgian England. The Lee family home, Stratford Hall, in Westmoreland County, Virginia, designed locally and anonymously soon after 1714, is one of the earliest and one of the finest of the great houses, with dual chimneys pinning down a central mass connected to the ground with a great stair.

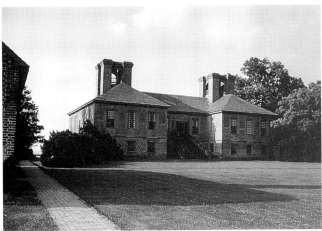

Stratford Hall, Virginia.

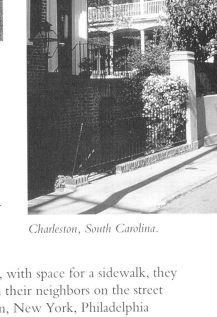

Charleston, South Carolina.

New house types were designed for cities with special sites. Charleston, South Carolina, crowded onto a humid peninsula and desperate for summer breezes, has single houses, perhaps three stories high, that are perpendicular to the street, one room wide with a porch beside it, and a garden, so that breezes pass through every room, brilliantly providing air and privacy all at once.

As cities along the eastern seaboard grew in population, space within the city became scarce, and they were built solid: houses came to the street, with space for a sidewalk, they shared side walls, and sometimes even collided with their neighbors on the street behind so as to leave no outdoor space at all. Boston, New York, Philadelphia (where remains the most intact section of all), Baltimore, Washington, and smaller cities in between and beyond them were built densely, mostly of row houses and tenements, through the eighteenth century and most of the nineteenth.

Then after 1870 a series of inventions changed all that again: the horsecar, the streetcar, the bicycle, and, most notably, the automobile opened up access to all that cheap land that lay beyond the towns. People were no longer confined to the dense urban centers, and across the country, the automobile cities grew, linked by networks of roads and then by new interstates: Detroit, Houston, Denver, and Los Angeles all were made mostly of freestanding houses again.

Perhaps the most important influence on the American house in the early nineteenth century was Thomas Jefferson's. He championed an egalitarian, rural America with every family in its own house, and looked for architectural models in the ancient republics of Greece and Rome (scorning the provincial Georgian buildings of Williamsburg, the old capital of Virginia) and helped usher in a Roman revival, which gradually became the Greek Revival and ennobled, with porticoes and classical detail, houses all the way to the Michigan frontier and the Mississippi Valley.

The Greek Revival, which had become an almost universal style in the new republic, was challenged, by the midnineteenth century, by proponents of Gothic design, with pointed openings, more verticality, more picturesque massing, and more overt romance. Pattern books described possibilities and strongly recommended a closer harmony with nature, with colors like russet and soft ochre and local materials to blend with the landscape rather than standing out from it as the pristine white Greek Revival houses had done.

After Gothic came just about everything at once, a myriad of house styles were illustrated in a myriad of catalogs, houses were even available from Sears, you simply ordered your selection, and its parts were shipped to your site on the railroad for assembly. When the U. S. Consul to the Sandwich Islands came back to Marshall, Michigan, he built a splendid pile recollective of the South Pacific. Henry Austin, the great and prolific architect of New Haven, Connecticut, built basic rectangular speculative houses, with limited applications of lavishly evocative detail, perhaps at its best when it essayed the "Hindoo." The Tuscan villas of central Italy enjoyed great vogue as models, particularly in lavish Florida suburbs, and Richard Morris Hunt, who had become the Dean of American architects, built Biltmore in Asheville, North Carolina, for Vanderbilt clients in the grand manner of a French château. But the "Battle of the Styles," as it came to be called, was surely won, if anyone won it, by the late Victorian exuberances of the new resorts, like Luck Baldwin's small but dazzling cottage in Arcadia, California.

There are, of course, many ways to make a house important: it can be made huge, like stately homes in England; few Americans had the resources and noble privileges to accomplish this. Or houses can be made permanent, built of stone for the ages; few Americans have tried this, either. Wood construction, quick and cheap (where there is timber), and relatively short-lived, is favored almost everywhere in the United States. But then there is ornament, which is an American favorite, and perhaps even more important, there is space around the house and in front of it: the bigger the dimension, the more important the house.

It is probably no accident, given the importance we place on the single family house, that when the architectural revolution came (and it came early), it was in the realm of the house. Frank Lloyd Wright was born in 1867, and by the 1890s he (and many others) were building houses for the midwestern prairie and the

Filipino House, Marshall, Michigan.

suburbs of Chicago that broke open the boxlike rooms they had inherited, sent windows in strips all around the walls, while the spaces flowed together under wide hovering roofs, perhaps pinned to the site by a central mass of masonry, as in Wright's Ward Willits house.

Forty years later Wright was still building innovative houses; his Fallingwater, in Bear Run, Pennsylvania, of the 1930s, is the most complex, and for some, the most thrilling house in America, composed of cantilevered trays and towers of native rock. Meanwhile, in the San Francisco Bay Area, a parallel revolution, more relaxed in its acceptance of existing idioms but equally innovative in its merging of the indoors and outdoors and in its mastery of flowing and surprising light, was led by Bernard Maybeck and others, then gently continued by William Wurster and a second generation of Bay Region architects.

More traditional architectural idioms would reappear, but the house would never be quite the same again. The typical American house came down to one story and opened up to a private inhabitable yard, usually in the back. The street, when those early Prairie Houses were built, was used by horses and carriages and an occasional horseless carriage, and the houses continued, across wider lawns, the tradition of opening up to it. Front porches had presented houses and their inhabitants to the public, and greatly enhanced life along the elm-lined streets of small towns spread across America. People felt to be members of a town. But when the automobiles came in ever-increasing numbers (and the elms died), dwellers were driven back into the privacy of their houses, where (worst luck) they would shortly be offered the comforts of air conditioning. Most stayed there.

The automobile, having driven dwellers off the front lawn, often took the space over, in a giant double asphalt driveway leading to a wide garage door that was generally by far the largest object on the face of the house. The face of the house, for the centuries before the twentieth, had been just that: the child's drawing of house, with a door for mouth, windows for eyes, a roof like hair, and maybe even whiskerlike shrubs flanking the front path. Now this alien aperture shape became what geographers call a "garage-dominant-ell," while humans have often resorted to the rear. Plans were frequently inverted, to situate the living room toward the back yard to view the private, often fenced-in play equipment, barbecue, and in Florida and California neighborhoods the swimming pool, and the other implements of outdoor family life.

In the early 1970s, with an unprecedented swiftness, all that changed. After the oil embargo energy was no longer cheap, and the glass walls started to become more solid again. About the same time cheap land, which had seemed like an almost infinite American resource, began to vanish. The typical suburban house, which might have been eight hundred square feet in area just after World War II, with two bedrooms and a bath, had grown to perhaps twice that size, on a larger piece of land, with three bedrooms, two baths, and a family room; some suburban communities, to maintain their gentility, required as much as four acres of land under every house, and setbacks from the boundaries of prodigious dimension. Even so, the elusive statistics suggest that in 1970 half of all American families could afford a single-family house. Then inflation in the building industry combined with soaring land prices sent that number plunging, and by the eighties, the number of families who could afford the single-family, freestanding house of the American dream was estimated to have dropped below 10%. And the numbers of Americans who can afford to build a traditional house continue to diminish.

Where then do we go from here? Stylistically it seems hardly to matter. The "modern" versus "traditional" controversies of decades past appear to have dissolved into a variety of combinations and persuasions in between. "Eclecticism," the impulse that Frank Lloyd Wright abhorred the most, seems to have swept the day, with some élan, as a look in any of the decorating magazines will show, as designers transform the historical ways of building and furnishing, even as they do not forget them.

Houses, it would seem, are just bound to get smaller and, perhaps, to come again up to their lot lines (in patio houses, zero-lot-line houses, and condominiums). Meanwhile the mobile home, formerly the trailer, which sidesteps most architects' inflated expectations, has taken over an increasing share of new housing and construction and, with its sense (it is generally only that, they are usually moored to the ground) of mobility, its simplicity, and relative cheapness, suggests that there are dimensions of the American dream that we have only begun to discover.

That leaves us at a time when only a fraction of the houses built today have anything to do with architects, and many wonder (forgetting that most people scarcely think architects are worth the expense), "What to do about it?" What might the future of architecture hold?

I think the answer is listening openly to the dreams of those we build houses for, and including them in the effort, so that they, having helped make their house, can more easily find them habitable.

There is also the dilemma in whether to follow the lead of the successful professions, like medicine and the law, and develop an extensive body of "professional" information, increasingly inaccessible to the public, arcane, and wildly expensive, or whether, more like the clergy, to loosen the profession, to open it to share with potential inhabitants the making of the physical environment, to try to tap the energies and images and memories of the people who will occupy buildings. I tend to lean toward the clergy, and house making, I believe, will be richer for the effort.

CHAPTER EIGHT

Centerbrook

"Fitting in" was and continues to be a fundamental Centerbrook principle. In an age of signature "look at me" buildings, especially in museum design, Centerbrook preferred to respect the context of cities, towns, and campuses. The firm began amidst the confusion of the late sixties, and weathered the deep economic recessions and energy crises of the seventies. It began in a tiny office close to Yale's architecture school. As with all of Charles's firms, there were close links between the "professional" studio and the academic studios across the street, which fostered transfers of rich ideas and a virtual revolving door of students working on the projects.

One Yale student, Bill Hersey, was an incredibly talented renderer, watercolorist, and perspectivist (he studied at Princeton under William Shellman). Hersey was a key figure not only in the Connecticut operations, but in Moore's later California offices. With only rough plans and sketches, Hersey could construct vivid perspectives that seemed to pull the viewer into the space of a drawing. Later, John Kyrk joined Hersey, and they worked as a team, producing drawings for many of Moore's projects and architectural competitions.

Two of Centerbrook's outstanding public buildings were the Williams College Museum of Art and the Hood Museum at Dartmouth. Both were masterful exercises in sensitive design. (Moore would go on to design several other museums with various partners, including the Cedar Rapids Museum of Art, additions to the St. Louis Museum of Art, the Palmer Museum at Pennsylvania State University, the Washington State History Museum, and the Monterey Peninsula Museum of Art.) Jacquelynn Baas, the acting director of the Hood when it was built, said, "Museum staffs are a notoriously cantankerous bunch, but the staff noticed a difference in how we treated each other and how we felt about the world after we moved into the building Charles designed for us. Somehow his spirit occupied that building."

The Centerbrook office thrived with a great variety of personalities; personalities, Mark Simon wrote, that eventually flourished in a variety of design paths. There was also a spirit of Yankee ingenuity that led, for instance, Bill Grover to invent a new process of designing a home for a client who had lost his vision. Bill conceived of a way to make raised drawings with a hydraulic press that could be read like Braille.

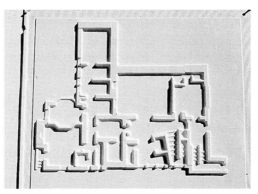

Braille House Plans Designed to Be Read with Hands, Made by Bill Grover.

Church Street South, MLTW/Moore-Turnbull with Marvin Buchanan and Donald Whitaker, 1966–69. Photo by Norman McGrath.

~

Mark Simon wrote in the next essay about the collaborations and work of Moore's Connecticut days.

Half of the current partners at Centerbrook were still his students at Yale when Charles Moore moved his offices from New Haven to the old drill-bit factory on the Falls River in the village of Centerbrook in the town of Essex, Connecticut, in the fall of 1969. He was stepping down as dean of the architecture program and had tired of urban stress (his home and office in New Haven had been repeatedly robbed).

In 1965 Charles had become head of the Yale architecture program and had begun to practice in New Haven independently of Bill Turnbull, first as MLTW/Moore-Turnbull and later as Charles W. Moore Associates.

The Moore office was above a bicycle shop just across Chapel Street from the Yale Art and Architecture Building, designed by Moore's predecessor, Paul Rudolph. The office was anything but Rudolphian. The A&A was a brutalist monument without color; its materials were all natural and raw — concrete, steel, rope shades, even sprayed asbestos ceilings. In contrast, Moore's office was small, ingeniously cramped and wild with colorful supergraphics. Cheerful as it was, it was also spare of luxury. Stools were unpadded, desks were doors. It was all on the cheap, as was the pay (for everyone, including the boss — "Our Fearless Leader," Gert Wood, his Yale secretary, called him).

The office was managed by Tom Rapp, who had started working for Charles in 1966, having quit Yale Architecture School before he graduated. Hordes of other students worked after school drafting and model making and fabricating custom elements for the many houses in design and construction. The bulk of the work was housing of some sort, condominiums, federally financed FHA low-income projects, or single-family houses.

It was around this time that New Haven's low-income Church Street

South project was designed and built along with its successful neighbor, Tower One for the Elderly. The Church Street project was built, as Charles said, to be defensible turf. It was originally planned that the apartments would be sold to their inhabitants, and the grounds would be maintained by the City Parks Department. They never were, and it became a slum.

Several extraordinary private houses were designed and built. Most notable were the Koizim and Klotz houses in New England. They sprawled, larger and more adventurous than prior work. Both were built with interior pavilions connected by large tentlike roofs. Wide steps meandered up and down in amorphous spaces between the pavilions. Handcrafted elements, like student-built fireplaces and stenciled walls, were lovingly constructed along with custom light fixtures made from standard industrial parts. Light poured in through walls of glass and layers of space.

Charles, as always, was constantly on the go, between classes, the office, and the airport. It was common to see him sitting on a step somewhere at school working on sketches with an assistant who had trapped him in desperation to finish a design. He did so much flying that the office purchased a private plane, piloted by Tom Rapp's brother; it was a luxury that he later found he couldn't afford.

Charles had always loved water; his thesis at Princeton was entitled "Water in Architecture." When student employee Bill Grover returned from a visit to a prospective job in Essex and reported seeing an old waterfall and factory complex for sale, Charles jumped at the chance to buy it for a new home and office.

Klotz House, MLTW/Moore-Turnbull with William Grover and Marvin Buchanan, 1967–70. Photo by James Volney Righter.

Koizim House, MLTW/Moore-Turnbull with Arthur Ballman, 1971. Photo by James Volney Righter.

Centerbrook Office.

The complex included a two-story T-shaped brick factory on the street with an attached house (the "Union Hall"), a neighboring house, a long forge shed to the rear, and a myriad of barnlike sheds and outbuildings. Behind it all was a wide dam and spillway with an underground head race feeding a huge cast-iron turbine in the subbasement that had powered the works making augers and drill bits.

Plans were drawn and a host of students working under the aegis of "Elephant Track Construction" renovated the central part of the grease- and metal filing–filled factory during 1969. A large upstairs loft was turned into the drafting room. First floor spaces were rented out to an antiques dealer, an interior designer, and a "Jack the Stripper" refinishing emporium complete with reeking vats of acid.

Charles turned the attached house into his apartment. The upstairs was a large meeting room (the old Union Hall) that became his bedroom and living room combined. He filled a two-story space next to it with an oversized freestanding staircase that included shower, sink, and water closet as landings over a tiny kitchen tucked below. A few years later the large room was to house a pyramid, built by the office after Charles awoke and sketched a particularly vivid dream. The top of the pyramid was lopped off to allow a mirrored "witch ball" to hang from the ceiling as the "all seeing eye" that is found floating above the pyramid in the Great Seal on one dollar bills. In further honor of cash, which never seemed to come easily, the Seal's Latin Motto was stenciled on the ceiling around the ball, and the outside of the pyramid was painted dollar green. It was a marvel.

Like the pyramid, the whole office was filled with verve and good humor. It was also a place with a mission. Charles had become famous as an architectural rebel — a "Postmodern-radical-eclectic" he had unfortunately called himself to a magazine writer in the '60s. Part of the tag stuck. People in the office knew they were changing architecture; new things were being invented every day with great excitement and electricity.

The office grew to a staff of fifteen; Charles kept flying around to lecture, tour, and teach. For one birthday he was given a drafting table with a chain and leg iron to remind him he needed to stick around more and do the work. He didn't. (It was ever so.) He also didn't pay much attention to business. When Richard Nixon cut off federal housing programs, which had been feeding the office, and those programs didn't pay until work was complete, no one was laid off despite the scarcity of work (and even greater lack of receivables). Charles returned from his travels in 1972 to find his business near bankruptcy.

Most of the staff left, unpaid, discouraged, or dismissed. Three stayed on, Bill Grover, Bob Harper, and Mary Ann Rumney, a Yale-trained graphic designer who operated out of the office semi-independently. Bill offered to be office manager. Though he had no business experience, he, like Bob, did have a mortgaged house just down the road, and there weren't any other architectural jobs in Essex. Bob, a former math major, helped Bill straighten out some very untidy accounting, and they started out anew, fighting off creditors and facing an uncertain future.

Of that time, Charles wrote: "Only some of the footsteps on the stairs belonged to the sheriff serving unpleasant papers. But we came to expect that every footfall was the knell of doom. We stopped refurbishing the premises, and I borrowed vast sums from my brother-in-law to keep the sheriff and other wolves from the door. Then with everything temporarily under control, I heeded the call back to California. The successor firm to Charles Moore Associates — Moore Grover Harper — picked up the pieces with enthusiasm and things looked up."

Moore Grover Harper started in 1975 with five partners, Charles, Bill, Bob, and two other licensed employees in the office, Jeff Riley and Glenn Arbonies. The other two architects, Chad Floyd and I, were promised partnerships as soon as we passed our professional exams. It was a clever way to keep us working for erratic pay. And Charles was leaving. It was an unorthodox beginning.

At first, during the late seventies, most of the work was brought by Charles. Jeff worked hard to get his own projects and eventually designed a dormitory at nearby Quinnipiac College where work has continued for over twenty years. Bill ran the office as president and oversaw projects at Cold Spring Harbor Laboratory, another long-term client. Chad invented televised citizen participation for urban design and traveled from city to city. Bob and Glenn worked on larger projects with Charles, and I managed most of his house projects.

The spirit of the office remained much the same as before. Despite a lack of work, everyone was enthusiastic and kept long hours. Several years later an old "pro," recruited to be a draftsman who could teach his young bosses a thing or two, noted after a week on the job, "Hey, you guys *work* here!"

No one knew how to run a proper professional office; the rules were being made up as it went along. In 1978, when Chad and I finally became partners, it was agreed all partners would be equal owners and paid the same salary and bonus except for Charles, who would be paid hourly as a consultant. With the hiring of additional employees, the group began to meet occasionally to discuss business. Many techniques were tried for assigning work and sharing of business chores. Bill, sick of administration, suggested that everyone get their own clients, write their own contracts, and do their own billing. Things became more democratic, and we younger partners began to demand a new name for the firm that would recognize our equal status.

Thus began a six-year argument that primarily ensued during the increasingly rare visits that Charles made to the office. Imaginary names were invented from our seven initials, as were some without any ground, like WAPMUNK, XYSTUS, The Ingenium, or Uther Pendragon (which eventually was given to the firm's painfully slow first drafting computer). Eventually it was decided that the best name would reflect the place rather than the people.

After some flirtation with "Essex Associates," the group settled on "CENTERBROOK, Architects and Planners." The factory sits in the village of Centerbrook within the town of Essex. The latter name seemed a little friendlier, and its acceptance was assured when someone noticed its felicitous suggestion of being mainstream, and Bill noted that nearby road signs already directed potential clients our way.

It was fitting that the name referred to the place. After starting as project managers for Charles, and after a period of unsuccessful collaborations, each of the partners was beginning to do independent work, stylistically as well as operationally. A general approach, however, learned from Charles, united us. Clients were listened to, not "sold," or lectured. The preexisting location of a building, its styles and site, gave direction to a design. Architecture was an additive process; for the most part buildings needed to fit in, not stand out. Tradition and invention were kept in balance. Centerbrook would stand for a place-first approach.

Times were still tough. There was a yearly argument about whether to spend the meager profits on starting up the long-abandoned air conditioning system, or on a big party. The October parties won out and became famous. Conveniently, Charles's birthday was on Halloween. These parties were always costumed affairs with a theme. The first, "Come As You Are What You Eat," featured a lot of vegetables including Bill starring as a giant asparagus. (James Stirling, whom Charles had lured to teach at Yale, brought two bottles of Wild Turkey in an apparent confusion between Halloween and American and Canadian Thanksgiving.) The next year, in honor of Charles's 50th birthday, a "gold" party included a *very* large tap dancer with her baton-twirling students leading a parade presenting him with a multilayered gold cake I had made. All of the parties demanded visitor participation for entertainment. The first year a band was far too expensive and so records were used. We built an empty stage wistfully filled with cardboard musical instruments. It became the site of an evening-long battle between two women clients who each wanted to lip-synch into the fly swatter microphone. Guest participation was born (well before we had heard the terms "Karaoke" or "Air Guitar").

The parties were held year after year, until success started to leave too little time for the increasingly elaborate production efforts. These included circus tents, a vibrating smoke-belching blast-off rocket for a *Star Wars* party, a complete TV studio for a make-your-own-show party, and a spinning time machine that sent its costume-changing occupants through the years (or minutes depending on their skit). Clones, clowns, and cowboys came and went while Charles would occasionally show up, wandering around or dancing with a bemused, shy look on his face.

By the 1980s all of the partners were doing their own work and were beginning to develop independent styles as well. All had their roots in Charles's work, but slowly different characters emerged. Early efforts at collaboration between the partners with-

Rubenstein Barn, Moore Grover Harper with Mark Simon, Landscape by Lester Collins, 1977. Photo by Norman McGrath.

Jones Laboratory, Cold Spring Harbor, Moore Grover Harper with William Grover, 1976. Photo by Norman McGrath.

Sammis Hall, Cold Spring Harbor, Moore Grover Harper, 1978–81. Photo by Norman McGrath.

out Charles were often disappointing or muddled in design, as well as financial disasters. As the office grew, collaboration began to occur more and more between the partners and employees than between the partners themselves. Given that, and to provide some sort of cross-fertilization, we decided to avoid a studio system that would have select employees working for each partner. Instead, at the weekly partners' meeting, whenever possible, we made work assignments to change the arrangement of players. That method carries on to this day.

Charles was always frantic on the fly. When he showed up, the office would be sheer chaos for the day or two he was here. His laundry had to be done, phone calls came in for him at what seemed to be ten an hour, he had inevitably lost something en route which needed tracking down, and his visit always turned out to be at least one day shorter than he had promised the week before. He managed this even if he had only promised one day; entire visits were occasionally held at the airport. We all learned to ask for two days if we wanted one. When he left the building, it seemed to sigh with relief along with the rest of us.

He would carry his correspondence with him unanswered for months at a time, until it had built up enough pressure (or weight in his bag) to demand atten-tion. We recently found copies of some of his 1975 correspondence. Charles had written many of that year's replies on the same day. I vaguely recall one beginning, "I am sorry that I haven't responded to your urgent letter a year ago . . ." I suppose that it is astonishing that he wrote at all.

Food proved to be a good lure to get work done. The anticipation of a great dinner could almost ensure a visit and keep him focused on work for several hours.

Williams College Museum of Art and Art Department, Centerbrook with Robert Harper and Richard King, 1977–83. Photo by Norman McGrath.

Despite worrying out loud about his heart and health, he rarely limited his intake. If asked what kind of sandwich he wanted for lunch, he'd say, "Gooey."

Charles seemed to invite time pressure. He would inevitably find enough delays so that designs were done at the last minute, in desperation. I think this heightened his adrenaline, or at least his attention. I once wrote of this proclivity:

"The work is frenzied and our mood is dark and we are designing. The problem at hand seems unsolvable and the scanty solutions that have come to mind are discarded with venom as useless. A deadline of some sort has unbearably passed. The future is clouded with imagined failure and recognizable doom. And this occurs during every job.

"We have come in this case, once again, to the point where anxiety will at last become reckless enough to stimulate our creative sources. Despite reassuring smiles to clients days or hours earlier, we find ourselves lost. We have no doubt just promised them that we will have no problem in mixing their rich and oily needs

Hood Museum of Art, Centerbrook with Chad Floyd and Glenn Arbonies, 1981–85. Rendering by Bill Hersey.

with a watery budget. Perhaps out of a sense of honor or duty ('This is what we're being paid for'), never with the memory that it happens every time, we sit sure of defeat trying again and again until, at the very nadir, one of us says something offhand, perhaps absurd, which sparks a jumping of brain synapses to an architectural concept as yet unthought or a scheme never before seen which might just fit the multitude of requirements, puzzle style, into a solution."

Hood Museum of Art. Drawing by Bill Hersey and John Kyrk.

I'm not sure, but it does seem that anxiety is a mandatory part of the creative process. I often think that Charles secretly knows that, not admitting it if he can help it, but pursuing it. I have often seen him putting off until the last minute enormous tasks or accepting for himself more work than he can possibly do, and my sense is that he is very carefully setting the scene for invention. I recall one evening in a Washington hotel where he listed thirty-eight jobs and five books, all behind schedule, which he was supposed to be working on. Rather than do that, we went out to dinner and had some fine wine, leaving desperation for the morning when, to our surprise, some marvelous work was done.

Charles brought an interesting assortment of assignments. In the seventies there were houses. I earned stripes working on my first house with Charles for Simone Swan on the North Fork of Long Island. I replaced Bill Grover on the job since Bill was insufficiently "Zen" for Simone. It was indeed a Zen cabin, spare but deeply roofed for solar collectors that never came, with a shed-roofed guest house and connecting deck. Simone selected Charles as a replacement for his own teacher, Louis Kahn (who died before he could start the commission). Kahn had agreed to use an old barn structure which we readily incorporated.

Charles and I produced a number of houses with similar barn themes and elements. The Isham House sits in the potato fields of Sagaponic, Long Island, as a trinity of barnlike boxes around a courtyard. The Rubenstein Barn, on the Eastern Shore of Maryland, was a renovation of a huge structure sitting on a first floor stone base. The original framing and siding were all left exposed to the interior of the addition of new insulated siding and roofing to the exterior. The Stanwood House, northwest of Hartford, Connecticut, though all new, had a barn-wood "cabin" at its core, as if the rest of the house were an addition. The clients were integral to their own designs.

Charles loved to collaborate. I think he was often lonely and work offered companionship, but beyond that I think he saw great results come from groups. He was willing to work with any need or idea as a premise for design. He never questioned clients about their stated needs. He said that he had enough of an ego to expect himself to do what *they* wanted well and to collaborate with anyone and still have it come out beautifully. That is not to say there weren't groans or rolling of eyes between the knowing. There were.

Larger jobs came as well. Bill Grover worked with Charles on Jones Laboratory at Cold Spring Harbor for

Williams College Museum of Art, Centerbrook. Photo by Norman McGrath.

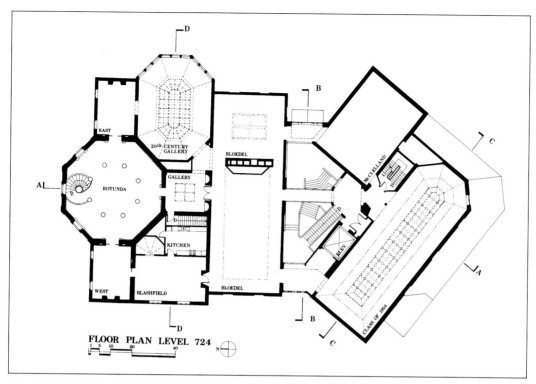

Plan, *Williams College Museum of Art*.

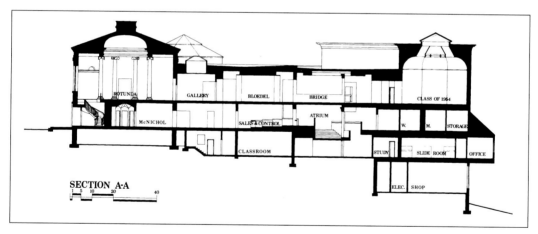

Section, *Williams College Museum of Art*.

James Watson, the Nobel laureate. The lab had been built in 1895. The exterior walls were preserved and new separate lab "pods," clad in aluminum skins, were inserted, each on their own foundation. These were inspired by the "Orgasmatrons" in Woody Allen's movie *Sleeper*. The lab won a National AIA Honor Award and much more work followed, including the Sammis Guest House, which Charles designed working with Bill and Glenn.

A few years later, in 1977, the chance for an exciting commission came up. Williams College was looking for an architect to design a major addition to the Art Museum. Work was slow at the time and the office went wild with eagerness, fabricating a handmade portfolio of large boards. Working day and night, Jeff Riley cut photographs into the cardboard to make them lie flush with the surface. The committee visiting from the school was wined and dined; Chad Floyd helped with presentations, and somehow the job was wrested away from others with more experience in museums. Bob Harper, the most skilled technician in the office, worked with Charles as the project manager, taking the job through several phases to an opening that starred a show of Charles's work.

In 1981, a similar opportunity arose. Dartmouth College needed a new museum and the Essex office mounted another all-out effort to get the commission. Chad masterminded the presentation with Charles and managed the job, when they got it, with Glenn Arbonies assisting. The schematic design was developed on site through a series of workshops that included Dartmouth faculty, students, and administration. More than fifteen site locations and schemes were considered before a final was chosen. This required a daring building that could tie together a complex, including the nineteenth-century Richardsonian Wilson Hall with the modern Hopkins Center by Harrison and Abramovitz. The design did just that and created a series of interconnecting courtyards in the bargain. It later won a National AIA Honor Award.

The participatory method used at Hood had been initially conceived by Chad with Bill Grover and Charles in a 1975 effort to win a riverfront planning commission in Dayton, Ohio. To beat out more experienced competition, Moore Grover Harper offered to open a downtown storefront office in Dayton to collect citizen comments during design. The selection committee thought the idea so laudable, they required all three finalists to agree to the method. Concerned that an edge had been lost, Chad secured the agreement of a local TV station to broadcast six "Designathons" in which the planning would be done on air *live* and the entire citizenry of the city would have easy call-in access to guide and critique the planning. We got the job. Charles and Centerbrook independently continued to use and refine the process thereafter for many projects, large and small. Many different workshop methods were devised for the variety of building designs and masterplans that resulted.

By the late '80s and '90s only a few of the projects at Centerbrook involved Charles. At Cold Spring Harbor, he worked on the initial designs for a large Neuroscience Laboratory with Bill Grover and Jim Childress. The two found themselves redesigning it alone, given his too-long absences and overextended schedule. The Stamford Center for the Arts went through several interesting revisions under Chad's oversight before the firm abandoned it in a second-phase fee negotiation with rough-and-tumble trustees. The Cedar Rapids Museum of Art was completed with Glenn Arbonies and Richard King. After an almost ten-year hiatus, I collaborated with Charles again on NAUTICUS, The National Maritime Center on the Norfolk, Virginia, waterfront. This museum of science and technology, offering a new project type, showed a science fiction character unlike any previous work. It promised new design departures. Sadly, it was not finished until after Charles's death. At one of our last site meetings together, Charles had difficulty walking, and so I bravely drove our rental car through the mushy sand under the huge open steel-frame of the building so that he could see the promise of the spaces being formed. "How perfect for Chuck," I thought, "a drive-through inspection!"

Today, the complex at Centerbrook has grown far larger than Charles ever imagined it would. Almost all of the buildings are occupied by the firm with a computerized staff of sixty. The old cast-iron turbine has been replaced with a modern plastic and stainless steel version which provides much of the needed electricity. Still the good humor and energy remains from the old days. And profits are occasionally wasted on great parties.

Centerbrook, Architects & Planners.

CHAPTER NINE

Involving People

Moore worked best when surrounded by people. His preference for collaboration extended to virtually all of his activities: he taught with others, he wrote books with others, he traveled with others, and, most important, he designed buildings with others. He did not regard architecture as a solitary act; rather, he relied on the energy and participation of everyone involved in the building process. In Berkeley, Moore wrote in an academic journal:

> Today, the architects are not in control of their environment; indeed, architects can rarely even affect the environment to any significant degree. Society no longer demands of the architect a responsible product, but the needs of the society must none-the-less be met, and they will not be met as the result of the "historical type" nice guys individually and individualistically at work. The day of the individual genius architect is pretty well finished.

Around a table, Moore worked with his partners and young assistants. All participated in the design process, using rolls of yellow tracing paper. Moore seldom relinquished his sensibilities, however. In design sessions his presence was strong, subtly firm, and those who strayed from Moore principles rarely wandered far before they were gently drawn back into the circle.

Donlyn Lyndon, one of the MLTW partners, continued his fruitful collaborations with Moore for many years in the ever-expanding realm of ideas. Moore's sense of collaboration, Lyndon believed, was so strong that it replaced for him a need to develop a personal, individualistic body of theory. Instead, Moore preferred looser, more easily transferable "principles and enthusiasms" from which architects could borrow, weave variations on a theme, and absorb. Lyndon wrote:

> Words were, for Charles, a means for taking pleasure in his observations, for sharing them with others, and stringing his thoughts across an experience of place. Charles was never careless with words, always tuning them to the nuance of interpretation, sharpening his intuitions with multiple layers of evocation. His words called into the presence of forms an array of associations that expanded the place for him and for the inevitable conversants accompanying him.
>
> These words were provocative for those who grouped around him, and many did. They were also, when set in print, with his long strings of loosely punctuated

Jamesian sentences, of enormous importance in leading others to see with something approximating the inventive connectiveness which was the hallmark of his personality. He hoped, too, that words could cast his observations and commitments in a form that would be independent of his presence. From very early on I can remember him speaking of the ambition to be able to set formulations that would reach beyond his person, setting a path that would be clear for others without his involvement. Perhaps he was conscious of how intensely his charm worked upon those with whom he worked, leading them to see, as it were, from his shoes. He aspired to more, I believe; without pretension he longed to build theory — especially to build theory that would not be pretentious, theory that would slip into consciousness easily, gaining authority from a persuasive connection with the human experience of architecture, rather than from borrowed linguistic trappings.

Charles was deeply suspicious of the confines of verbal category, just as he was wont to break open the boundaries of rooms and felt compelled to subvert the simplicities of any single encompassing order. In this his thought is seamless, whether invested in words or in the configuration of places; systematic order exists to be challenged; presuppositions form the basis for the unexpected; rules are valuable when broken — or at least distended; the general is given spirit by the particular, sometimes the peculiar. Life is present in invention; true invention springs from a penetrating knowledge of conventions. Nothing worthwhile is devoid of complexity. (Reader beware, these are my words, not his — very likely much more categorical than he would consider apt.)

The dynamics of this impulse on the one hand to formulate and on the other to resist are perhaps most cogently illustrated in a passage from *The Poetics of Gardens,* coauthored with Mitchell and Turnbull: "It would have been fun perhaps to build a grand synoptic system — to distill a set of rules from them [the gardens discussed], collapsing all the overlapping and conflicting principles that formed most of them, but it wouldn't have been fair: we have discovered too many ways to make a satisfying garden, too many ways to design a building, too many ways to construct a poem or a melody, to presume to select just one way to proceed. The lessons that we can learn are all morally shaded, with mights and shoulds, maybes and maybe nots, and there is always another, perhaps contradictory or at least demurring, view to consider." The passage makes clear that it is the range of his observations and the fecundity of imagination which overcomes the impulse to codification.

Yet there remained a commitment to being more than a personality — to becoming part of something larger. It was evident in his enduring commitment to teaching and writing, in his incessant interest in collaboration and participation, in the invention of a succession of architectural firms, in his architecture which sought to be a part of the place in which it was lodged, to belong emotionally to the people for whom it was built. Each of the several firms of which he was a part was initially centered on his leadership, but they evolved, each in a different way, into fertile ground for the development of independent careers, spawning groups of people bonded by shared sensibilities, and a core group of ideas and convictions — by a legacy of images, witticisms, passions, insights, catalyzing phrases, and processes. At no point did he, or we, lay out an encompassing, carefully constructed theory, answerable for its own internal consistency. In a sense, participation with others in a collaborative act of making replaced the wish for theory.

In articles and books written with various collaborators Charles did attempt, however, to lay out lines of thought that could guide others in the creation of places, places that would provide the intensity of satisfaction which he envisioned as humankind's proper fate. For the most part, I would contend, these are based in several fundamental principles:

1) The primary act of architecture is to create a semblance of territory — a dedicated place apart; an inside, differentiated from the more ubiquitous outside and imbued with special qualities. This is much more than building mere shelter, and more humanly pertinent than visual rhetoric.

2) The specialness of that inside should be rooted in the affections of its inhabitants — their interests, as expressed in images and particular requests, in the things which they collect, in the investments of craft and care that they are willing to support, or in the ways which they take possession of the place should give rise to its particular qualities.

3) Each act of making a place apart must be cast in terms that also draw connections — buildings should be fixed to their sites and bear traces of the heritage of buildings and ideas in which our minds are formed. They should allow their inhabitors to know where they are — tempering recognition with enough surprise to awaken slumbering perceptions.

4) Valuable places reveal (and thereby encourage) an irrepressible human spirit — they are deeply invested with human energy, imaginative energy that is waiting to be discovered by the attentive observer and which is the ultimate source of architecture's interest for us.

5) Human spirit itself is but another evidence of the wonders of existence — wonders also manifest in those things which have an inherent liveliness and which may be incorporated in the places we build; the mysteries of water, the flux of light, and the intricacies of the geode.

In practice all these were informed by the conviction that places themselves hold more promise than the words we can speak around them; we can learn more from illuminated example than from explanation. Hence the profusely illustrated articles and books; hence the incessant travel, often with students and companions in tow; hence the generous places he designed, so full of invested energy.

A summary of this sort does not do justice to the process of Charles's thought, to the incessantly playful, multiple, probing, and allusive quality of his conversation, lectures, writings, and buildings. Nevertheless, I would hold that these are the foundations from which his work and thought evolved, branching and elaborating as he encountered new conditions, engaged new clients and companions, became engrossed in changing circumstances, or spun new tales from the tangled strands of his searching imagination.

Important influences affected Moore's sense of involvement, the first reaching back to the

Princeton years, during which there was a shared sense of discovery. At MLTW, there was a sense of "one pencil, four hands," and later at Yale, collaboration led to the construction of buildings by Moore and students with their own hands. Independent of Moore, Lawrence Halprin wrote in the early sixties an important book, *The RSVP Cycles,* and with Jim Burns developed the "take part" approach to design in which participants would gather and act out their dreams through site walks and design workshops. Chad Floyd, one of the Centerbrook partners, was also a key figure in the evolution of the collaborative design process. Together, Moore and Floyd would host call-in public television programs, allowing citizens to participate in the urban design of their cities.

In his studios, Moore always involved young students and architects, which gave them the sense that they were more collaborators than employees. Young architects, hesitant with inexperience, were often amazed at Charles's eagerness to sweep them up and readily include their ideas in the design at hand. Ideas, not status, had merit. Moore customarily gave young people extraordinary responsibilities, letting them handle, fresh out of architecture school, important buildings. While he knew that they probably would not be able to cope with everything, and would doubtless make many mistakes, he also knew that it was the best way for young people to learn how to guide a building through the design process. As a result, the Moore studios were very intense, many often worked throughout the night, "en charette."

But the most intimate sessions were those in which Moore would work with the inhabitants of buildings. When Moore Ruble Yudell was selected by an Episcopal congregation to build a new church (and required its congregation to accept the design by vote), Moore saw it as an opportunity to let the people design the building. He did the same when his Texas firm, Moore/Andersson, was hired to design an Episcopal cathedral in Fargo, North Dakota. There they built a soaring carpenter gothic cathedral that rises from the plane of the prairie. Involving people was not an easy operation, as the architects often had to come together to satisfy an array of ideas about what a place could be when produced by a community of individual personalities and tastes.

Jim Burns, the organizer of the "take part" sessions once said: "Charles's nourishing qualities took the form of expanding people's lives as well as their waistlines. As Shakespeare's Falstaff described himself: 'I am not only witty in myself, but the cause that wit is in other men.' That's accurate about our Falstaffian friend Charles, and can be paraphrased into 'Charles was not only creative in himself, but the cause that creativity is in other people.' That slyly, shyly smiling round face shone both with witty responses to people and encouragements for us to excel, to do it better."

∽

Here Moore recounts the trials and joys of making places with others.

Buildings require prodigious amounts of energy in order to be able to give satisfaction. Great buildings have the energy of countless craftsmen and workers as

Chad Floyd in the Storefront.

Televised Design.

well as the spirit of designers and ambitious patrons. Buildings in our own time need the energies not only of the architect but of the users, their builders, even the financiers and official sponsors. The users are an especially important group — no people feel so passionate about buildings, so involved with them, and so proud of them as the people who have given them shape, and it's likely the shape people themselves give to their buildings will pass the urgent test of familiarity. Architects through most of history have hung on with some desperation to whatever prerogatives they have scratched together and have made the independence of the users into a symbol of their virility. Most appallingly perhaps is Ayn Rand's *Fountainhead* where the hero, Howard Roark, destroys a high-rascacielo-rise building because it violates his artistic principles. Clearly a building so closely held is not going to serve well as the open receptacle for the energy and love of others.

For many years now it has seemed to me that buildings need to be designed by more than just their architects. The notion starts from a perception of Donlyn Lyndon's that buildings are repositories of human energy and that if they get enough energy, they will pay it back in satisfaction, but if they don't get enough energy, they remain incapable of paying back anything to people. The kind of participation that once caused barns to be built by many, each contributing their particular craft, has always been a strong influence, which we called upon in Kentucky when those Yale students built structures they had designed themselves.

Another opportunity to involve the people for whom we were designing came in Dayton, Ohio, where Chad Floyd organized a series of design charettes focusing on reinvigorating a stretch of land along the Miami River, about which there was considerable controversy. Many people in the city were suspicious of others, mostly outsiders, who they thought were doing the wrong things, so we had to come in as openly as possible and introduce the people to their river.

First we hired a gypsy violinist to perform at a picnic lunch along the river, so people would come and walk and see the place. Then we set up shop in a storefront window where some two thousand people came by with suggestions about what should be done to their river banks. And then on six television programs we acted like architectural short-order cooks with rows of telephones so that people could call in and say what they would like to see. It was very exciting to design things right on television with the cameras whirring and the lights on and people jumping up and down. Out of the thousands of ideas and suggestions, there were almost none which invalidated the others.

Group Design.

Another instance of participatory planning was at a smaller scale without the benefit of television at a nine-acre site where the San Gabriel River meets the sea between Long Beach and Seal Beach. There was a piece of public land once occupied by the Department of Water and Power that had opened for development. When we found out that condominiums were just about the only things that would make enough money to be built, everyone got discouraged. But their depression turned around when we appeared

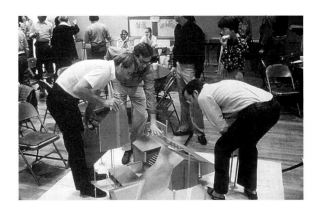

Parishioners' Models with Moore.

with drawings, some Baroque and some Spanish, that led one of the engineers to say, "I've dealt with architects all my life, but it is the first time that I've dealt with architects who didn't assert their scheme, their values — so it's all ours."

One of the really critical things about all of this, I think, is that if we, the architects, enter with hidden agendas, we've had it. That is, if we want a set of things and we let that show even a little bit, kiss them good-bye. If, however, we drift in with an open mind and an avuncular smile and the desire to have people have what they care about, then the chances for getting it are very good. What follows from that surely is that a building which has the energies of all the people interested in it is more likely to succeed than the masterpiece of a skilled designer operating alone. We had a chance to push this notion even further than we might have otherwise in the parish of St. Matthew's in the upper-income Los Angeles suburb of Pacific Palisades.

The farsighted bishop had early bought about ten hectares of land in a coastal area which by then became very valuable, and it had served as site for school and church. The church was a much beloved little A-frame of wood which burned down in a forest fire, leaving only an adjacent prayer garden which survived the

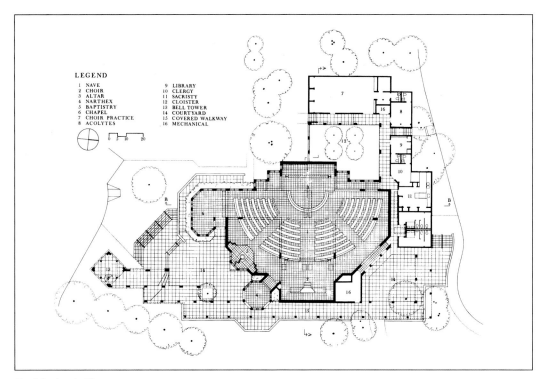

St. Matthew's Plan.

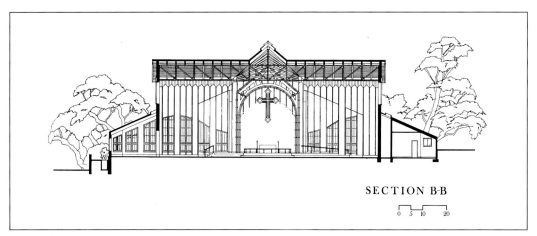

SECTION B-B

0 5 10   20

St. Matthew's Section.

flames. Just after it lost its building, the parish also lost its rector of many years, and
the process of replacing him had revealed fresh the passionate differences of view
which are normally hidden by the discreet manners of I guess every Episcopal
parish. The views in general can be categorized as high church (close to Roman
Catholic) and low church (more kin in spirit with left-wing Protestantism). Because they were aware of their differences, the parish set into their contract with

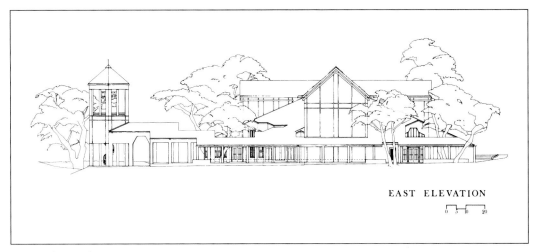

St. Matthew's Elevation.

the architects their requirement that at least a two-thirds majority vote must approve everything about the new building. Our friends in the parish were not confident that even a majority could be found in favor of anything.

When we were selected to do the job, we thought that the only way to get such a majority for any scheme would be to have the scheme designed by the interested members of the parish, hoping we could get enough interested to carry the day voting for work [for] which they felt responsible. We have repeated this process now, in part and with changes, often enough so that I'm convinced that it works: that people in a creative mode, whatever their differences, are much more positive and cooperative and ready to do something than the same people in the kind of critical mode that a committee structure implies.

A key player was, and frequently is, Jim Burns, who with Lawrence Halprin developed the "Take Part Process." Jim choreographed four Sundays of workshops, spaced about a month apart with the interested parishioners. The first Sunday, we met after church and had an awareness walk (as these things are called in California) around the extensive site with a notebook for everyone to fill in with verbal descriptions, questions to answer, sketches, and diagrams to help figure out where the new church might be placed. Nothing was taken for granted. After the walk we came back, had some lunch on the very pretty lawn of the parish house, and worked together, often using butcher paper to draw ideas for the siting of the church. Afterward we went into the temporary church/basketball court and were confronted with sets of model-making equipment which Jim had assembled: Froot Loops, cellophane, colored paper, scissors, tape, and parsley. (Parsley is wonderful for model-making material since it wilts in a few hours and doesn't let people fall too far in love with their creations.) Then people made singly or in groups models of their ideal churches. Froot Loops usually represented people. The designers of all these models then presented them to the group which was there, as in subsequent sessions, about 150 strong out of the 350-person parish.

That perhaps was the magic day because each table, convinced it was going to be unique and at odds with all the other tables, produced what was basically the same plan of seven rows of pews in a semicircle or half-ellipse around the altar. We were astonished at the fact that all the answers were the same. I guess we needn't have been since they'd already said they wanted to sit as close to their altar as they could but not surround it because they didn't want to look at each other, but to focus on the altar and what lay beyond. No other configuration allowed so many people (288 was asked for) to be so close to the altar. Of course there were discrepancies, mostly in the location of the choir, and our role as architects was to make clear the areas of agreement and minimize the differences which could get ironed out later. The important thing was to seek and find consensus.

Another action that we tried for the first time at St. Matthew's which has since become a standard part of our process was to show a carousel of eighty slides of various kinds of buildings that had something to do with the problem at hand. We handed out sheets that gave each viewer the chance with each slide to say "I like it" or "I don't" and then separately to say "this is appropriate for St. Matthew's." We tallied the results and presented them at the third meeting on another Sunday a month thence.

They told us interesting things: the most popular pictures (three of them), interspersed among many others, were all of Alvar Aalto's Vuoksenniska Church in Imatra, Finland, which is white, although most everyone had said they preferred dark wood, but the church at Imatra does have windows that look out at fine trees. The least-popular church was St. Peter's in Rome, whether for reasons of doctrine or of cost it seemed unfair to ask. Another thing we noticed was that concrete surfaces, even masterful ones by Louis Kahn, scored very low and that plants casting dappled shadows in a forest or on a wall scored always very high.

Given so dramatic a mandate on the plans and attitudes shown by the responses to the slides, we came back a month later with four large models showing roofs that would fit variations of the plan. Five out of six tables that day chose the same roof, a relaxed Latin cross. I'd been swept away with an architect's fervor and also had made what I thought was a wonderful model, for instance, of a four-postered baldachin in bright colors. It was rejected out of hand by everybody. The groups at the tables also produced that day a set of more specific directives like "more glass to the ground," providing opportunities for continuing skirmishes between parishioners who were anxious to see the prayer garden, which was their link with the past, and the rector who was concerned about establishing, for instance, the sacred sobriety of Good Friday while the squirrels were exhibiting fecundity in the bushes outside.

Behind the altar I was to draw in the next weeks a series of little houses like an advent calendar occupied by saints which unfortunately reminded the rector of a *Laugh-In* program he had seen with comics in such a set of niches. The next iteration kept the wall behind the altar simple and blank which everyone found boring. In the subsequent weeks, after meetings with the liturgical consultant, a wonderful man with whom I swapped C. S. Lewis stories, we came up with the four evangelists including St. Matthew as they are found in the Book of Kells in Dublin which parishioners said were weird. Finally John Ruble designed a tree of life which hit the desired note.

There were many issues brought up at this stage and discussed four weeks later in which it was important to please both high church and low church parishioners. The floor, for instance: in southern California the most economical and appropriate surface for a floor is Mexican tile, usually large terra cotta squares, but that had some of the wrong messages. Mexican meant Roman Catholic. We proposed and they accepted that the corners of the square tile could be sliced away and a small square of blue slate be inserted at every intersection carrying the mind across the Bay of Biscay to Devon and home. (Somehow it seemed all right that the blue slate for reasons of durability had been replaced by blue-green tile.)

Even the crucifix was a much-debated issue. The rector was anxious for a large cross over the altar "brooding," as he put it, like a hen over her chicks. There was no objection to the cross, but there was considerable discussion about whether the body of Jesus should be on it. I made what I thought was an ingenious solution that involved a giant board with the silhouette of the corpus visible from the side and just an abstract thick line from the front which I thought gave viewers their choice of corpus or noncorpus, depending on their point of view. As it turned out though, the cross was a gift of a low-church lady who banished the two-dimensional corpus.

A more complex issue and one that brought on considerable discussion was the material of the wall of the church. The previous A-frame had been wood, and many members of the parish wanted natural wood again. The group however that was looking for a fine organ wanted superior acoustics, which required, according to the acoustician, dense walls of heavy plaster. We ended up proposing deep wood battens on a plaster wall so that the wall seems mostly of wood if you view it from a raking angle and mostly plaster if you or the sound waves address it head on.

One of the tenser moments came during a discussion of the plaster wall nave, which we were drawing with a high ceiling. I was vigorously attacked during the fourth meeting when this was being presented by a woman who cited Jesus's belief in energy conservation with the attendant supposition that the ceiling be low lest heat be wasted warming up the organ in too big a room. Fortunately for me, parishioners interested in the organ responded vociferously, reciting how the organ needed to be cool with therefore a high ceiling. I therefore didn't have to put forward any defense of the high ceiling, which I probably would have on architectural grounds.

Afterward the rector, who had been fairly dubious about the participatory process, said he was becoming convinced of its worth and that an important part of the reason why it was working was that we architects never had become defensive. He noted that for us to even once become defensive about the scheme would have killed the mood and sense of involvement of almost all the people taking part. I agreed but laid it to slow reactions on my part and my partners: we don't get defensive until much later, when the crisis is over.

The architects' role may seem diminished, but I don't think any of us felt that our involvement was less critical or less satisfying. We left the fourth session with a detailed set of worked out requirements, produced final schematic drawings which went up in the parish house a month later. Ballots for the required vote came out 87% in our favor. Not very many people were going to vote against a scheme in which they had had so major a hand, and I for one felt far more comfortable with this effort than I would have with peddling a design that we liked, about which they were unsure.

Almost a year after that triumphal moment of trying to be responsive to the various committees which, no longer unified in that creative thrill of making something, lapsed frequently into sometimes long and bitter disagreements, we found that the impetus was still there from the act of creation which this time included not just the architects but a great many of the people who would inhabit the church.

The church got built and even won an AIA award. It's important to note that all of this was achieved through the combination of skills and interest, including Tina Beebe's work on the colors and Richard Peters's lighting design. I'm often asked if we as architects haven't felt a diminution of our creative satisfactions in sharing all these design decisions, and I have to note that part of the province left to us involved putting a Latin cross roof over a half-elliptical floor plan which seemed like something Alberti would have responded to enthusiastically.

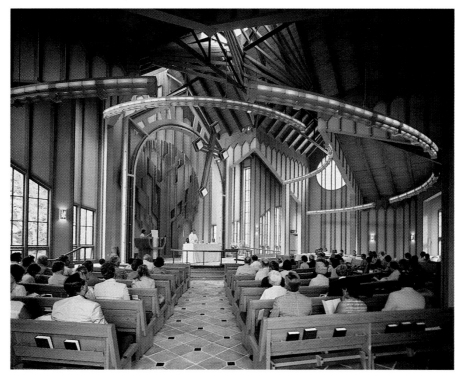

St. Matthew's Church, Moore Ruble Yudell. Photo by Timothy Hursley.

CHAPTER TEN

My Own Houses

$\mathbf{M}$oore often quipped that the houses he designed for himself were "chances to pursue chimera to the possible discomfort of no one but myself."

Each time he moved he either renovated or built a house. His houses were fantasies, theaters for living, filled with stairs climbing and turning, windows and gates and doors, stupefyingly complex ceilings (with which the myth was kept up off the floor), columns and layered cutouts and repositories for toys and books and furniture. All of the houses were inexpensive. Familiar objects leapfrogged from house to house, such as the cherished portraits of Eliza and Allen Willard, which were always hung in prominent places. There were common themes too. Most important was the geode — the simple, unadorned stones concealing surprising inner worlds of magic.

In Salt Lake City Moore lived in apartments that were decorated on the cheap with painted planes of color. Moore returned from Korea smitten with Eastern architecture and the skillful rendering of simple materials with simple tools into extraordinary decorative systems. When he designed a house in Pebble Beach, California, in 1954, it was unabashedly Eastern: shoji screens, floating planes, and a Zen rock garden all beckoned to Katsura and Daitokuji. Moore spent his Princeton summers living in the house, and his mother stayed until she died in 1958. Roger and Betty Bailey, who always wanted to live in a Moore-designed house, moved in next, and spent many years there.

The Japanese influence followed Moore to Princeton, where he first transformed an office into a Japanese tatami room to the apparent dismay of the janitorial staff. And when Moore moved into an apartment on High Street, he described his redecorating in a letter to his friend Carol Selby:

> Alas it is weeks after your birthday for which the card was bought — and even more weeks since the Germaine Montero album, which is magnificent, arrived. Thank you very much indeed; it is a real joy and manages to carry superbly even through the anguished death moans of my poor old phonograph.
>
> Happy birthday, too — I hope it was a good one. Are you ever coming to New York? I await word of this. Awaiting, as a matter of fact, seems to be what I do most of, at this stage. But there's lots of news.
>
> The summer was hell. On August first the thesis which had to be done by Sept. 23 had one chapter written, fifteen to go. But somehow I got it written and

off (with 65 pages extra of footnotes and bibliography, yet, whose typing is still unpaid for) by Labor Day, then drove to Princeton from California, had a 10-day charette with much help, and managed to present the thing on time and with enough success to squeak me through. I still haven't seen the color of their sheepskin, but may yet. The fat manuscript is — and has been for weeks — in the hands of the editor of the *Arch. Record* who does not send me daily telegrams. It will need lots of work to become a book, but has, they all announce, some hope. I've put it aside for a few months, to let it all simmer down. It's awfully general — the title never got past *Water in Architecture,* and would need sharpening and my OWN NEW PHOTOGRAPHS (how do you do, Mr. Guggenheim?) to make it work. I might try some articles, then put them together.

The six, seven weeks since the thesis have been, as you would suppose, strangely (my god) at sixes and sevens. I'd been putting off the amenities for so long to be a graduate student that I had, I guess, vaguely supposed that a Whole New Life lay on the other side of the thesis. This was not so — romance did not swarm into my life — I haven't even been asked out to dinner by any of the faculty, with one minor exception. Social life, such as it is, involves graduate students I knew last year, whom I now teach, who wander into my newly swank slum apartment (just across the street from the campus) and stay very late. I'm anxious to break out a little, and should have the bills paid off by January so as to be able to.

I teach one class — 2nd-year graduate students, doing a set of designs for Newport, R. I., which is to be sure a fascinating place. I've managed to make it up there twice with considerable rice paper sketching and walks by the sea. I had the class for the six weeks before Enrico Peressutti appeared, now help him until Christmas, which is fine, have a *long* vacation, with work, then have the 20 or so Senior Theses in the spring. This is supposed to leave me practically free to do original research, which currently involves thinking about starting a book called *The Sense of Place* which worries about the character of architecture — everything from bulldozers to water symbolism — and uses Monterey and Newport (old-new, sort of) to focus it all. I've just arrived at it and am quite excited — just takes writing is all.

On the side, Jay Ritchie and two others have just opened up an office in Princeton, and I work for them — for money — working on the historical part of a study of lath & plaster they are doing for the lath & plaster industry. It's all very prestigious for them and might be thus for me, as well as dragging in the absurdly important groceries.

The apartment is kind of pleasing — top floor of a ratty old University-owned house, but it has high ceilings, white walls, round-headed windows

Moore's Princeton Apartment, 1957.

in deep reveals, and (now) tatamis on the floor, couches on slab doors, a huge table covered with white marble chips, rocks, and the chessboard, walls full of *Vitruvius Britannicus,* and an air (if I do say so) of undeniable swank, perilously close to the sort the American Institute of Decorators specializes in, all made of things found lying around campus.

What will come of it all?

Moore built his next house in Orinda, California. One of the earliest references to Moore's thoughts about the house are contained in a letter to Felix Drury, dated February 28, 1961:

My pieces of news hinge mostly on a two-week trip to Guanajuato, just north of Mexico City, which turns out to be the best place this side of Spain. A wonderful silver-mining town with one automobile street and lots of small pedestrian lanes and steps, baroque churches which used up sixteen rolls of film and actually caused the watercolor brushes to swing into action. The best part of it was the smug feeling, sitting for two weeks in the same place while harassed American tourists roared through on their way to somewhere else, trying all the while to see all of Mexico in ten days flat. I acquired a rest, a tan, no diseases, and — based on some houses carved out of the ruins of old mining towns — a powerful desire for a house of my own.

Disastrously enough, I came right home and implemented this desire with an acre and a quarter in Orinda, just fifteen minutes from the University behind the hills on the side where it's hot in the summer, with the only lot in northern California of that size that has a full-fledged sense of place. It involves a driveway sweeping around a ravine filled with oak trees and up to a hundred-foot grassy circle with the land falling sharply away on almost all sides, again full of oaks, and with long views through them to the Valley and hills behind. A vast rickety financing scheme is expected to net me the lot and $5,000 cash, free from the scrutiny of banks, to build a house, including a swimming pool, so I am presently neglecting all my other work to find out about cheap swimming pools or whatever will produce an underwater whirl for no money at all. I seem to have located some Etruscan columns from a torn-down warehouse for $2 each, and somehow they are going to be the basis for this incredibly cheap and incredibly elegant establishment.

A few years later, Moore purchased Unit #9 at Sea Ranch, a place that he kept throughout his life as an escape for vacations, academic holidays, and design charettes.

When Moore resigned his post at Berkeley to teach at Yale, he bought a house in New Haven and transformed it into a fun house of 1960s pop imagery, with Shirley Temple cutouts, neon, plastic pillows, a false dome above a star-spangled bed (before there were cotton clouds above with dangling putti), and giant backlit masonite supergraphic numbers. The "pad" was even featured in a 1969 issue of *Playboy* magazine. But after the house was broken into several times, Moore fled New Haven for Essex, where he installed an apartment within the renovated mill at Centerbrook.

Pebble Beach House, 1954–55.

Soon, however, Moore heeded the call back to California to teach at UCLA, and he built another house with two other academic families, this time a condominium. Also, in the mountains outside of Los Angeles he kept a tiny cabin with his childhood friend Martha Kirkpatrick.

Finally, Moore moved to Austin in 1984, where he and Arthur Andersson transformed an existing house into a Texas "spread" including a home for Moore, a smaller house for Andersson, and two design studios. That house would turn out to be Moore's last, and would be the fullest expression of his quest to completely integrate his spatial motives and his now overflowing collections. The house was literally a geode. Its mild-mannered gray exterior encased an absolutely stunning pink interior (that glowed like a jewel box at night) beset with cluttered magnificence. More carefully interwoven than his previous houses, this house had floors that were painted with a Pantheon-scaled pattern, toys arranged in scenes, pilasters decorated with student-painted ornament, and the architectural library organized on built-in shelving.

Most of Moore's houses were impermanent, fleeting images that signified his brief stays in places. The watermelon pyramid was long ago dismantled and the plywood tubes were removed and piled in heaps on a New Haven sidewalk. But for Moore that was fine. He had no reason to impose his sensibilities on others. The houses were only shells, ready for the next inhabitants to come along and make them their own.

In this next essay, Moore traces the history of making his own houses.

My own houses have given me opportunities, spread over forty years and stretching between the coasts, to test theories about establishing my presence without threatening the comfort or sensibilities of anyone but myself. Most of my houses I built with a minimum of means, and they often benefited from decorative surges involving the energies of friends and students who helped me transform with jigsaws or brushes, plywood and paint into pleasing shapes.

A meager veterans' loan provided the means for my first house, and was as close as I could get, with those limited funds, to the kind of wonderful shapes and layers and details I had seen in Japan. It was a simple plan of a line of rooms facing the sea, strung out to catch rather handsome panoramic views of the Santa Lucia mountains, Carmel Bay, Point Lobos, and the south light. We based the rooms on a module to allow ease and cheapness of construction (it was all built for $10,900), and during the summer I built the decks, fences, and gardens.

Inhabiting, as I mentioned earlier, is a basic human endeavor, not far behind eating and sleeping, though far less universally achieved. While touted theoretical or linguistic abstractions have been the basis for some architects' houses, I've tended toward the idea that a house can be a stage where the inhabitant can act out his or her life. (When I proposed this to Harvard architecture students they angrily snorted "Bah! This is theater!" and I said, "So be it.") For me it has involved establishing as potently as I could manage a sanctuary not only for me but for my possessions, trying to evoke the feeling of well-being that Indonesian dancers call being centered.

My condominium at Sea Ranch, where I spend my vacations and academic holidays, has been my most consistent sanctuary, the house that I've kept the longest, where I go to work, but most often to recharge and gather my energy. The climate is moody, so a clear distinction between outside and inside was critical. Inside the 24-foot frames we inserted "furniture" containing beds, bathrooms, and kitchens, sometimes three levels high, and made of smooth wood to achieve further contrast between inside and outside. Over the years, as my moods changed, I repainted the interior and have most recently added a red and white checkerboard in homage to Katsura. The bed, atop a four-poster aedicula, was meant to become private by means of canvas drapes that would fold down, making a tent that I thought quite Rudolph Valentinesque, although the flaps are seldom folded down anymore.

When I built a small house in Orinda, I needed less a distinction between inside and out, since relentless winds and thick fog were not regular factors in the local, inland climate. When I came across the little piece of land just over the hills from Berkeley one afternoon I was immediately smitten. The site consisted of an open, quite pretty grassy meadow, with oak trees all around, where a circular pad, about eighty feet in diameter, had been bulldozed long ago and had since grown soft around the edges.

At once I began dreaming about a square house in a round meadow that an ancient Chinese poet, Li Po, had once praised the virtues of. I'd also read of aediculas in Sir John Summerson's *Heavenly Mansions* and for heaven's sake had to do it! (Once Summerson said I couldn't, and so I did two of them because it was my own house.) Louis Kahn's Trenton Bath House was also fresh in my mind and so I designed an open volume, square in plan, with a roof supported by interior aediculas made from salvaged architectural columns. I made a second, less-monumental aedicula to shelter the bathtub and celebrate the act of getting wet, a special temple of the self.

With the columns providing structural support for the roof, I was free to break open the walls, so I made them with large barn doors, which could slide on tracks and open

Orinda House Site.

half of each wall to the meadow. That the corners stayed free was the clearest indication that the walls were conceptually not quite there, or not there at all, helped along by the light in the house moving, following the doctrine that the myth ought to be kept up off the floor, and the space slipping in and out from under the aedicular structures. Shelves were built for reasons of economy but also to try to enhance this business of layering the inside. Orinda proved that even the simplest of structures, built of humble materials, could still establish a potent sense of place; a place where I could feel at that comforting center.

When I moved to New Haven I bought a workman's little house of the 1860s on Elm Street, very near the campus, that closely resembled a typical child's drawing of a house. It seemed important not to destroy the whole inside (it was common then to gut these houses) but to make in it furniture of a size so ridiculously large that the whole house sort of split its sides, with a surprising set of leaps of scale of relative size. In order to make it work it became important not to lose the house itself, but insert three tubes or shafts of layered plywood, which we named Howard, Ethel, and Berengaria.

Moore House, Orinda, California, 1962. Photo by Morley Baer.

Shower, Moore House, Orinda, California. Photo by Morley Baer.

Moore House, New Haven, 1966. Photo by John Hill.

Moore House, New Haven, with Vertical Tube and Shirley Temple. Photo by John Hill.

We saw the shafts as furniture, each with a series of circular and semicircular forms; they were made out of two layers of plywood the thickness of a two-by-four apart, with the opportunity for bright color between the two layers with the color that all the rest of the house was — a sort of soft green, gray putty on the outside and with white on the inside to give it importance. What the circles did was make it possible within the limits of the little tubes to have circles of eighteen-foot diameter, a size that you would scarcely think you could afford for a piece of furniture for a house so small and funny. Shirley Temple looked on in slight re-membrance of her own preposterous small size. All that was done with an eye to making the place, the dinky little place, look giant.

The parts that didn't contribute to that expression we downgraded or turned into a joke, like the act of supporting the house on jacks resting on columns, which seemed quite appropriate since the columns, which were the only ones I had, weren't high enough to fit. And then Bill Hersey, who worked in my office, had a dream one night that he had been to my brand-new house and had seen numbers on the wall. It seemed to me perfectly legitimate that the numbers should be cut into very thin masonite and caused to slide back and forth in approximation of my bank deficit.

When we moved the operation to Essex, I made a little apartment in an end of the space where we inserted a pyramid cut away in section to display some of the things that I collect. The object was the major piece of furniture in my living room. It was a big living room and it seemed important, although some friends say mercenary, that the motif of the U.S. one-dollar bill should be built twelve feet

Moore House, New Haven, with Masonite Number Cut-outs, 1966. Photo by John Hill.

high. It also seemed important that many of the little things I owned might be in galleries inside that pyramid, because that's the way pyramids are, and actually I slept in it on the back side because I read that if you slept in a pyramid close to your razor blade you get sharp. (But it never worked out.) And it also seemed important that if you had something that was cut open and had a chance to paint it like a watermelon you'd better not pass up that opportunity. But I think that pyramid, dumb as it was, was as full of the images that I had been cheerfully stealing from all over and as full of attempts to duck the images.

In Los Angeles, I built in a neighborhood near the university a condominium containing three units. The idea for mine was a giant stairway that cascaded through three levels like a waterfall, and had several landings. Entering at the lowest level one caught a long diagonal view up through the entire house where everything was made of a mix of cheap (often) and fancy (seldom) materials. Movement up the stairs was animated by places to be and put things in, and at the top a nineteenth-century pediment framed the final ascent up a precarious stairway along a great wall of books.

Moore House, Centerbrook, with Watermelon Pyramid, 1970–75. Photo by Robert Perron.

I also had in that condominium a big panel covered with shelves, and I wanted something special on the back of them which was the main feature of the high living room so I went to a grocery store in Chinatown in San Francisco. They had a book of gold and silver squares and I bought lots and cut them out, and Tina Beebe and I glued them up into a little gold and silver checkerboard that covered the whole back of those shelves, which I thought was very pretty. One night some Chinese friends from Singapore were there with Tina, and looked at it and turned pale. It turns out those little squares are what you fold in a very special way in the Orient and then light for funerals. Apparently you don't glue them on walls.

A notion that often got left behind in most of these houses was comfort; either I left out the heat or had too little space or made places too vertical. So when I

Moore Rogger Hofflander Condominium, Exterior, Los Angeles, 1975–78.

Moore Rogger Hofflander Condominium, Los Angeles. Photo by Tim Street Porter.

moved to Austin I took it upon myself to make a place considerably more comfortable and inhabitable than its predecessors.

When I arrived, we had a vision for a spread, fittingly Texan, but in the days of Austin's high-priced prosperity we were unable to find anything worthwhile or affordable on the real estate market. Suddenly, Eden, the wife of Hal Box (the dean of the architecture school), found a site with an old house on a gently sloping acre of impressive trees in a pleasant old neighborhood, Tarrytown, near to downtown, where fancy and modest houses mingle comfortably. (Some people had tried to put multiple housing condominiums on it, and when it turned out there were something like forty-four lawyers within shouting distance in the neighborhood, the developers pinned their ears back and we were able to get it.)

Like my house in New Haven, this was going to be an act of renovating the existing small house that had been built in the 1930s and then added on to in the 1940s. In addition, we built a house for Arthur Andersson, a swimming pool, a studio, and a second studio was later added.

There was something really sort of semisinister about the house, it looked like some minor mafioso had built it for his moll in central New Jersey, so I thought it was very important to change the character of the house as far as I could, by opening it up and making it brighter. But at the same time it also seemed to me some-

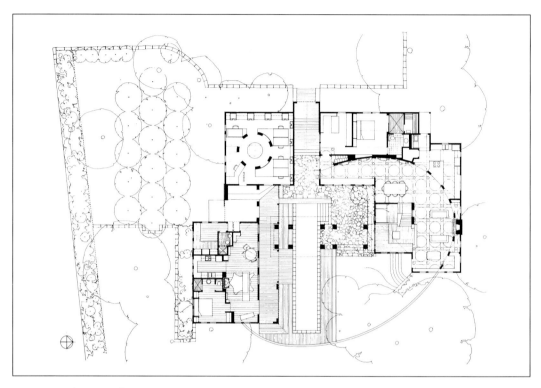

Quarry Road House Plan.

what morally incumbent to leave some traces of the original, leaving us with the task of selective erasure.

Arthur Andersson, Richard Dodge, and I spent many months thinking about and revising our designs. There were important images and ideas: in a courtyard, away from the wind, we would have a lap pool reminiscent of Geoffrey Bawa's tank in Colombo, Sri Lanka; the wagon entrance to the Sherwood Ranch in Salinas, California, was another important image that would support our idea of the act of arriving; and the wide, spreading stairs in Bantry House in the west of Ireland was another persistent image that I wanted to include in my living room.

Most of the windows we left as they were, and I added one big wall of glass, and the low ceilings were removed along with their many interior partitions, opening up spaces characterized by colliding gables. My shower was the only addition to the original house, and is separated from my bedroom by a sliding glass door. A translucent roof of fiberglass admits light into the shower, and a door in its galvanized metal wall leads to a sauna.

That left the act of adding something, to dramatize our act of inhabitation, the gesture that would settle us in. It had to be a big gesture to include my house, Arthur's house, the studio and the courtyard. That gesture soon became an ellipse (the "Lazy O") in plan in which we arranged the public half of the spaces (my living room for instance), and then kept the private rooms (my bedroom) outside. In

Moore House, Austin. Photo by Timothy Hursley.

Quarry Road Entry Gate, Charles Moore, Richard Dodge, Arthur Andersson, 1985. Photo by Timothy Hursley.

Moore House, "Opium Den," Austin. Photo by Timothy Hursley.

Moore House, Austin, with Moore-Designed Adirondack Chair. Photo by Timothy Hursley.

my house the ellipse is a wall sweeping through the space that Hal Box compared to "canoeing along the steep bank of a curving stream toward a point out of sight."

Just inside my front door a set of steps leads to an attic, then the curved wall takes over. Its passage is marked by pilasters, with bookshelves between, then openings for the kitchen, an alcove, the fireplace, and then more alcoves before the curve sweeps outdoors again. The shapes for the pilasters are suits of armor (gleaned from Karl Friedrich Schinkel's Neue Wache in Berlin) cut from plywood, topped with Mexican masks, over pilasters or bodies of galvanized metal with dowel faces that opened to reveal Kachinas made by my sister, Mimi. Graduate students in my Texas studio designed and painted patterns on each of the plywood surfaces using the colors of the kilim in the living room. Last, we used lightbulbs with silver tops to make the insides and layers glow at night.

We painted the wood and concrete floor with a uniform pattern of overscaled squares and circles, and when we peeled the green asphalt tile from the floor in my dressing area, we found a grid of handsome mastic patterns, which we liked enough to keep.

Just behind is the opium den with low seats and cushions all around and the big window we added to admit a generous amount of light, shaded outside by summer wisteria. A stair leads to a little bathroom, unchanged from the previous occupant, while another stair leads up above, close to the ceiling, to a little sleeping loft for guests or napping interns with views cut out of the wall to the living room.

The wall of the dining area seemed the most prominent place, so that's where the portraits of my great-great-grandparents Willard, whom I first remember hanging in my grandfather's stair hall in Battle Creek, were placed, and now they seem to take in Texas with the same equanimity with which they faced the rest of my houses.

And everywhere are shelves jammed with books and objects — awash with objects — and that is its most notable characteristic. All of these things, souvenirs of places I have visited, miniature cities and scenes with staggering leaps of scale, all of these things contribute by default to the ornament of my house.

It's important to note to that ornamentation, far from being frivolous, is one of the very serious and urgent needs of an architecture that people can have any connection to. That whole attitude that sought to strip buildings of their ornament yanked a generation or two away from interest in their buildings. I think it's a dangerous and wrong attitude that we have to do everything we can to get over.

CHAPTER ELEVEN

Urban Innovations

The Urban Innovations Group, or UIG, was a teaching arm of the school of architecture at the University of California at Los Angeles; it opened in 1971 and closed in 1993. UIG was a design laboratory of architecture, in which faculty members could bring "real world" building projects and involve students in their day-to-day development. UIG had an interesting link with Moore's past. Roger Bailey & Associates was its precursor in miniature. Bailey opened the practice in Ann Arbor so that his small group of wartime students could extend their learning into projects actually being built.

Typically, students in architecture schools are given design problems, usually based on fictitious building programs, and are limited to the initial design phase. However, UIG broke that practice, and drew students into a live office with projects actually being built, so all could participate in the design, the development, and construction monitoring. What better way to learn how to design buildings than to actually do it?

One might think that the projects handled by students were insignificant. But they worked on buildings of great importance. Perhaps most famous was the Piazza d'Italia, a building that, with Michael Graves's Portland Civic Center and Philip Johnson's AT&T Headquarters, became an internationally famous icon of postmodernism. When it was featured on the December 1978 cover of *Progressive Architecture,* with a glowing article by Martin Filler and gleaming photographs by Norman McGrath, it aroused reactions from architects that ranged from those declaring the death of architecture to those celebrating the piazza's jubilant sense of abandon and public life. Students also helped win an intense architectural competition for one of California's most coveted projects of the 1980s, the Beverly Hills Civic Center. Later, UIG designed civic centers for Oceanside and Pleasant Hill, California. One very important design that many believe would have "changed the face of Los Angeles" was Bunker Hill, a grand vision for redeveloping a cultural and residential district in the city.

Few people knew Los Angeles better than Charles. Both his experiences of the "old" L.A. and his witnessing the vast changes the city had undergone, infused his encyclopedic knowledge of its buildings, places, history, and folklore that ultimately led to his own guidebook to the city, *The City Observed: Los Angeles,* coauthored with Peter Becker and Regula Campbell.

John Echlin was a student of Moore's at UCLA and worked in the UIG office. He remembered:

The L.A. Spectacular was the name of an urban design studio at UCLA in 1980 featuring as teachers a host of architectural stars active on the L.A. scene, including Charles Moore. Along with seventeen other gullible graduate students from around the globe, I signed up. Our task was to design a new subway system for L.A., a much debated topic at the time.

Charles would teach the spring semester after a fall semester of supposedly rigorous preparatory studies in urban design theory. Numerous lectures, seminars, design exercises, and tough-minded criticism delivered by the other stars on the roster preceded Charles.

Charles didn't have to use the soapbox method of teaching to promote himself, since every student in the class knew his ideas and his personality before he ever walked through the door. He was relaxed, modest, accessible, eager to answer questions, reluctant to give lectures, and merciless in his critiques when he was cornered into giving one.

What distinguished Charles most from his predecessors was his avoiding the classroom like a morgue. He left no doubt that after a lifetime of teaching, writing, and practicing, giving a desk-crit just didn't interest him in the least. There were too many places to visit and too much learning to be done in the world outside. Having been cooped up in the studio with all of the theory we could stand, we proved very willing collaborators.

As the Pied Piper of Selby Avenue (when he was in town), Charles was only too happy to lead us to all his favorite spots around California. What about the L.A. subway system? Well, we would design that too, somehow, in good time. Charles did have his requirements though. He insisted that we keep a sketchbook of our adventures, and there was his reading list, books such as *Ramona* by Helen Hunt Jackson, or Nathanael West's *Day of the Locust,* not exactly your typical architectural theory.

Every week it seemed we had another meeting place. Someone would pick Charles up at the airport and we would ren-

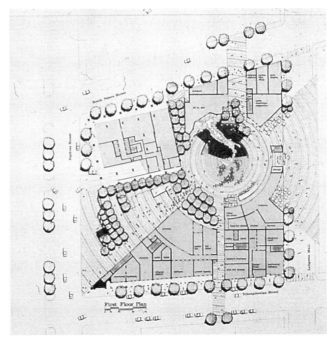

Piazza d'Italia, New Orleans, with Contour Map of Italy, Urban Innovations Group and August Perez Associates.

dezvous. One day it was to Pasadena for a tour of L.A. past, the next week a tour of Disneyland for an important lesson in why everything phony in L.A. seems so real. Often we had accompanying guests, such as Elias Torres for a true Spaniard's perspective of Catalina Island. Or, on another occasion after a personal tour of Kresge College with Charles, we had a seminar with Reyner Banham on the Four Ecologies of Los Angeles. Sometimes the person was synonymous with the place: a visit to the Eames House with Ray Eames, or the Sea Ranch with Larry Halprin. The latter hosted an unforgettable week of perceptual workshops, conducting us on blind walks through the woods, building driftwood cities, and allowing us in on a highly restricted Pomo Indian kiva ceremony.

So what did any of this have to do with designing a subway in L.A.? And what kind of a teacher was Charles Moore anyway? Many professors of architecture use a reductive method of teaching, narrowing a number of factors down to a few primary essentials which through correct application can yield satisfying but predictable results. Others teach additively, using principles like Lego blocks, building up step-by-step. Charles's approach was not so much reductive or additive; it was a leap into another dimension — call it teaching through proliferation.

Charles's method worked like the story of King Shiram of India, who wanted to reward his Grand Vizier for inventing the game of chess. The Vizier asked the King modestly to reward him by placing one grain of wheat on the first square of the chessboard, two on the second, four on the third, and so on, each time doubling the amount up to the 64th square. Unknowingly, the King readily responded to the simple request and summoned a bag of wheat. But after the twentieth square the bag was empty and he ordered more bags. Unfortunately the quantity required to fill the 64th square would have been some four to the tenth power bushels of wheat, more than the world's entire production. The King had the Vizier beheaded.

Studying with Charles was like gathering grains of wheat, collecting a proliferation of experiences: people, places, books, adventures, events, encounters with other senses and dimensions — more than one could possibly assimilate in a semester, probably more than one could work with for a lifetime.

So how did our semester end? Four of us formed a group and made a film of our proposed subway route. We worked like mad day and night building props, filming, splicing, scoring the soundtrack, trying to convey the character of each station along the route, using the quintessential L.A. medium. It was a mess. Charles was the first to say so, loud and clear, at our final crit. As for the L.A. Spectacular, I can't recall a single lecture, seminar, design exercise, or critique from the first semester. But I still have that sketchbook with sketches of fountain details in Pasadena and strange scribbles in charcoal from the kiva ceremony. The rest, each a memory of a particular but very different learning experience had with Charles Moore, are things I'll never forget. In fact, I'm still working with them.

≈

In this essay, Ron Filson, a former director of architecture of UIG, writes about his experiences with Moore designing such important projects as the Piazza d'Italia in New Orleans and the unrealized project, Bunker Hill.

Urban Innovations Group, the brainchild of Harvey Perloff, was conceived in 1970, and was formally organized in 1971 with strong support from William Mitchell and others.

At that point the school of architecture was young, and had been initially conceived of as a somewhat radical blend of curricula in urban planning, urban design, and architecture. The idealistic goals of the school (which grew out of 1960s idealism) were that the common ground of the planner and architect was the field of "Urban Design" and that UCLA would focus on the radical fusing and advance this almost new discipline. George Dudley, the school's first dean, was an urban designer who gave the school its initial strong focus.

His successor, Harvey Perloff, a dedicated planner and educator with considerable vision, was able to see beyond his own background as an economic policy planner to a future for these combined disciplines. Perloff was firmly convinced of the need to link academic education with professional experience, so he began a teaching office of the school, where students would work with faculty on "real world" projects. He also believed that research and professional work with the University could and should be used to solve pressing urban problems in the community. The school could draw upon Los Angeles as a unique laboratory of late twentieth-century planning and design concepts. The office would be known as the Urban Innovations Group.

The original architecture faculty included urban planners and designers, although Tim Vreeland, a well-respected architect from Louis Kahn's office, came in 1969 to head the fledgling architecture component of the program. A number of interesting faculty members with interdisciplinary and "frontier" urges also came to UCLA in the early 1970s. These included Marvin Adelson and George Rand (both psychologists), Gene Kupper, Helmut Schulitz, Jurg Lang, Thomas S. Hines (the American cultural and architectural historian), and Bill Mitchell, the person who ultimately became most instrumental in bringing Moore to Los Angeles. An early pioneer in computer applications in architecture, Bill had completed the MED program at Yale in the late 1960s (where he worked in Moore's New Haven studio), and then taught at UCLA, Harvard, and is currently the dean of the School of Architecture at M.I.T.

Under its first two directors, Ralph Ireland and Al Swanke, UIG attempted to bring planning theory into the focus of actual professional projects. The first projects came from friends of Perloff and members of the board established to govern UIG. They included studies for Twentieth Century Fox in Culver City, and several "development potential studies" for Victor Palmieri in his role in reorganizing Penn Central's land holdings in southern California, including a beautiful 5,000-acre ranch, Coto de Caza in Orange County. Along with other faculty and students, Bill Mitchell focused on investigating development options, and Moore and I later developed recreational housing proposals for the project.

Another contemporary issue at UCLA, due largely to Mitchell's intuition, was a strong interest in strengthening the architecture program. Since the fusion of urban planning and architecture into urban design had not been as thoroughly successful as early visionaries had hoped, a strong renewal in mainline architecture had begun. Once convinced this slight shift in direction was necessary, Harvey Perloff wanted the biggest "name" architects possible. He and Bill Mitchell were both familiar with Moore's interest in returning to California, and they played shamelessly on his weakness! (Charles Moore was the first of many well-known architects, historians, and critics whom Harvey actively recruited, including Barton Myers, Ricardo Legorreta, Cesar Pelli, Charles Gwathmey, Richard Meier, and Charles Jencks.)

By 1973, Moore had ridden through some tough years at Yale as Chairman and Dean, and his practice (which had moved to Centerbrook) had, either because of or in spite of recessions and other problems, dwindled somewhat. His partners at Moore Grover Harper (later Centerbrook) had become increasingly independent and capable of individually obtaining commissions and developing their own work. The time seemed ripe for a change.

It was also in many ways a homecoming. Chuck's fascination with Los Angeles dated from his boyhood; he wrote fondly of trips to southern California from his home in Michigan, and also of his time in San Francisco in the late 1940s.

Moore had experience with a number of projects in the Los Angeles area. The earliest of these dates to the 1950s and was interestingly a project for his cousin Martha Kirkpatrick. MLTW/ Moore-Turnbull's Kresge College at UC Santa Cruz was one of the most significant projects of the late 1960s and his Faculty Club at UC Santa Barbara is considered one of the high points of his midcareer. In addition, Chuck built a psychiatric office building for six doctors in west Los Angeles in the early 1970s, which he always referred to as one of the most "interesting" but difficult buildings of his career. Ironically, when he built his Los Angeles residence (after designing a truly fantastic house for Lee Burns in Santa Monica Canyon), he found a site on Selby Avenue, across Santa Monica Boulevard from the L.A. Psychiatry Clinic, both under the shadow of Moroni, guardian angel of the nearby Mormon Cathedral. The Selby Avenue Condominiums (which had three units for Moore and two acquaintances) were in many ways emblematic of his return to Los Angeles. (It is important to note that Chuck had drawn upon Dick Chylinski for construction monitoring for both the Burns House and the Condominium.) The Selby condominiums played (with a vengeance) massing and fenestration conceits that would later inform much of his work. Its liveliness was rare even for southern California, and the soaring spaces of Moore's unit stunned all who entered; characteristics which would also appear more and more frequently in his work.

Years before, I had worked in Moore's offices in Connecticut, but left to spend some time at the American Academy in Rome and North Africa. I expected to return to New England to work again, but the economy was not very vibrant when I returned to the United States in 1973, so I headed west. Things were also slow in San Francisco, but I managed to meet with Tim Vreeland and others at UCLA and was offered the directorship at UIG, which I thought an ideal balance between academic and professional worlds. My principal responsibility was directing architectural projects at UIG, but I also taught and was appointed Assistant Dean as well. Best of all, it was a chance to work with Chuck again on major projects.

The working method at UIG was both exhilarating and frustrating. UIG's function as practice arm of the school was many times at odds with the demands of an architectural practice. Real clients, real budgets, real schedules, issues of liability, and other concerns often made projects with inexperienced students and faculty (often with a wide range of interests and agendas) complicated and difficult. Although I found that my role as Director of Architecture was to work with a number of faculty members and students on a diversity of projects, my heart was in the projects that Chuck had brought to UIG or that we were able to attract after his arrival.

The Piazza d'Italia in New Orleans was in many ways the most exciting and the most successful project at UIG, given the diverse goals of the organization. A hot topic of discussion with Chuck was how we could win the Piazza d'Italia competition. The limited competition began in 1974 with six other firms including Charles Colbert, Jack Cosner, Perez Associates (with R. Allen Eskew and Mac Heard); Cashio Cochran, Conrad, and Stewart Farnet of New Orleans; Robert Brambillia of New York, and Caldwell-Turchi of New Orleans. Moore was the sixth competitor, and his work on the project began at Moore Grover Harper in Centerbrook. The scheme presaged the later development at UIG with a central piazza, although it was elliptical in the first proposal. Other competitors' schemes ranged from the fascinating to the mundane. The jury, held in spring 1974, chose the Perez & Associates' scheme as the winner, but, in an unprecedented move, the jury strongly suggested that Moore be involved as a creative consultant. Everyone agreed, and after the contractual arrangements were made, work transferred from Connecticut to Los Angeles.

UIG had the principal design responsibility, while Perez Associates in New Orleans assumed the day-to-day management of the project. They also made all of the technical drawings, and Robert Kleinpeter was invaluable in converting our sketches, often quite flaky, into substantial and believable construction documents. As a result of this arrangement (which we used in subsequent projects), we were able to more easily integrate the professional and educational missions at UIG. One of the only regrets of this type of organization was the relatively small number of students who could be involved, perhaps three or four students had the benefit of working with Moore. Marty Schwartz was perhaps the most active, following the project from the initial design concepts to construction.

The project was important for me since it was an introduction to New Orleans. During the course of the project I got to know the city and the people in it, and I found myself drawn to the character of the place. (Years later, when I was offered the Deanship of Tulane, taking it was an easy decision.)

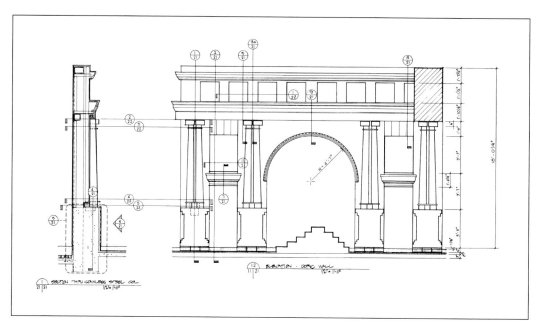

Piazza d'Italia Construction Document, Robert Kleinpeter at August Perez Associates.

Piazza d'Italia, Perspective by Bill Hersey and John Kyrk, Urban Innovations Group and August Perez Associates, 1975–78.

The way that we worked on the Piazza and other projects at UIG was, if any-thing, flexible, given the hectic teaching and working schedules of everyone in-volved, in addition to Moore's intense travel schedule. We needed to be very flexible yet rigorous in structuring design sessions and other project meetings. Typi-cally, we would work on a project and schedule review and design sessions with Moore whenever time was available. I found myself torn between wanting to meet with Chuck alone (out of selfishness, I am sure) for the sake of efficiency and want-ing to involve as many students as possible in the most intimate aspect of our pro-fession, sitting around a table and designing with someone like Moore. I am pleased with the number of students who, because of UIG, had the opportunity to do exactly that.

Students worked on a fixed schedule at UIG, although we had to limit the number of hours per week. We had a system of residents and interns made possible by a grant from the University that let us hire one or two students on a full-time basis for a year after they completed their degree requirements. Often these students had previous professional experience and provided valuable expertise as job captains and project managers. John Ruble was working at UIG in this capacity when Buzz Yudell came west from Connecticut to assist on a number of projects. That associa-tion grew into Moore Ruble Yudell, which continues its successful operations today.

Throughout the UIG years, Moore was protected and assisted by Marilyn Zuber, the administrative assistant who kept his calendars and made sure (in the early days) there were a couple of martinis in the small refrigerator in the office for those 6:00 P.M. design sessions that we would schedule for just one or two people.

The project that represented, for me, the culmination of the early years was the Bunker Hill Developers Competition, completed between 1979 and 1980 by a stel-lar group of architects assembled by Harvey Perloff. It began when the City of Los Angeles solicited proposals from developers for a redevelopment area (a little over four blocks) situated between downtown and the Music Center. The project clearly achieved the best of Harvey's goals and visions, and was a masterful organizational and pedagogical experiment.

As the competition began, a number of important changes were occurring at UCLA and UIG. First, Perloff convinced one of the founding partners of Gruen Associates, Edgardo Contini, to join the UCLA faculty and become the executive director of UIG following his retirement from Gruen. Contini was a major figure in planning and architectural circles in Los Angeles. He had worked with Cesar Pelli on the Pacific Design Center and managed the Fort Worth Master Plan, along with other important projects of the 1960s and 1970s. Contini was also a man of commitment and vision, and shared with Perloff an interest and a belief in the po-tential of UIG to affect positively the community as a whole. His impact on a wide range of projects, including Bunker Hill, was huge.

In addition, Perloff continued to strengthen the quality of the architecture pro-gram and brought Barton Myers, a well-known architect from Toronto, who had worked with Louis Kahn in the United States, to teach design studio in 1979 and

Piazza d'Italia. Photo by Norman McGrath.

act as the overall coordinator for the Bunker Hill team. Perloff had convinced Rob Maguire, one of Los Angeles's most accomplished developers, that such a major undertaking could benefit from a symphony of different voices that would include Charles Moore, Cesar Pelli, Hugh Hardy, Lawrence Halprin, Ricardo Legorreta, Robert Kennard, and Frank Gehry. Committed to architectural quality, Maguire felt that this would not only be a positive and powerful team, but the whole effort a worthwhile conceptual undertaking.

Harvey was closely involved with the entire process and worked with Maguire and Edgardo to flesh out the full team and find roles and responsibilities for everyone. Barton Myers brought Bruce Kurabowa, Mike Payne, and others from his Toronto office. Bruce especially proved to be invaluable to the overall coordination of the project. Barton assumed the role of Master Planning Coordinator and took on design responsibility for some of the major housing components. Contini directed the overall effort for UIG, and acted as the infrastructure planner and designer, coordinating vehicular and pedestrian circulation and parking utilities. Not until later in the project did I fully appreciate the complexity of this task, and the mastery that Edgardo brought to it.

Charles Moore was responsible for one of the major housing pieces, "Angel's Flight." Around the country, architects were working on various pieces: Cesar Pelli was sending drawings from New Haven, Hugh Hardy was sending proposals for the museum from New York, and Ricardo Legorreta was popping in and out from Mexico, forwarding very exotic ideas for the hotel. During Bunker Hill the UIG offices were being renovated, and we moved into warehouse space in Frank Gehry's building on Cloverfield Avenue in Santa Monica. Gehry's involvement in the project produced a fascinating station for the Angel's Flight funicular that was to be restored to its earlier site on Bunker Hill. The opportunity to work with Frank Gehry, adjacent to the other projects going on in his office, was quite stimulating for everyone involved.

The design sessions for Bunker Hill were some of the most exciting events any of us ever participated in. In one of the most dynamic, electric, and productive collaborations I've ever witnessed, Moore and Lawrence Halprin designed the public spaces. The quality of the design work was absolutely stunning and the ability of Moore and Halprin to forcefully advance ideas while understanding and accommodating each other was an absolute joy to behold. Given the cast of characters, division of responsibilities, and the tight schedules, it was amazing to see the strength of individual ideas and the collaborative spirit flying as fast and loose as they did.

Capital-Fountain, Piazza d'Italia. Photo by Regula Campbell.

Moore's Angel's Flight with the Funicular, Drawing by Bill Hersey and John Kyrk.

In retrospect, it is very fascinating to look back on UIG's activity throughout the 1970s and 1980s. The fact that it no longer exists is more a comment on the rampant reshuffling and downsizing of the 1990s, prevalent in major American universities and corporations. It was, to be sure, a vibrant experiment. It was a progressive and adventurous attempt to broaden architectural education, both for faculty who could have opportunities to relate their teaching to professional projects and for students who could expand their education by working on real-world concerns. It was, for those students who had the opportunity to work with Moore on a wide range of projects, a once-in-a-lifetime opportunity. When I meet students of that period, they constantly comment on the impact their time with Charles Moore had on their education and subsequently their careers.

When one goes back and looks at the original goals, the mission of UIG, and wonders how well it lived up to them, it is important to place the vision of George Dudley and Harvey Perloff into perspective. The 1960s looked for relevance in architectural education. Certainly, there was a naïveté in the urban design dream of pulling together willing and contented planners into a new realm of city design. It

Bunker Hill View, Drawing by Bill Hersey and John Kyrk.

was, I guess, an inevitable backlash to traditional visual architectural values and stale policy planning. But it is wonderful that the vision was pursued and UIG persevered for twenty years.

Much of this success had to do with the attention paid to Moore's work and the notable projects he brought to UIG, most of all, the Piazza d'Italia. The frustrations of acting as a professional firm on the one hand, and as an atelier in a school of architecture on the other, was hard felt by all of us. The frustrations led to a number of spin-offs, Moore Ruble Yudell, principal among them, which went on

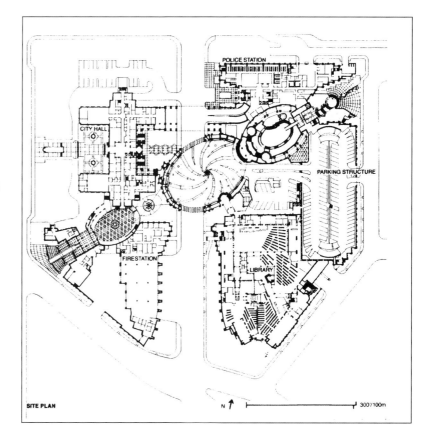

Site Plan, Beverly Hills Civic Center.

Beverly Hills Competition Model.

to produce significant work. Barton Phelps and Steve Dumez became Directors of Architecture at UIG from 1980–1986 and 1988–1993, respectively. Both produced important work during and after their tenures at UIG. My own decision to leave UIG for New Orleans and Tulane was somewhat sad, but I felt that my seven years had been valuable and productive — it was important to move on to other opportunities. I had always admired Chuck's never-ending quest for new challenges and interests and wanted to consider this a lesson learned.

UIG will be regarded as an important and successful educational effort. It is distressing to note that the documents, records, and especially drawings are in disarray. It is unlikely that any comprehensive review or analytical history of UIG will ever be done, given the condition of the material.

But it will be remembered as an important time, due in great part to Charles Moore.

Beverly Hills Civic Center, Urban Innovations Group with Albert C. Martin & Associates, 1982. Photo by Willard Hanzlik.

CHAPTER TWELVE

Water and Stone

Moore's interest in water in architecture began with his Princeton Ph.D. dissertation. At the heart of Moore's fascination was water's ability to connect — the notion that all the water in the world is linked, drops of water or cups of tea possessing the same qualities as the Mississippi River or the Indian Ocean. He saw magic in the paradoxes of water: its ability to transform but be shaped, its usefulness but threat, its delicacy but power.

Friends, colleagues, and students always nourished Moore with new water spectacles, sending postcards or snapshots or tourist pamphlets.

In 1956, Charles's mother wrote the following:

> Know how busy and anxious you are about the thesis — once the 'that' jells, then you'll be on your way.
>
> When you think of the word *water* there are so many facets — life, its importance; the means of getting it — wells; Ruth of Bible times; the River of Life — the Ganges; the aqueduct, fountains, their religious significance; the great canals, famous bridges.
>
> You know I enjoy going to Burton Holmes Books & in the "Paris Exposition" found that the Palace of Electricity was the core of the Exposition; from it went forth along the myriad endless nerves of wire, the thrills that gave it light, life, and motion. Yet *without* water, there would be no sheen, no power, and no electricity. The fountain, therefore, is first wholly ornamental; the waters of the jets, cascades, and pools, flowing in such graceful wastefulness, will return to serve a serious utilitarian purpose, in the boilers of the great machinery hall . . .

Dona Guimares wrote from the Alhambra in Granada, Spain:

> Now I know where you got so impressed with water — and how I wish I'd seen the movie you did on it — only thing is, how did you ever get all those tourists *out?* It's in full bloom right now, the most delightful spots, every one I can't help contrasting it with Villa d'Este. Here water is a natural gift, almost gently led, it's quiet water, no bravado or show-me quality — more reflections — it's *guided,* not *led*. This whole town sounds of rushing water — even the hotel. Your guides on what to see where are excellent. I have a few more choice spots to add, however, like the great Arab Baths here — somehow reminds me of the Gallia Placida Tomb . . .

And in 1957 Moore received the following letter from Hugh Hardy in Washington, D.C.:

Oh Charles,

Well, La Grande Fontaine de Trois Mademoiselles ne marche pas. Then there's the silly group of allegorical figures in front of the Library of Congress being spit upon by turtles; a large terraced affair by the station where water begins to sprout in the shape of a Jell-O mold and ends drooping over granite lips into a green-tiled pool. (At night this is lit in *the* most horrible colors — puce, mauve, pea green); we have then empty granite dishes commemorating the Christoforo Colombo and McKim Mead & White: the Mellon's are perhaps the best of all because they really have enough water — it crashes and rolls, sprays and foams.

There's one on Pennsylvania to call upon the memory of A. Mellon, benefactor-to-Art. It has a perfectly smooth circular roll of bronze so that the water hangs off in a fluttering conical sheet. There are the great slobbering things by the Federal Reserve and the shameful dribble at Dupont Circle.

The little ones in the Dumbarton Oaks Gardens are fun, and that whole place becomes a greater delight with each visit. Mix Capability Brown with Le Notre, toss in an axis-and-jet from Tivoli — all at small scale — and the result is constant fun. Discovery. Not much space but lots of Time.

I am heartened by the thesis progress, not so much in size of output, but in QVVVALITY. Seems to me you have successfully banished the papier-mâché-look-how-they-uncouple-themselves-with-the-touch-of-a-button-there aspect of the original plan. It all seems ideally suited to your SENsitive type presentation technique of the studied Parker 51 wiggle. Frightening to think of having to sustain SENsitivity over the period of time necessary to get it all down on paper, however. Do think models should be bits of things glued, much white paper and LINES.

You do seem worn down. Come to Washington. Bask in Georgetown backyards. Be STIMulated by fascinating bureaucratic crooks. You need new fields to conquer. Everyone in Princeton KNOWS how clever, how witty, how facile you are. There's no challenge. Come wither a new group.

Absorbing all of these dispatches, Moore constantly went to see more, and photographed, sketched, and watercolored seascapes, fountains, canals, and pools; sometimes he even dunked his brush in coffee for earth-toned washes.

When Moore was able to include water in his own designs, he drew upon sources from around the world. The Lovejoy fountain cascade in Portland, Oregon, that Moore designed with Lawrence Halprin was meant to recall the crashing white water of Sierra cascades; its noise and foam and mist were meant to lift burdened minds away from the city. His Oceanside Civic Center featured a court filled with water in which a grid of islands each had a palm tree, a double-coded composite of Spanish patios, islands, orchards, and pools of water. Sometimes the water feature was a cause for humor: in the Santa Barbara Faculty Club, the fountain was made with an oscillating lawn sprinkler — the kind used on suburban gardens — set to slick sloping planes of tile. And in New Orleans, at the Piazza d'Italia, Moore summoned the lessons of the Trevi and created a monumental stage-set backdrop against which water once played: tiny squirts (wetopes) sprung from the column capitals and bases, and then collected in basins surrounding a relief of the Italian peninsula.

World's fairs were perfect opportunities to celebrate water. Jean Labatut had designed water and fire spectacles for the 1939 New York Fair "that employed more than 1,400 water nozzles and 400 gas jets; it was illuminated by a three-million-watt lighting system, with 585 colored drum lamps and five giant spotlights, supplemented by 350 firework guns." Moore planned an elaborate park along the edge of Lake Michigan for the unrealized 1992 Chicago World's Fair, with a stream winding through a Piazza Campidaglio-like pattern, its frayed edges slipping into the formal edges and harbors pulled in from the lake's shore. But for the New Orleans World's Fair (the theme was "the source of water"), Moore designed an even more elaborate spectacle that included a number of water features arranged along a "Wonderwall" of brightly painted aediculas, shops, animals, and lights, set under the rotating magnificence of a giant Ferris wheel.

In Charles's own Austin house, Mexican terra-cotta dragons spill water through their mouths into the swimming pool, helping to mask noise from the nearby freeway and railroad. At the University of Oregon Science Center, Alice Wingwall, a friend and collaborator of Moore's, designed a courtyard cascade that contrasted the splashy fluidity of water with a collection of geological specimens. Even the act of taking a shower was elevated. Moore always rejected the stale practice of mounting a showerhead on a bathtub wall. Instead he made rooms for showers usually bathed in sunlight and always under great nozzles spilling plumes. In Orinda the shower was in the living room, guests remember soaking their feet while having cocktails, and in Austin, a nozzle the size of a sunflower spills water into a galvanized metal shower room with a translucent fiberglass roof.

But some places Moore only had to take advantage of the presence of water: at Sea

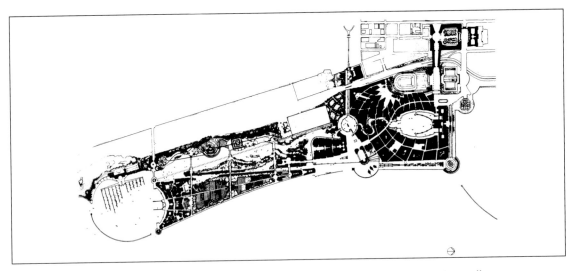

Plan, 1992 Chicago World's Fair, Moore Ruble Yudell working with Skidmore, Owings, and Merrill.

Oceanside Civic Center, Charles W. Moore and Urban Innovations Group with John Echlin, Robin Hayne, and Danielson Assoc., 1985. Photo by Jane Lidz.

Ranch the edge of the cliff dramatically falling to the constant surge of ocean and the endless, hypnotically rhythmic crashing of waves below are a constant source of fascination.

In this essay, Moore celebrates the magic of water.

Water is amazing stuff. It has no shape and yet it can erode the hardest rock and make things of very different sorts look fluid by casting its own aura on them. Water has even been instrumental in shaping the world's national organizations of humans, from Romans to Californians, and for the Egyptians; when the Nile flooded annually smearing property lines, they had to be redrawn each season after the waters subsided.

For millennia, water has been, in the hands of poets, a symbol of life, health, and fertility (even chastity), of blood, even of death and life's rhythms. Flowing

University of Oregon Science Complex, with "Cascade Charley Fountain" by Alice Wingwall. Photo by Timothy Hursley.

water speaks of time and sometimes of delight, of splash and sparkle and cool breezes and human comfort. But when water is uncontrolled, it is a menace in the shape of floods and tsunami and leaks slowly filling the hulls of sinking ships.

Water, at least in its architectural manifestations, seemed to me an exciting subject when I was looking for a topic for a doctoral dissertation in architecture at Princeton. It seemed then, even more urgently than it does now, that our ways of thinking about the stuff of which architecture is made were too confining: that the symbolic and the expressive were viewed with suspicion and that only the functional (in the narrow sense) and the geometric were admitted. It seemed then, as it does now, that water, with its extraordinary range of qualities, represented one of the magic substances that could lead us back to a rich and expressive way of building.

Most extraordinarily of all, water has the power of connectedness, so that any water, anywhere on earth, reminds us of all other water. Even a small stream or a pond or even a bowl of water can stir powerful connections to the great rivers and the sea and the mysterious deeps.

One vivid example is said to have existed in a tea master's garden at the edge of Japan's inland sea. Although it looked down on the extraordinary drama and beauty of rocks and waves and the surf and horizon, the garden was surrounded by a hedge and separated from the view except for a small opening, through some branches, above a washing bowl. Here, the visitor would glimpse the flash of the vast sea at the same moment he saw his own reflection in the tiny bowl, reminding of his own links to bigger things as he made the visual connection between the tiny body of water, cooling his fingers, and the larger one outside.

Such poetics lie at least in part in the age-old human mystery about where the water is all coming from. We know now that water evaporates up into clouds, falls back to earth as rain onto the hills, rushes through streams, gathers into rivers, and then flows back into the sea, from which it evaporates again. But for the ancients, such a cycle never seemed really satisfactory; nobody could see the water going up in large enough quantities to make the system work and where it went underground produced in their minds complex networks of subterranean waterworks. Plato imagined terrestrial seesaws that slogged the water down the streams from one side to the other and then a major tipping of the earth sent all the water splashing down the other way. Medieval visionaries imagined huge spouts of water out beyond the pillars of Hercules, at the edge of the flat world, that pumped the waters of the ocean up into the sky. In fact, no theories ever gave much satisfaction until the eighteenth century, when the water cycle was clearly explained by Giovanni Poleni.

The Trevi Fountain in Rome, the most magnificent exhibition of water on our planet, was built in celebration of this newfound knowledge by Nicola Salvi. There the giant basin of water signifies the sea, and jets of water represent evaporation, and then the cascades, falling past Neptune, complete the water cycle. Even though the water cycle is commonplace, the magic endures.

If water is to move us, we must be able to get as close to the magical substance as possible. Forty years ago, Gordon Cullen in the *Architectural Review* summed this closeness up as "mental-leaning-out-over" — the chance to feel a direct link with the water at those enchanting places along the sea, along the edges of rivers or even lakes. This can happen on a dock or pier with water underfoot (it's best when the floorboards have spaces between them) or lapping at the edge, where it is possible to imagine, laced with danger, yourself leaving solid land and being suspended over the sea.

Harbor towns that were made before modern industrialized ports sometimes had their very hearts at the edge of the water or even within it. Portofino, on the Italian Riviera, has a little bay that comes right up into the central square of the town. A wall of buildings hugs the sea and wraps around the back of this piazza with sidewalk cafes and people sitting at little tables. The stone pavement of the square slides almost imperceptibly into the water so that even people gliding by in small wooden boats can mingle with people walking along the edge.

Streams flowing through the countryside toward distant oceans have stirred writers for millennia in the way the water, always moving, offers us escape, in our

Cotswolds, England.

minds anyway, from our crowded cities and towns. The pretty village of Lower Slaughter in the British Cotswolds has a stream that floats away and carries our minds to the distant sea, where mermaids are. An asphalt road might beckon us through this space and away, but it's unlikely that the power would be anywhere near as great — asphalt isn't magic.

Water has served through history as an organizing spine as well. In Cambridge, England, the Rivers Granta and Cam flow by the so-called backs (which are really the fronts) of the residential colleges. These rivers flow past dramatically varying conditions — grassy banks, low walls, buildings coming straight up from the water, and, occasionally, even bridging over it. Thus, there is a rhythm of things to see here that makes a trip, usually made in a punt — a narrow boat poled by a standing oarsman — a complex delight.

In the medieval German town of Bamberg the water serves as a kind of base for the town, which is built solidly along and over the river. The river suddenly

Bamberg, Germany.

turns into rapids at downtown places, almost as if the rug has been pulled out from under the ancient fabric of this town. The same intimate, almost confronting connection was preserved earlier in this century by San Antonio ladies who insisted that a loop in their river, which had been flooding and soaking shops, be kept when the politicians wanted to fill it in. Now that the water is controlled, the river — known as the River Walk — is by many accounts one of the most successful downtown places anywhere. People can watch from above on one of the many bridges the water sliding through the city, or can go down to the edge and follow the winding course along restaurants and shops. Sunkenness, moving down to the level of the water, makes it all the more potent; once below the streets of San Antonio, we feel even more connected to the fluid, especially since there are no railings along the edge.

In desert climates, the environment takes its shape from the routes of water brought to plants and people. The orange trees in the garden of the Koutoubia in Marrakesh are irrigated from little channels made simply out of grooves in the dirt. In the mosque at Córdoba a complex pattern of channels was created out of stones to supply the different needs of orange trees and the palms that grew up high enough to shade them. In Seville, in the Patio of the Oranges, this gets developed further into patterns crossed over by single bricks, where on a hot summer day, water glides under-

Seville, Spain.

foot in the shadows rendering the place a cool delight.

The preciousness of water in the desert makes an oasis, a place where water miraculously appears, seem to be a magic place. Sometimes people can swim there, as at Sidi Harazem, near Fez. Or, the magic of water can be altogether artificial as in a remarkable fountain at the Portuguese royal palace at Queluz near Lisbon. Un-clothed nymphs emerge from these waters in ways that remind us of the old days of moviemaking, when the crash of waves on the beach served as an altogether under-stood symbol of unions being achieved on the shore. (The alternative, of course, was fireworks.)

Water makes a place in a much stricter way in Coimbra, Portugal, where a sixteenth-century fountain, which used to be in the courtyard of a nunnery, achieves extraordinary distance from the city noises and traffic all around by placing a pavilion in the middle of a square body of water. Access to this pavilion is down

some steps, so that you walk under the level of the water (and therefore, in a sense, through it) and then back up steps to the central building where a tiny fountain sprinkles the center. Then little bridges go even farther away from where you started, to four tiny chapels poised above the water in four diagonal quadrants. The use of this center pavilion as an island, set off against the world by water, has been used from the times of Hadrian in his villa, or later, at the base of the Spanish Steps in Rome, where a

Coimbra, Portugal.

sinking stone barge surrounded by a thin channel of water makes enough separation so that you don't feel connected to the traffic pouring through the square.

An amazing thing about water is that it is, of course, the source of life on our planet as it was its original home; and it still supports all manner of life. In Pompeii, a fountain, adequate for donkeys to drink from, was made special for humans since there was a little carving of a rain god reminding them where the sustaining water came from.

Another kind of power is water's capacity to erode over time the hardest stone and cast it in a shape we think of as fluid and waterlike. Antonio Gaudi's Güell Park in Barcelona has a lizard made of tile that slides fluidly over a streamlet making its way down a hill. When the sea engages in superhuman rages, objects made to confront it must be shaped to meet this shapeless force, from the fluid shapes of ship hulls to mooring bollards. Bollards along the edge of Portofino are streamlined smooth with the taut elegance of truly functional objects, without protuberances that could be knocked off. On England's much moodier coast, a masonry dock curves out from Lyme Regis around a little harbor and into the teeth of the waves with massive, fluid, and strong shapes. On top, pipe railings that people can hold onto grow very thin, so that the water can crash over and through them without sweeping them away to sea.

Four Rivers Fountain, Rome.

The fluid qualities of water have been an inspiration to sculptors for centuries. Roman fountains probably offer the richest available catalogue of sculptured surfaces made in response to water. Gianlorenzo Bernini, in the Four Rivers Fountain in the Piazza Navona, carved the muscles of humans and horses out of smooth marble, but made the rocks and plants out of porous travertine. Bernini polished the travertine smooth where the water runs, but where it doesn't flow, he left the stone rough and jagged. Much like it are the natural shapes formed by water in tidepools along the shore, such as Calpe on the Spanish coast where a miniature world of rocks and water and little creatures has its calm punctuated by the giant crashing waves. The rhythms of erosion here, as with the waves on a beach, are at once recognizable and unpredictable, so that we stay fascinated.

Some sculpture with water takes it the other way around, literal to the point of flat-footedness. The pilgrimage stair at Braga, Portugal, has Christian manifestations on it where water symbolizes blood and healing, all at once, flowing from various landings of this long stair and out of the eyes, noses, mouths and other orifices of the human visages, as well as onto rocks under Noah's Ark and out of the nail holes of the cross. Equally literal, in Copenhagen, a fountain celebrates the legend of Mother Denmark, a woman who apparently was promised all the territory she could plow in a short period, so she turned her six strong sons into oxen to accomplish the job better. They are depicted plowing frantically.

One of the most powerful aspects of water comes from our knowing a great deal about it. We know, for instance, that it always seeks a flat surface in basins. When we see a landscape in which the water appears to be tilting, rather gently at Versailles or more pointedly at the Medici Fountain in the Luxembourg Gardens of Paris, we enter into the scene with more vigor than we otherwise might. At the Medici Fountain one set of signals causes us to expect the masonry to be horizontal and another set causes us to expect the water plane to be horizontal, but the two are not the same. I've seen visitors enter into the sphere of the thing by throwing up.

A more comfortable entry into the sphere of things and a more moving one, certainly, comes in Japanese gardens, especially the kind that offer a stroll around a lake on a path along the shore that sometimes goes inland or even occasionally on rocks out over the surface of the water. Kiyosumi Park in Tokyo has stepping stones with little shallows recollective of the famous islands visited by Marco Polo in the great lake at Hangchow in China. Visitors would marvel at the still surface of

Medici Fountain, Paris.

Villa d'Este, near Rome.

Trevi Fountain, Rome.

tiny lakes on the islands, high above the lake, where one could look and see the moon far below while all around was the big lake with its choppy waves in which no moon was visible.

The Villa d'Este, outside Rome, which was developed in the sixteenth century and has grown luxuriant with planting and suitable decay in the centuries since, is one of the world's major manifestations of water. Water becomes an organizing force, a display piece, and the main point of a garden which cascades down a hillside fed by a river that is now dammed up every morning so that, during the afternoon, it can keep all kinds of big and little fountains running. When it was first made, you entered from the bottom of the hill past very gentle, small fountains and then ascended paths and stairways beside increasingly wild and tumultuous exhibitions of water, up and up past water running by you in the opposite direction through the handrails, past fountains that recollected ancient Rome, and past cascades that you could walk behind. A final flight of steps led to a quiet courtyard and the villa above, where one tiny jet recalled all the wonders below. Today, entry to the garden is from the top down, so it's all backwards, but still the orchestration of all manner of water effects, big and little, is still the theme on which the garden works.

Perhaps still the greatest display of water ever built is the Trevi Fountain. As noted earlier, it was built to celebrate the discovery of the water cycle. Here the cycle is personified by Neptune, on the facade of the adjacent palace, who rides high and commanding as though he had pulled the waters up out of the sea, into the sky and back down into the world. Below him, river gods ride horses, which are made of marble, like themselves smooth and fluid but strong. Around them water falls in every conceivable pattern on travertine made smooth by its flow in sheets, in trickles, in gushes, and in tumultuous cascades, down over edges and into a set of tidepools and then into a basin. The last recalls, of course, the ocean, made more evocative by being sunken in its piazza, well below the level of the surrounding streets. All the water so far has been falling, but, in the tidepools, little jets throw some of it skyward to suggest the completion of the cycle.

These are only a few, of course, of the thousands of places on our planet where water has been celebrated, enjoyed, dramatized, and made to organize human efforts — at the scale of a fountain or a garden or of whole cities. It offers us chances, as few substances do, to place ourselves in the world, to figure out where we are, and, by some kind of extension, who we might be.

CHAPTER THIRTEEN

Moore Ruble Yudell

Moore Ruble Yudell has its office in Santa Monica, California, but its work is international; the firm has designed buildings throughout the United States, Japan, Sweden, and Germany.

As with all of Moore's studios, everyone was bound in a spirit of collaboration. Tina Beebe, a color specialist, began working with Moore on the Santa Barbara Faculty Club project. The reintroduction of color back into architecture, after a long absence, always was a cornerstone of Moore's architecture. For Beebe's master's thesis, Moore invited her to help design the Burns House in Santa Monica, for which she developed a broad palette of subtle gradations so that every wall was a different shade of color, each shifting chameleon-like as the light changed throughout the day. She continued on many projects — again threaded throughout Charles's myriad associations — including the color design for the Piazza d'Italia, the Rodes House, and Tegel Harbor Housing. Beebe once wrote: "At a point during the painting of the Piazza, I asked Charles how the painting was going. He replied that the colors were 'absolutely eye searing!' As my throat sank into my stomach, he followed with 'just heaven,' his eyes sparkling with delight. One of the great joys of working with Charles Moore has been and is, in ways, oddly similar to the greatest reward of working with color, his ability to be consistently and reliably unpredictable."

Color only exists for the human eye in the presence of light, which leads into another important collaborator, not only at MRY, but with virtually all of Charles's other firms: Richard Peters was Charles's lighting designer, fellow Princeton student, Berkeley colleague, and lifelong compatriot. Deeply influenced by Jean Labatut (who had devised that elaborate spectacle of light at the 1939 World's Fair), Peters went on to design his own spectacles, and together, Moore and Peters shared a luminent odyssey of traveling and designing ways to manipulate natural and artificial light. Like Moore, Peters was also deeply influenced by Louis Kahn ("the sun never knew how wonderful it was until it shone on the face of a wall"), as well as Alvar Aalto and his ability to manipulate the subtle glint and gleam of silver northern light. Perhaps most important, Peters believed light could accentuate layers, gradations of shine or shadow, that could pull visitors into dim spaces, then suddenly urge them from the shadows into "light rooms." Peters's and Moore's light worlds were not limited to Finnish restraint however; there was the adrenalined American exuberance of the Piazza d'Italia, experimenting with "Doric light columns" and "neon acanthus leaves," the lighting

Burns House, Moore Ruble Yudell with Richard Chylinski and Tina Beebe, 1972–74. Photo by Morley Baer.

jazz of the Santa Barbara Faculty Club, and the awesome computer-controlled million-light extravaganza of the New Orleans World's Fair. Their work together spanned decades. Peters often contributed to the lighting designs for Moore's own houses, and then continued to work on projects such as Kresge College, Church Street South, St. Matthew's Church, the Beverly Hills and Oceanside Civic Centers, Tegel Harbor, Gethsemane Cathedral, and the Washington State History Museum. Peters writes:

> I believed that every space should contain 'focal glow, ambient luminance, and a sparkle of brilliance' to use the wonderful words of the late Richard Kelly, America's most influential lighting consultant, and Charles understood what I was trying to say in my work with him, especially in the opportunities to explore the relation of light to enhance space and its effect on people. Working with Charles on all the projects was a carefully considered balance of daylight and artificial light. He understood and talked 'light' and thus every idea was worth exploring. He always believed in the accidental effects which could happen and wanted to be very accommodating to the whims and fancies of his clients; he always seemed to have a second sense about making a world to fit his clients' dreams in which light was a part of the total conception. Nothing was ever viewed as bizarre, and consequently nothing ever ended up exactly as was initially planned. One never knew what Charles would bring back from his many trips that would eventually be incorporated into the buildings, from Italian or Mexican chandeliers to fanciful paper shades or tin wall sconces.

In this essay, Buzz Yudell writes about the work of Moore Ruble Yudell.

Rodes House, Moore Ruble Yudell, 1979. Photo by Timothy Hursley.

It is not at all surprising that Charles was so entranced by the power of cosmic dualities. At the level of philosophy, the coexistence and mutual definition of yin-yang in Eastern thought was a model sympathetic to his understanding of the world. In his own life, the dichotomy between his considerable intellectual and creative confidence and his simultaneous vulnerability shaped his work and relationships.

Charles took particular pleasure in the vulnerability of other architects whom he admired. I recall his delight in reading David Gebhard's book on Schindler, with its descriptions of his vulnerability and complexity. He also identified with H. H. Richardson's confident eccentricity, his emotional and physical vulnerability, and his need to be surrounded by protégés even while working in waning health in the comfort of his boudoir-studio.

Charles's great self-confidence propelled his ability to explore, experiment, and be iconoclastic. On a more practical level, he was seldom intimidated by an intellectual or social setting. It was said in New Haven that the only two persons Charles found the least bit intimidating were the IRS agent and Yale's president Kingman Brewster — it was noted that these were the only two appointments to which he was certain to be punctual.

In contrast, his vulnerability and sense that the world was uncertain and truth probably unknowable was fundamental to his exceptional ability to listen and to his lifelong commitment to collaboration. All relationships were personal for Charles. Intellectual and creative collaboration was inseparable from long-term emotional connection. It is therefore not surprising that as Charles moved to each new home, his web of relationships kept expanding. He did not sever the earlier friendships and partnerships but rather let them transform, mature, and mellow while newer and greener connections were being nurtured.

I consider it a great gift to have become enveloped in Charles's extended family. From 1969 until his death I had the pleasure and challenges of being student, architectural apprentice, protégé, academic colleague, partner, and friend. Along the way this wonderful force field of creative and emotional relationships led me to the other pivotal relationships in my life: with my wife, collaborator, and muse, Tina Beebe, and with my partner and great friend, John Ruble. Throughout this span, other creative and personal relationships have been woven into this sphere with inspirational colleagues such as Kent Bloomer and Stephen Harby.

Moore Ruble Yudell started from the combination of sympathetic vibrations with the chance of time and place. I recall Charles visiting Tina and me in our fledgling office, "General Eclectic," on a gray New Haven winter day in 1975. Charles's wanderlust had taken him to Los Angeles, and he was beautifully tanned and flush with excitement. When he suggested that I come and help with some new projects, the temptation outweighed our preprogrammed antipathy to Los Angeles. Perhaps after two years of tasting the strange fruits of California we could safely come back to the cocoon of the Northeast.

Moore Ruble Yudell started with an abundance of energy, enthusiasm, and shared visions for architecture. John Ruble, whom Charles had spotted as a sympathetic soul, joined us early on. John was getting a second degree at UCLA after graduating from the University of Virginia and working in the Northeast and in North Africa for the Peace Corps.

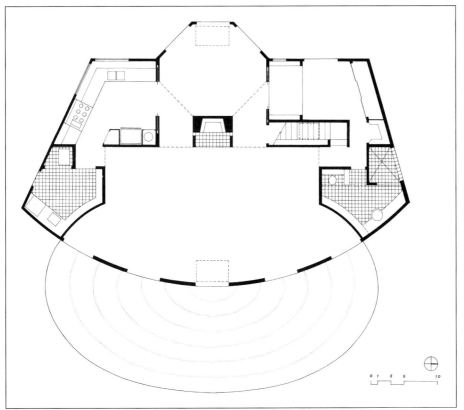

Rodes House Plan.

Tegel Harbor, Berlin, Moore Ruble Yudell with Thomas Nagel, 1987. Photo by Timothy Hursley.

We also began in opposition to any textbook advice on forming an office. Barton Phelps, another of Charles's protégés, used to give wry advice to those about to take the rather onerous California registration exam: "When you get to the professional practice section, think of what Charles would do, and select the opposite." Admittedly, we were all innocents about organization and finance, but our pleasure in designing together sustained us through the hard knocks of learning how to create a professional practice.

Our first office was as modest as the setting was vivid, as Charles had enthusiastically proposed that we take over the second bedroom in his new condominium! We collected hollow-core doors and trestle bases, pooled our drafting equipment, and, with just enough start-up "capital" for leads and paper, we launched ourselves happily into the unknown. In retrospect, it's rather amazing that Charles, who had been through two similarly fragile beginnings at MLTW and Centerbrook, had so gleefully stepped into uncertain waters. Tina was swept up by the Eameses' office, and soon we were both so busy we forgot that we weren't supposed to like nor stay in Los Angeles. By the fall of 1977, we decided to cancel our return fare and officially start a partnership.

Tegel Harbor Promenade with the Humboldt Library, Moore Ruble Yudell with Thomas Nagel, 1989. Photo by Timothy Hursley.

Charles loved beginnings. He loved the challenge of the new, the infinite possibilities of the tabula rasa. As a corollary, I suspect he was repeatedly energized by the presence and collaboration of younger partners. In the Centerbrook office he tended to veto his associates' desire to bring in more "trained" architects. He was suspicious that they'd go around detailing with butt-jointed glass or costly corporate "reveal joints" and not care about the humanity of the buildings.

Our first years as Moore Ruble Yudell focused on house design. We were delighted to closely collaborate with clients and develop unique responses to the particularities of place. The Rodes house and the Kwee house, while geographically and programmatically worlds apart, shared the tensions of important dualities.

The small and tightly budgeted house for a marvelously eccentric and erudite gourmet-cook bachelor professor of English, the Rodes house evolved in response to the pull between modesty and grandness. In eighteen hundred square feet, the house needed to accommodate splendid parties, visiting literati, and theatrical productions. David Rodes, an admirer of Palladio and Thomas Jefferson, was willing to balance one grand space against a poché of support spaces, including a Jeffersonian bed box and dressing area. Unstable soil suggested a highly disciplined and

Humboldt Library Interior. Photo by Timothy Hursley.

simple geometry to reduce the foundation and framing costs. An underlying geometry of cubes and double cubes played against angled sidewalls (following the site's geometry) and a bowed front that made for the greater formality and scale the owner sought. The geometry reached into the landscape in formal front and informal back gardens, important extensions of the life of the house.

The Kwee house in Singapore, while considerably larger and more comfortably budgeted, was also based on the collision of strict geometries with a countervailing sensuousness. While the house was approximately five thousand square feet, the site was quite small and neighbors close by. In Singapore the family lived with a degree of formality yet sought to feel the comforts of informal living as well. The exterior of the house was purposely quiet and unassuming. The tropical climate was central to the conception of the house. One entered the deep shade and began to move through the geometry of overlapping squares and rectangles, creating a series of layered spaces that filtered the strong equatorial light. Tina Beebe's colors provided a sense of moving toward coolness in the processional courtyards. The first court, lushly landscaped with water, provided a counterpoint for the formal living spaces,

University of Oregon Science Complex, Moore Ruble Yudell with Stephen Harby and James B. Morton, 1989. Photo by Timothy Hursley.

and the second court, irregularly shaped and eroded by the glassy wall, was situated within the bedrooms and family rooms, the informal center of their lives.

In these early projects there was a kind of tense duality between logic and intuition, or Euclidean geometry and fluid form. Collaborative design helps to keep such a dynamic tension in balance. Like the tripartite form of government (which Jefferson helped to form), working in ensemble provides checks and balances, and allows each participant to feel free to make intuitive leaps because there are always others to catch him. It's not design by committee, as some who have not experienced this might fear, but rather like a jazz group: improvisation with shared melodies and rhythms, but the chance for individual expression, all in a flexible but structured ensemble.

As we were working on these houses we had our first opportunity to work at the scale of a community with the citizens of the small town of Seal Beach, California, who needed a consensus plan for a nine-acre parcel of Department of Water and Power land where the ocean and river meet. It was so polarizing that the community was literally divided between extreme positions of gross overdevelopment and total preservation of what was actually a degraded brown field with fragments of old industrial foundations. Each side was demonizing the other. Working with Jim Burns, we involved the whole community in weekend workshops on and near the site. While they began with "developers" and "environmentalists" at each other's throats, certain magic moments of consensus developed along the way. In one workshop people agreed that development should neither cost the taxpayers nor produce inappropriate private profit. As we began to show alternate use plans, it became apparent that a certain amount of carefully situated development could pay for long-desired public open space and cultural amenities. In another magic moment an elderly participant who came to every workshop pointed out that there

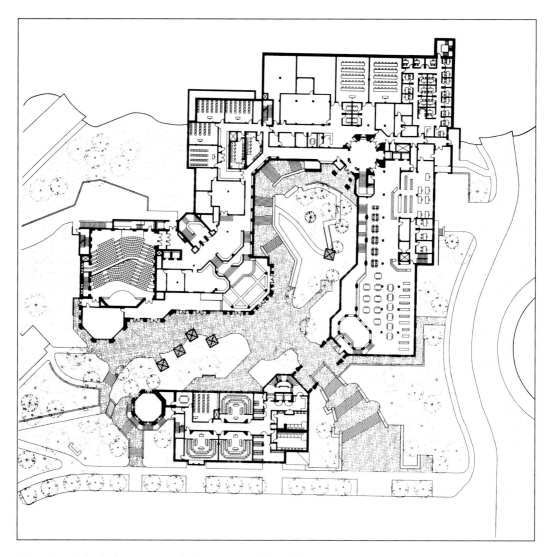

Plan, Haas School of Business, Berkeley, Moore Ruble Yudell.

was a line somewhere defining where X amount of development would exactly subsidize Y amount of public improvement, and if we could find that line the first consensus about the tax/profit balance could be met.

We then developed an economic game, working with Lee Burns, an economist from the Planning Department at UCLA. Dubbed "SeaBopoly," the game modeled an almost infinite range of development possibilities in terms of use type, cost, revenue, and location. We consciously calculated the currency ("Seals") to have an obscure dollar value. Players were given a certain number of Seals at the beginning as well as a board that divided the site into 100 equal squares. We acted as bankers as people bought uses that cost money (public and cultural amenities) or generated income (private development). Working in small teams, participants had to fill out their boards with land uses that would exactly balance expense and revenue. By the end of this process extraordinary consensus was achieved, the demonization and polarization were mitigated, and we were convinced about the power of an open and inclusive process.

While the Seal Beach experience was a matter of only a few months in the work of our fledgling office, it was pivotal to our growing interest in working at the scale of communities. The workshop method worked especially well in the St. Matthew's project, described earlier in this book.

Another pivotal project for us during this early period was the competition-winning scheme for housing, cultural, and recreational facilities at Tegel Harbor on the edge of Berlin. Unlike the previous projects, this was an exercise in the making of a community where there was no access to a client. The scheme developed as a synthesis between urban typological precedents and a bold gesture of specific place making. We built half of the housing as a composite of villa and row house types relating to adjacent tower buildings, and the rest were designed by an international group of architects under our master plan. We extended a narrow canal into a long sensuous promenade. A library came later, along with cultural buildings that were hybrids of industrial wharf structures and the taut classicism of Schinkel's nearby Villas. The gardens, promenade, and library have become a weekend destination and vital community center.

Other important community building opportunities followed. At the University of Oregon we collaborated with the Ratcliff Associates to master plan and design four new science buildings. Here, Christopher Alexander's *Pattern Language* had been adopted as campus policy, and the community was well versed in participatory decision making. Through workshops, we studied the making of community at three scales — the campus, the department, the laboratory or office — so that we could heal rips in the campus fabric and encourage personal and academic interaction. A great atrium at the heart (first suggested by physicist John Mosely) has become a campus-wide focus for colloquia, special events, and celebrations. We believe that the American campus is one of the healthiest paradigms for physical and spiritual manifestation of common values, and without the intimate involvement of the academic community, we could not have intuited the culture.

Subsequent projects built on these lessons. In Pasadena, we were able to restore the axial geometry of the original city plan in a large mixed-use project in the center of the historic district. Working with Lawrence Halprin and Maguire Thomas Partners (an enlightened developer-client), we shaped a series of public spaces around the great 1927 City Hall by Brown and Bakewell. A cross-axial matrix of gardens and fountains became the urban armature for the office, hotel, and restaurant elements.

If we had started off learning how to crawl when we began our office, we found ourselves sprinting by the mid- to late eighties with many architectural and urban-design challenges, many new associates, and a full professional office. But in keeping with his ten-year cycle of wanderlust, Charles was lured to Austin with new challenges at the University of Texas and an opportunity to spawn another fledgling studio in the rooms of a new house.

Since Charles's perpetual travel kept him in the air more than in Los Angeles for the previous ten years, we developed ways to optimize our creative time together. One particularly successful technique was to have three- or four-day design retreats in inaccessible and somewhat exotic spots. One of Charles's favorites was the Two Bunch Palms Spa near Palm Springs, since a mix of soaking in hot springs and succumbing to various herbal massages was meant to wash away the wear of traveling. Amazingly, it worked most of the time.

From those spas we launched designs for the Haas Business School at Berkeley and a new chemistry building at the University of Washington. At the Berkeley Business School, we reinterpreted Bay Area arts and crafts traditions and made a sequence of courts linking the building to the landscape and deferring to adjacent structures while creating an inner campus. In Seattle, the chemistry building frames a favored view of Mt. Rainier. Inside, halls and meeting spaces provide a social counterpoint to the isolated work in the laboratories.

Potatisåkern Housing, Malmö, Sweden, in Construction, Moore Ruble Yudell with Cecily Young and Renzo Zechetto.

A parallel thread of community making continued in housing design, particularly in Malmö, Sweden, and Kobe, Japan, and in our collaboration with a team of architects for the new community of Playa Vista in Los Angeles. Strong connections to all of the sites and climates generated the forms. In Malmö the tension between the scale of local villas and the grand scale of the adjacent sound led to a synthesis of discrete typologies and crescents of housing sweeping toward the water. In Kobe, a spatial narrative of gardens became a metaphor for the site's transitional place between mountains and the sea. In Playa Vista the precedents of southern California landscape, bungalows, and courtyard housing combined with contemporary imperatives of environment and traffic created a plan which revived a sense of community while celebrating the benign climate.

Throughout these years we have continued to design single-family houses because they connect us to our own beginnings and to the generative ideas of habitation and place making. We remain committed to the act of place making at a hierarchy of scales. We are still fascinated by learning about the primal act of dwelling from other cultures and past times, while maintaining the freedom to explore new ways of expressing these lessons. We wish to found our buildings on the logic of powerful geometries and orders. However, their specificity and much of their memorableness comes from the response to the particularities of our clients, communities, and places. As we have continued to work in Charles's absence, we hold as strongly as ever to the humanistic values for which he stood and the collaborative manner in which he created.

From Left: John Ruble, Buzz Yudell, and Charles Moore. Photo by Rob Lang.

CHAPTER FOURTEEN

Soane, Schinkel, and Jefferson

Sir John Soane (1753–1837), Karl Friedrich Schinkel (1781–1841), and Thomas Jefferson (1743–1826) were rough contemporaries whom Moore looked to for inspiration. Of the Soane-Schinkel-Jefferson troika, Moore wrote:

> And here we are in the midst of another dizzying advance, our powers vastly extended in an electronic revolution, trying to place ourselves. We are, to boot, the immediate inheritors of the modern movement in architecture, which seems to have thrown the historical baby out with the admittedly murky bathwater. So it is no wonder that the generations of Schinkel, Soane, and Jefferson make fascinating models for us: they latched onto the past to get their bearings in the present, and the courage to plunge into the quickly changing future, and they seem, whatever their other problems, to have found a dazzling amount of joy in it.

How Moore absorbed their influence is key in understanding his work as another example of his Princeton-era "looking to history for parallels." None were copyists. All sought to derive, transform, and adapt.

Moore admired Jefferson's willingness to tear things down and rebuild at Monticello in an ongoing quest to get it all right. Architecture was to be an exploration of constant renewal and invention and surprise. Schinkel's depictive and compositional prowess has seldom been equaled; his architectural engravings (which Moore owned a set of) were a tour-de-force display of romance and inventiveness with the classical forms of antiquity. The sense of place that Schinkel could evoke in two dimensions far surpasses the sense of place that most architects ever achieve in three.

Perhaps most influential was Sir John Soane. James Volney Righter, a Boston architect and former student of Moore's at Yale, said the impact of Charles's introducing images of Soane's London house was astounding, both for the zeal with which Charles described the place, and for the fact that students were simply not exposed to places like that in those days. It was a revelation.

Moore studied Soane's ingenious ability to squeeze into cramped London lots complex series and layers of spatial experiences, both in plan and in section. The way the light worked, subtly shading the breakfast room, or flooding from skylights into the galleries, and the control of views and axes and termination points were all enormously influential. And

220

Soane's urge to collect a mountain of objects, which he integrated into the architecture by arranging and cramming and spreading throughout his chambers certainly was a model for Moore's own insatiable drive to accumulate.

Moore assembled throughout his life a vast collection of toys and folk art, each object a memory of places he had been. Most of it was not really valuable. Soane shopped in Greece; Moore in Mexico. Where Soane collected marble busts, Moore collected Hopi kachina; where Soane collected venerable European paintings, Moore collected little architectural models sold in street markets. Charles collected series of similar things: St. Michael angels, Balinese puppets, Mexican masks, or bamboo bird cages, and then laced the series with a myriad of objects, bric-a-brac, fragments, baskets, rocks, doodads, boxes, shells, fabrics, and pictures. Everywhere he went, Charles would cart back more; for instance, a year before his death, he crossed from Mexico back home to Texas — his Chevrolet Suburban literally packed with new acquisitions.

Everything Moore stuffed into his houses. Like the Soane House, they were not arranged chronologically or stylistically. Rather, everything was mixed up, so that colors and textures contrasted, valuable objects democratically were crowded by the cheap, figures and buildings were arranged in unexpected leaps of scale, and things from one nation juxtaposed with objects from another. An Aalto tea cart was matched with a richly upholstered Victorian chair; an Eames chair (designed so that minimal material would achieve maximum effect) contrasted a Moore-designed, art-deco, Mexican-colored Adirondack chair. Tina Beebe once remembered looking for drinking glasses in Charles's kitchen cabinets, but only found kachinas. Rolled Navajo carpets lurked like alligators under his bed. Baskets contained baskets that contained baskets. Spanish chests were loaded with dozens of scrolled Chinese ink washes, medicinal cabinets were full of tiny figures and race cars and buildings, and glass-topped tables were designed to accommodate painted dragons and water scenes with floating armadas of wooden ducks and ships and miniature Torii Gates and seaside fantasy cities.

And everywhere were books. Shelves were loaded with thousands of volumes on the history of garden design, architecture on every continent, journals and pamphlets; monographs of architects and artists, student dissertations, histories of housing and urban design, and then scattered throughout were favorite books, histories, and authors: Henry James, *The Book of Tea,* Jose Ortega y Gasset, T. S. Eliot, Robertson Davies, Italo Calvino, Jorge Luis Borges. (When someone asked Charles how he organized his library, he quipped, "By size.") Finally, tucked in one long shelf was Moore's extensive collection of more than one hundred children's pop-up books!

≈

Moore describes his personal tour of the cultural horizon of Soane, Schinkel, and Jefferson in the next essay.

> The chief reason to rummage through the past is to find some friends, people
> who shared some of our hopes and even some of our limits. For several decades
> now many architects have looked to the generation which matured in the 1920s —

Le Corbusier, Gropius, and others — for models and support. I find it difficult indeed to see how our current concerns coincide very closely with those of half a century ago. Instead I think I spot a close connection with members of the generation which practiced about 1810, including John Soane, Karl Friedrich Schinkel, and Thomas Jefferson. These architects found in the Classical past a deep reservoir of shapes and meanings which they made their own, willfully and lovingly misunderstood, transformed to face the extraordinary new challenges of the industrial revolution of the nineteenth century. They made, in the course of coping with these challenges, some buildings to which some of us can feel very close, not only for their low construction budgets, but also for the great pressure on them to say something, to speak to a new world anxious for their message.

In the course of looking at them, I hope to allude to the nature of influence: that is, what it is like to borrow and lend. The major source here is a book by a poet, Harold Bloom, called *The Anxiety of Influence*. His model is an arrangement wherein the young poet (read architect) seizes on the work of an older poet which he extravagantly admires. He heads toward that body of work with his own, and then at the very last second, in a poetic game of chicken, swerves slightly to the side and hits some other target. If he does this just right, he makes the target itself seem to have moved to his point of impact, leaving the older poet with a near miss. If he doesn't do it just right, the target won't budge, and the world will note (if it notes at all), "Oh God, another one." The chance willfully to misunderstand one's predecessors, immediate or distant, is a chance which anybody who is trying to make something (buildings, for instance, which say something) is entitled, indeed obliged, to take. This account of three architects will engage, accordingly, in some willful misunderstanding.

Thomas Jefferson was intent on developing an architecture that would make the rest of the world proud of his undercapitalized new frontier republic. I find it thrilling that he thought architecture might be helpful. Karl Friedrich Schinkel, similarly, was using architecture to make something important, a visible flowering of humanism for a humanist monarch in what might otherwise have been thought of as a muddy garrison town very near Western Civilization's Eastern Front. John Soane, meanwhile, from his London base, was sympathetically and seriously giggling through those building years, making structures of such deep triviality that they command our thoughtful attention.

I am not the first, certainly, to consider these worthies, and what I see is apt to differ strikingly from what others have discerned. Mies van der Rohe, for instance, when he completed his museum in Berlin, said that he hoped he had done something worthy of the Berlin Schinkel. And I have to suppose, from the evidence of Mies's museum, that he saw a different Schinkel from what I see. But Schinkel remade the face of Berlin, and gives us a rich storehouse of works to consider, even after the destruction of the Second World War. Jefferson, who found time during his busy architectural career to be President and Minister, and to pursue other interests, also has made some inroads into the minds and hearts of our forebears. John

Soane's career was rather more limited, but again, has meant different things to succeeding generations.

These three gentlemen, so far as I know, were not close to one another. Jefferson's bias, for reasons known to us, was not pro-British; Schinkel is said to have been a friend of John Nash, whose opinion of Soane's work, I gather, was rather like mine of, say, the current work of Minoru Yamasaki. So the chance of establishing a personal connection among the three is not open to us. What does link the three is not just contemporaneity, but a shared capacity to elevate the simple, the cheap, even the trivial, to works which speak; to make out of the pressures of the world, of pressed time and restricted budgets and the tumult of social and industrial revolution, a group of buildings with meaning, for them and for us.

Sir John Soane's Debt Redemption Office in London has a complexity of geometries in plan worthy of the Emperor Hadrian or of Louis Kahn. Various geometric room shapes are overlaid and moshed together without losing the clarity of the recognizable parts. It all bears very little resemblance to standard classical planning; but note how effectively the peekaboo qualities characteristic of Soane's work allow the architect, just by opening up a crevice in a very modest surface, to concentrate the inhabitants' attention. He achieves a magnificent effect with a very minimum of means.

This, like most of Soane's work, has vanished. But one wonderful, perhaps the most wonderful piece of Soane's work is left to us. It is his own house in Lincoln's Inn Fields in London, left by him as a museum for his collections. It is actually the center row house in a group of three which he built. He lived at first in the left-hand one, then moved to the center, which he spread out in back, behind the flanking houses to give space for the museum, his personal collections of antique trivia. The mind boggles at the cache of disparate objects packed into this tiny bright space, even layered in one rear corner, where overlaid panels flop out to reveal view after view. Next to that is the breakfast room where a handkerchief dome settles down over a space within the tiny space, allowing what's left to squirt up around the outside to light. There are models of buildings and Classical pieces of every size, mostly tiny, but hovering around an enormous Egyptian sarcophagus.

A century and a half after its construction, the outside of the house continues the London rhythms of getting sooty and then being cleaned, revealing in the chiaroscuro a series of little Classical surprises. One enters first a small vestibule, then an entry hall, which makes use of a big mirror to dissolve the space, to make it altogether impossible to figure out where you are and what's going on, though seconds ago you were on the sidewalk. Beside you (or is it?) is a dining room with red walls and mirrors, the slight curve of arcades, windows somewhere in the background admitting light but indoctrinating it instantly into the rich dark red mysteries of the space, faceted, encrusted with paintings and models and objects congealed but somehow not stilled, caught up in the dance marshaled by light, the changeling.

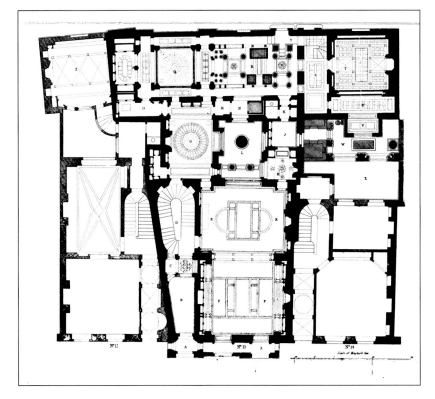

Soane House Plan.

    Just above this dark dream is a pair of drawing rooms all in ivory, where light is admitted to a brighter mystery dance. Here the wonder is geodic. Taut ceiling planes break open to suggest infinite distances in the six inches behind their surface. The light that plays on them has poured through two front walls, and danced and dodged between glass panes in the space between. Little Gothic stalactites hang in the openings pricking the light into frenzy, so it is not Le Corbusier's pure, serious Hellenic light that washes these models of Classical buildings (which set on every surface), but a giggling demon light. It seems to be friendly but it is not domesticated.

    Back downstairs, next to the dining room is the breakfast room, whose tiny space, as we've noted already, is greatly compressed from above by a shallow handkerchief dome, itself relieved by a miniature lantern at its center, but seeming to have an altogether disproportionate effect on such space as there is below which shoots up the narrow slots at the edges of the room, into light. All this squirting space is being goaded, like the light was up above in the drawing room by dark stalactites, here by convex mirrors at the pendentives, which give it no peace. And half the spaces are, of course, not spaces at all, but only illusions made by mirrors, though some are real, up around the edges, where little extra worlds crowned by skylights are crammed with paintings you can't see until you flatten yourself against a wall. Many other paintings, of Pompeian persuasion, hide themselves in their tininess and make one long to fashion a room like this all out of postcards, whispering their trivia in unison ("not to the sensual ear, but more endear'd, Pipe to the spirit ditties of no tone").

In a nearby corner is a room you must now enter with a guide, who will reveal layer after layer of paintings (Hogarths, and Soane's own buildings) by flopping open and then closing a set of big doors on which the paintings are hung. Once all the doors are swung away on one of the sides, you are surprised by a tiny two-story space which opens onto the little courtyard which has given light to the other rooms we've seen, in spite of its being packed with such solidities as a substantial memorial mourning the passing of an ancient dog. Next to all that is the tiny, crammed full but brilliantly lit urban galleria of a museum, with Classical fragments stuffed into every conceivable space, and appearing in places you wouldn't have thought of at all.

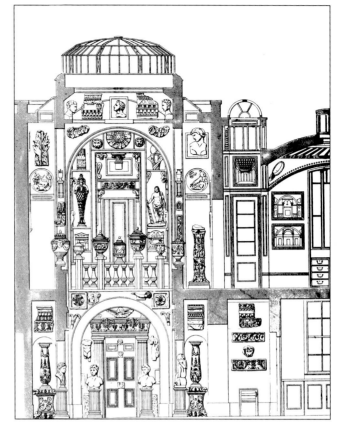

Soane House Section.

People dressed for London come as such a surprise on this compression that it is a full astonishment to come upon someone with no clothes on (though he's marble) more than fully lit under the focused skylights of this gallery. The same skylights are pouring energy into the fragments from excavations across the known world, brought out of the underworld and into the light — with a vengeance. The place breathes life into these shapeless Classical stones, and Soane's lifelong passion for collecting them and fixing them here, like his passion in his buildings for breathing strange hot new life into cool, cool ancient forms, has made of the Classical past a living Present.

Meanwhile, in a much newer, smaller European capital was unfolding another career which shared with Soane's chiefly its base in the late eighteenth-century Grand Tour of Italy and a continued passion for the forms the young architect had seen there —a passion too strong to admit of rote copying. Karl Friedrich Schinkel came back to Berlin, where the presences of the architect Gilly (for whom he [once] worked) and a remarkable cultivated royal house were transforming what had been described not long before as a forlorn muddy town full mostly of military barracks into a pleasant capital still, for a European capital, surprisingly middle class.

Pictures of Unter den Linden, Berlin's treed main street in Schinkel's time, astonish us with their bourgeois modesty: the houses along it were only occasionally palaces of nobility. Mostly they were the dwellings of bankers and bakers and clothing merchants, comfortable, but not at all grand.

Schinkel's little pavilion at the Charlottenburg Castle is altogether chaste and simple and controlled. Inside, it has an exhibition now of some of Schinkel's concerns, especially early industrial ones, like the establishment of a Prussian ironworks. Outside, the Classicism of the square structure is established with the most disciplined and delicate illusion. It is hard even to see the thin line which runs along the top of the column capitals and alone marks off the entablature. But that is all it takes to make this box into something far more than a box, a whispered recollection of all kinds of Classical riches. The same impulses create the precisely incised porches within the building's cube; reserved for its outside is the altogether modern iron balcony, also lovingly handled, its underside painted blue with stars.

A pair of Schinkel's urban sketches cheerfully mix Classical and Gothic elements. They reveal in picturesque hilltop siting, city squares with towers and flags, concerns that were soon to be applied to making a special place on the little island in the Spree where the monumental heart of Berlin was developing and was yet to be. The impulses we see here had a Classical base but were at heart Romantic and theatrical.

Perhaps the most moving passages of Schinkel's Romantic imagination start from Tuscan country villas, with spatial warps. My favorite is capped flat on top with an arbor, the spatial splendors achieved entirely by diving down, around a little four-columned temple, the downness reinforced by the presence of Germanic Styx-crossing mechanisms that propel the whole scene to the very edge of the infinite. Consider the problems, which will require magical intervention, of that boat entering the almost-underwater arch which lies just ahead of it.

Breakfast Room.

Soane Collections.

Schinkel Pavilion.

Bocages, Louisiana.

On another surprising spatial construct, we have a hunting lodge, which combines the Gothic possibilities for drafty vertical gloom with a cheery fire, in a Classical chimney plunging up through the center of the central space, encrusted with stags' heads.

More domestic, the country house at Tegel for his friend Wilhelm von Humboldt (the brother of Alexander, for whom the current was named) envelops an older smaller Baroque palace, supersedes it without insulting it, and shows a new face to a garden allée worked out by Schinkel, von Humboldt, and their sculptor friend Thorwaldsen; French on one side, English on the other (where there is a hill) with the statuary of a Prussian family graveyard at the end of the allée, it is a piece, in the fading light, of Romantic Northern mystical eclecticism without peer.

It does not hurt, on the other hand, to note the points at which our sympathies do not make it back across the years. I submit Schinkel's scheme for shaping up the Athenian Acropolis whose irregularities our generations have come to extravagantly admire. He lines up the recalcitrant stones like recruits on a Prussian drill field, then domesticates the whole. When he was at home his urban improvements, held in line by small budgets, were more modest and, for us, more congenial. I show one of the gates for Berlin, the Leipziger Tor, where Classical buildings, less charged than the Parthenon, flank an opening in a fence which leads you from one circle into a smaller one, from which streets radiate.

Two alternative (both fortunately discarded) schemes for honoring the Prussian monarch with astonishingly overscaled statues of himself don't transmit a serious message to us either. It is, rather, the smaller pieces, even in the larger work where the architect engages in serious play, skilled and supple, with the size of things, with shaping and — especially — miniaturizing the scale of the pieces which in their modesty and precision speak to us. The theater in Berlin recalls a little the house

Tuscan Villa.

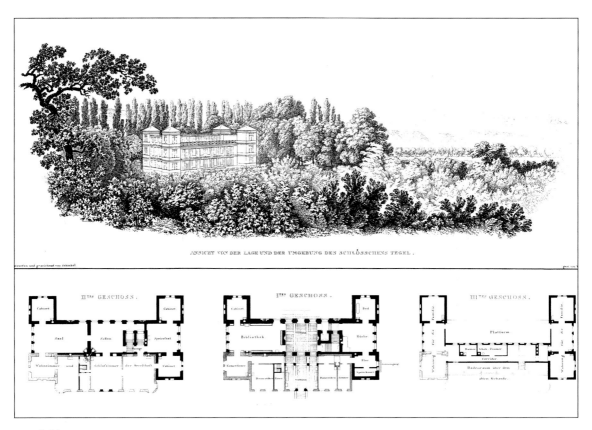

ANSICHT VON DER LAGE UND DER UMGEBUNG DES SCHLÖSSCHENS TEGEL.

II.ter GESCHOSS.

I.ter GESCHOSS.

III.ter GESCHOSS.

Humboldt House.

Leipziger Tor.

Bocages, in Louisiana (which it antedates), with a double entry of Classical piers big and little which engage in lively syncopations. For the designer of Bocages, as well as for Messrs. Schinkel, Soane, and Jefferson, the rediscovery, after the middle of the eighteenth century, of what was left of the real sites of Classical antiquity supplied a source more robust and more poignant than anyone had seen since Hadrian.

Another monumental building in Berlin, the Old Museum, develops at its entrance the same sort of vertical surprises that transpired in the shadows under the arbor at Charlottenhof. Here you slip in between the bases of the Ionic columns and sweep up, in ways which enhance your dignity as a human inhabitant of the space, expanding your stature and your importance as you enter.

Nearby is the powerful little Neue Wache, purely and simply a monument, full of power. But my favorite is an unexecuted scheme for the same project, surmounted by mad skeleton signpost-armorials, a proto-Calder throbbing to the rhythms of very distant Northern drummers. A wall that I have worked hard on, representing the Doric order in a fountain in the Piazza d'Italia in New Orleans, slits into almost-armor a pair of stainless-steel Doric columns in homage to these skeleton warriors of the North.

Thomas Jefferson was born a little sooner, on an even more distant frontier. His formal education occurred not in Italy but in Williamsburg, the tiny capital of his province, which he (unlike Rockefellers after him) thought was architecturally hopeless, composed of wretched misshapen piles of misunderstood English barbarism. It was essential, he believed, while throwing off the political ties with England (to which ends he authored an eloquent document in 1776), to loosen as well the cultural ties which had caused his forebears to make these pathetic little

Monument for Frederick the Great.

buildings. His own models were French and Roman and Palladian. He stood in the
street in Paris while the Hôtel de Sâlm was under construction, looking on it, he
said, as a lover would his mistress, and then he came back to his beloved hilltop in
Virginia to make Monticello, making first a scheme he thought too Italian, not
French enough, then tearing that away to make for his home the powerful and personal structure that now graces the nickel. It does not hurt to notice that the
scheme for the house of the most populist of our Founding Fathers is an unabashedly elitist one, which puts the proud public rooms and the seat of the master
in a highly visible pavilion, fitted with the Classical splendors of column, pediment,
and dome, astride an almost invisible podium, an H in plan, the vertical bars of
which reach daylight in verandahs over the edges of the hill. The work of the
house takes place in this extensive podium, so that what seems above like a simple,
small Classical temple is really the tip of an iceberg, except that below very un-
iceberglike, cannily considered well-running episodes of complex frontier house-
keeping were taking place. The tiny house to which the youthful Jefferson brought
his bride became, with its later reflection, the visible pavilions at the ends of the
podium which very simply state the theme of the house, while the domed and ped-

Schauspielhaus, Berlin.

imented portico in the center takes on more public tasks, even the development of an architectural idiom suitable for the whole new republic.

Now it is a time when architects are trying to use in our work with pleasure and without guilt the shapes we like and respond to, without engaging in an absurd cult of originality which supposes that we have never seen anything in our lives and have each invented every shape unaided. At such a time, it is a great comfort to see Thomas Jefferson, too, finding architectural excitement in Paris or Nîmes, and bringing it back across the ocean to his mountaintop in Virginia. Once he got it home, he had no hesitation about mixing the imported forms with the products of his native inventiveness, like the triple-hung window which allows you to slide up the two lower sashes, so you can walk upright from indoors to out. More directly still, a new capitol for Virginia at Richmond, free of the colonial burdens of Williamsburg, is meant to be as close an approximation as was possible to its model, the Maison Carée at Nîmes.

Most powerful of all, some of us think the most important group of buildings on the continent, was Jefferson's part of the University of Virginia. It was designed, on a hill near Monticello, as an open U, a bay of space that opened to the vastness

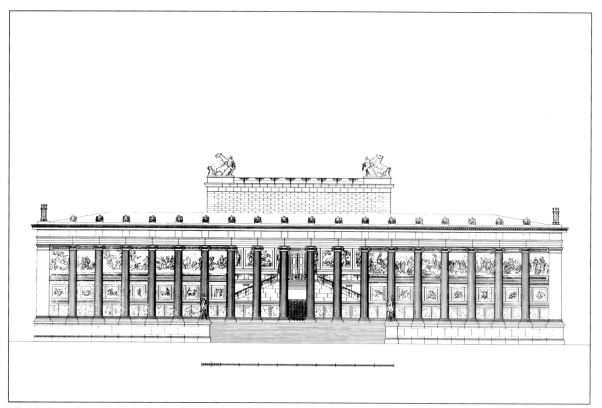

Altes Museum.

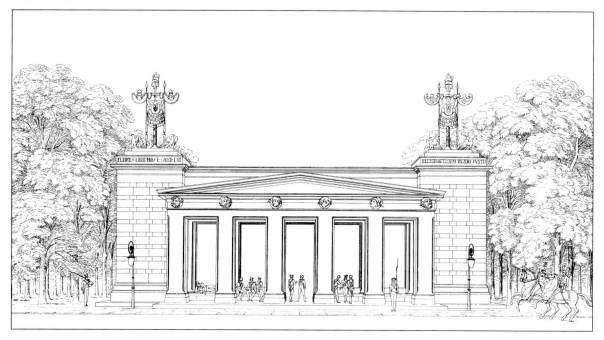

Neue Wache.

University of Virginia.

Monticello.

of the broad mountain valley. The sides of the bay are continuous colonnades, along which are placed ten professors' houses, where classes would meet. At the head of the bay is a central building, with formal antecedents in the Roman Pantheon (a library not a church), set not to dominate the lawn, but to center the embrace of the vast valley space beyond. Behind the colonnades and pavilions, on both sides are private gardens, enclosed by ingenious walls, one brick thick, serpentine in plan with an additional row of modest habitations beyond.

The wonder of these buildings, it seems to me, is that they are talking, speaking about a great many things. One of the things I imagine they are talking about is a thoughtful coexistence of the populism of the continuing colonnade, behind which students live, and the elitism of the mannered, altogether exemplary ten pavilions which served as homes for professors, classrooms, and expositions of the glories of the five architectural Orders (and then some) to the young persons who were having their minds formed in these precincts. Each pavilion signals a different drama of accommodation between its Order and the continuing colonnade. Sometimes the colonnade is interrupted by a big porch, sometimes it glides right on through, sometimes it overtakes the pavilion, and slips right on in front of it. The colonnade steps down, to cope with a falling away of the land, or becomes for awhile a little arcade so that another colonnade the same size but ennobled by its elevation can sit on top.

Along the colonnaded porch are perhaps the most desirable student dormitory rooms on the continent, and at the most elegant of the pavilions, Pavilion IX, is surely one of the magical architectural moments of any time. The apsidal porch, presumably influenced by the contemporary works of Ledoux, contradicts in its height and grandeur the comfortable shelter of the colonnade in front, to set up a complexity of passages from shelter to expansion to front door that achieves clear and powerful monumentality, that tells us what we hoped to hear about the democratic republican new land.

If I were someone else I would have seen other qualities in these three oeuvres. But for now, the simultaneous elitism and populism, the coexistent high art and low, and (especially interesting I think for us) the extreme economy that gave the successful gestures in this work the maximum effect with a very minimum of means, these are some themes about which buildings can talk, and did, when their authors counted on them to help establish a new order in a new century.

Pavilion IX, University of Virginia.

CHAPTER FIFTEEN

The World as a Garden

When Charles Moore was a postdoctoral assistant professor with a Council of the Humanities Fellowship at Princeton University in 1958 he was intrigued with bulldozers. And when faced with developing a design problem for his architectural students, what better combination could there be than bulldozers and Byzantine mosaics? In his program syllabus for his students, Moore wrote:

> Linus Tessera is internationally known for his fine mosaics. His work has heretofore been very small, but he has just returned from a trip around the world, and the tiled domes of Iran are still on his mind. The greatest impression of all, however, was made on him by small Byzantine churches in Greece and Turkey, where mosaics cover interior walls and vaults whose curves and countercurves have introduced Mr. Tessera to a whole new world. Accordingly, he has bought several acres of flat well-drained desert land in southern Arizona, and hired you as his architect. His desire is to use a bulldozer to carve the desert floor into a shape against which Steel-Tex paper-backed steel mesh can be laid as reinforcing for concrete, which is to be shot on by the Gunite process. He has no idea for the roof.
>
> The local earth-moving contractor (there is only one in Ajo) has a bulldozer with a blade width of 6 feet, and a very small dozer with a 3-foot blade. Hand labor is difficult to find. The soil presents no special problems; it is remarkably firm, but easy to bulldoze, and water collecting in pools drains in a few minutes into it.
>
> Mr. Tessera's wants are simple. He lives alone, though he often entertains. He needs a studio with about 600 square feet, which will double as a living room, and a small kitchen, bath, and sleeping area. He does not want to feel sunken into a pit, but any extensive glass areas must be carefully protected, since the summer sun is blistering, although the winter sun is welcome. A "Swamp cooler," which requires a 3' x 3' x 10' high tower, is the standard cooling method in the area. A well provides some water. Mr. Tessera enjoys plants.
>
> You are, in effect, the sculptor of this land. Mr. Tessera will wait and see where he wants to put large mosaics (new to him) on the surfaces you create for him, but he is open to suggestion.

Moore's fascination with bulldozers didn't end there. He was also hard at work on a book concerned with the shaping of large-scale pieces of land. In a grant proposal, Moore described his project:

Kobe Nishikamoto Housing Gardens, Designed by Charles Moore, Moore Ruble Yudell, with James Mary O'Connor, 1993. Photo by Tetsuo Hanawa.

Structures, land, water, and vegetation are the elements of the visual environment susceptible to design control. Structures, on the one hand, are the special province of the architect; vegetation, on the other, is intensively studied by the landscape architect. But land and water, those much larger forms, whose visual importance increases as our speed of travel exposes us to more of them, fall into an area which is largely neglected by both professions. It is precisely in this area that the chance lies to bring our visual environment back under control; but so far the most noble gesture we have been able to muster is to leave the land alone. The twentieth-century earth-moving equipment that could allow us to compose the large forms of our newly enlarged environment is still a symbol of the land's desecration. As an architect and teacher I have become concerned for our carefully designed buildings loose in the increasingly chaotic landscape; as a scholar I can use the lessons from the past to throw some light onto the problem, to find some beginnings for the control of what we now can see.

The method of this book is to juxtapose examples from the present with those from a number of other civilizations. If the older examples will not always demonstrate the use of mechanical equipment, they will show a concern with visual problems which is of the utmost importance to us. The movement of the ground in Central Park to separate pedestrian and vehicular ways and the reshaping of the hill at the Villa d'Este in Tivoli to create the gardens, for instance, are both useful to the study. Of particular importance to it, however, are the great "earth civilizations" of Middle America. The Mayan and Toltec compositions of earth terraces which served as temple bases have received some homage (most recently in Frank Lloyd Wright's *A Testament*) but not yet much careful analysis, as they relate to one another, to the buildings on top of them, and to the surrounding landscape. Since these compositions were achieved through the movement of large quantities of earth rather than the building of large masonry structures, they are particularly germane to our own situation, in which huge quantities of earth, even (in California) whole mountains, can be moved with relative economy, while the achievement of the same kind of control of form with masonry walls, since it is still partly a job for hand labor, is prohibitively expensive.

Moore never completed his work on earth moving, but his interest in landscape and gardens never diminished.

Another critical influence was J. B. Jackson, an important figure in American architecture and landscape scholarship. Jackson was among the very first to celebrate the vernacular, commercial, and "cultural" landscapes; in his *Landscape* magazine he featured many groundbreaking articles well ahead of their time. Moore's interest in Jackson's work continued for many years; he always stressed the importance of Jackson's ideas in his studios, assigned his essays on his reading lists, and often organized seminars with him in Santa Fe or Austin.

The nature of change was the important quality that drew Charles to gardens and the landscape. He loved the idea that in the landscape nothing is static, always expressed by changing foliage, erosion, moving water, and shifting light.

Bonham Cabin, Moore with Warren Fuller, 1961. Photo by Morley Baer.

~

Moore's ongoing collaborations with Lawrence Halprin, one of America's foremost landscape architects, is an important spoke in the wheel of Moore's creative life. In the following essay, Halprin recounts his collaborative friendship with Moore, which spanned several decades.

I first met Charles Moore because of a photograph. In 1963 I was on a *Sunset* magazine jury assigned to examine a large number of entries submitted for awards on houses built on the West Coast. The architects and designers on the jury were a distinguished group from all over the country, and we met for several days at the magazine's headquarters. As usual, the first cut was made by *Sunset* staff, but some of us rifled through the rejects which had been stashed face down against a wall.

I spotted one, perhaps subconsciously, which said a lot to me. Its major image was an enormous elderly redwood tree at the foot of which was a tiny, almost childlike cabin with a metal chimney and factory-glass windows. It looked exactly like a child's nursery school drawing of a home. I pulled it out and brought it back to the jury's pile and then spent the rest of the day trying to convince the jury members to give it an award. I remember having a very hard time of it! Amusedly, the jury finally agreed to give a special award to the tree if I insisted. I did!

The house was designed for the Bonhams. And, the architect, whom I did not (it turns out) know, was Charles Moore whom I had never even heard of.

The next year I was hard at work on an extremely exciting commission, a wild eleven-mile stretch of coastal sheep ranch, about one hundred miles north from San Francisco. I had been asked to master plan a coastal community in an area where I have, over the years, gone to hike and fish and whale watch with my family. The quality of this incredible landscape resonated with all my feelings about wilderness. Logging was still a major factor; redwoods and Douglas fir were still being cut from second-growth redwood groves seventy-five years after their ancestors had been logged to build San Francisco.

In discussions with the client, Al Boeke of Oceanic properties, I had proposed a unique development which would be based on ecological principles as well as aesthetic ones. I hoped to find ways to allow people to live on this land without destroying it by suburbanization or, even worse perhaps, by improving it with lawns and flowers and exotic garden plantings (thus taming it). I wanted to reinforce the strong and austere relationship between the open landscape and the indigenous architecture, like the barns which dotted the coast and strengthened its character by echoing its power and simplicity. I was searching for ways to allow the landscape to envelop the architecture and remain, as much as possible, in its natural state.

As I searched for ways to accomplish this, the photograph of that small cabin at the base of the magnificent redwood came to mind. I asked Al Boeke to hire Charles Moore and Joseph Esherick (who had the same quality of strength) to join me at the Sea Ranch. It was one of the most important choices of my professional life. Together we evolved a new approach. As Charles has written, "neither buildings nor people should dominate the landscape; rather they should live together in harmony with it. Trees, views, paths, and meadows were not regarded as things to be cut down, destroyed, or bulldozed indiscriminately to make way for buildings . . ." We wanted them to "come into a partnership with the landscape, to make something new that would be at home with what was there."

Regarding the design of the Sea Ranch buildings, Charles said: "Fixtures and decorations were kept to a minimum. Only some venting pipes, skylights, ships lamps, and strips of copper decorate the roof. Building materials are allowed to age naturally so that they blend into the landscape's gray and brown rocks and golden grasses: thick posts are connected to lintels with bolts and steel plates that are rusted to blend with the wood, and planks are attached to the structures with metal nails that streak rust down the vertical grains of wood."

What evolved as a result of Charles's design was a kind of profound architectural aesthetic, linked to the morphology of the landscape itself — buildings whose exoskeletons, like those of insects, express austerely the origins of their development. As a result land, landscape, and building blended together into an ecological whole.

It was a great adventure, full of creative enthusiasm and searching, full of the joy of "making something new." Charles was looking for something beyond style, something inherent in the linkage between specialness of place and how architecture could enhance it. I believe that one of our greatest disappointments has been, that in lesser hands, this specialness has disintegrated into a cliché of a style now copied inappropriately around the world — copies which lose track of the essence and copy the forms as decoration. Overall, however, Charles and I so enjoyed our shared experiences at Sea Ranch I asked him to join my office.

It was during that time, the summer of 1966, that my wife Anna and I began developing the notion of exploring the creative process. We called this "Experiment and Environment," and we invited students of dance, theater, design, architecture, and landscape architecture to join with us for a monthlong workshop at the Sea Ranch. Charles joined with us as we explored the notion of environmental design as an archetypal human need in a series of happenings on the beaches of Sea Ranch. Below the great cliffs, aggregations of driftwood which had piled up on the rocks served as materials for primitive buildings. In a series of "scored" activities the students joined in building first personal structures for themselves, and then common concerns for the group as a community.

As they built, subconscious feelings about needs, emotions, and fantasies emerged and were expressed in the built structures. As the days passed the structures became venues for dance; seaweed and kelp were used for costumes, drums were formed from the driftwood, and dances threaded through the beach community.

Community itself was expressed in the structures and platforms facing the sea. Couples dug out organically shaped rooms and on the cliffs above scouts and lookouts, like ancient warriors, guarded the driftwood villages. Charles was enchanted

Sea Ranch Workshop.

Sea Ranch Beach Workshop.

and saw here for the first time the emergence of deeply felt architectural symbols. "What got built over a couple of days," he wrote, "was a set of individual constructions which added up to a village much fuller of symbolic implications than real architects were building at the time, much more expressive of the dreams of the temporary inhabitants."

These experiences were like three-dimensional dreams expressed in built forms. Like dreams they were, we felt, expressive of human desires and hidden feelings pointing the way to a universal language. Many years later Charles and I conducted similar workshops at Sea Ranch for architectural students from UCLA. Through this process of active group creativity, groups which Charles felt had "failed to coalesce" quickly merged into a vigorous community stretching from cliff to cliff in an expression of common purpose.

Charles has since been widely instrumental in the use of this process called "Taking Part" in real-life communities. His own nature is vividly expressed in Taking Part, which destroys the normal, ego-centered design method of "I am the great man" architecture. His own way is interactive and exploratory, influenced by place and purpose. It is joyful! It always seems to involve large aggregations of colleagues and assistants who working together with him evolve, it seems, incredibly innovative and special solutions to ordinary human design problems. That certainly has been my experience working with Charles. In all those years, working with him has been a great creative joy. The process itself has been as important as the projects which we have designed and built together.

Many of these projects are based on water as a dominant element. At Sea Ranch the Pacific Ocean dominates the great rock shapes which lie offshore like abandoned pieces of landscape left behind by the incessant crash of the waves against the cliffs. All this formed a background for our work.

Halprin and Moore with a Pioneer Square Model. *Pioneer Square.*

My next water opportunity came in Portland, Oregon, where a large portion of aging housing stock was taken over by urban redevelopment. Skidmore, Owings, Merrill had been chosen as the architects and I was asked to develop the landscape matrix of the environment. The dominant element of the plan was a road grid which we turned into a series of pedestrian ways. Since the Portland grid is an unusually small one of two hundred feet by two hundred feet, this left the possibility of leaving several modest, one-acre courtyards at some of the intersections. These courtyards, surrounded by buildings and linked by the pedestrian ways, form the basic structure of the scheme. They humanized the environment, providing gathering spaces as well as pathways which link them to downtown. We hoped they would also allow for a variety of environmental experiences which would develop a unique character in each of the small neighborhoods.

I immediately urged Charles to join with me in designing the first of the water-centered courtyards. I knew of his obsession with water; it matched my own. I had reveled in the unmatched variety of water forces and types in California's High Sierra, where I had hiked for weeks each summer. I intended to make water take the central role in Portland. So Charles and I started. I had two ideas. The first was to base our designs on the essence of water as it existed native in the high country. But I wanted the design to capture and abstract the natural erosion process, not imitate it. In the second, I intended to make a place where people would be invited to come in and physically use the water and not just look at it.

Charles was delighted. I remember as starters, I put together hundreds of slides I had taken in the High Sierra. For hours Charles and I sat together in a dark room with others of our group showing slides and discussing the inherent messages of the images I had captured: forms, shapes, cascades, weirs, sprays, tumbled rocks, erosion forms, sounds, channels, and runnels. As we watched ideas emerged, and Charles, with Bill Turnbull and others, worked at the erosion form which became the Lovejoy Fountain. Since it has been realized, people have luxuriated in it, fantasized about it, and just plain enjoyed it. People have gotten married in Lovejoy, overrun it, run unclothed through it, and visited it for the simple joy of watching neighborhood children play in it.

Lovejoy Fountain Shelter.

Dazzling Water at Portland.

At the top of the waterfall Charles designed a beautifully convoluted shelter echoing in architecture the forms of the waterfall. I was charmed by it, but as he pointed out, when it was done some of his Yale architectural colleagues asked, "who threw that tantrum?"

Charles and I have worked with water again and again. In competitions which have never been built, and in projects which have. In particular, I remember Charles's delight in using water runnels in Plaza Las Fuentes as a device to point at the city hall whose open architecture and airy dome by Arthur Brown he so admired.

Even when we did well, however, we sometimes unfortunately lost out. One of our greatest regrets (shared with many of our colleagues and our client Rob Maguire) was not being chosen to build our team's design for Grand Avenue in Los Angeles. Because we knew that traffic flows followed many of the same attributes as streams, we treated the street front as a long pedestrian quayside, paralleling the flow of cars. Along the way courts penetrated at right angles to the quayside, and in each court great and varied displays of water cascaded from buildings, aqueducts, and walls, down steps and through buildings. We lost the competition because of what Rob Maguire has since characterized as, "having little to do with the talent of our team but much to do with our political inexperience." But, he continued, "the process, from the joy of creation to the anguish of defeat, forged a special relationship."

As I think back at our years together, I remember, of course, Charles and his travels. He was a voracious traveler with architecture (and food and drink naturally) as his focus. Travel formed grist for his creative mill. My own memory was of his very special interests in the gardens which he visited and admired greatly. They were an obsession with him perhaps more so, in a way, than the architecture that,

Plaza Las Fuentes Fountain.

he perceived, embellished them. In the early 1960s, when Charles worked in my office, he wanted very much to be a landscape architect. He could have been a superb one. I think he treasured gardens because they placed fewer limitations on him than did the technical demands placed upon architecture. Charles felt that the creative excitement of design occupied more of a landscape architect's time. He also appreciated the fact that gardens are not as finite and fixed forever as buildings. Gardens accept change, for change lies at the core of nature's way. Charles sought change as a way of life, a kind of inevitability which the creative process needed to accept, not prevent. That is how he lived his own life. He moved around, he did not stay put, he did not work alone, he interacted with people, sometimes whole communities. Charles accepted the idea of outward forces — variations, mobility, aging, erosions of water and wind and mosses and lichens. I never did, however, hear him admire earthquakes. Perhaps that much instantaneous violence violated his inexorable search for rightness.

All of this linked Charles to gardens as, he said, "an extension of architecture, a fragment of a city and a natural paradise. Garden possibilities are shaped and suggested by the balance (or tension) found at a site between natural growth and the artifices of man." Actually Charles's houses were like gardens, gardens of fantasy and delight. His own house in Los Angeles, starting at the street, climbed up a hill of interior stops (which incidentally turned out to be rooms) at various levels for resting and views. On the way up, small mementos of his travels embellished the journey. There was a kind of arbor of books and a secret small place behind a steel door (his own grotto) in which I can imagine Charles, like a hermit straight out of Capability Brown, reclining at his leisure.

I remember so well a trip we took together through Bavaria looking at the wild architecture of the mad Ludwig. Charles's knowledge of all the beautiful jewel-like churches there was astounding. He knew each church, each architect, when it was built and why, how the gardens surrounding the palaces came to be, their designs, their materials, and how they fit into their times. He knew as well about all of the gossip that surrounded their building and the stories of the major players in their lives. It was more than enjoyable to travel with Charles. It became a novel: brilliant, evocative, searching, deep, and fantastic at the same time. Charles in his travels was a genius, just as he was in his work. All the world was his garden!

But perhaps my warmest memories of Charles are of our working and being together at Sea Ranch. It was there that we made what has been called wonderful examples of ecological planning come alive at many different scales. The great

Moore Painting at the Halprin Cabin, Sea Ranch.

scale of eleven miles of coastline was preserved for a group of remarkable inhabitants in the architecture of the first condominium which sits like a great imitation as well as an outgrowth of the natural land form. I remember Charles's genius at designing our own first small cabin. I remember how just as Matti Sylvia, our contractor, was about to break ground, I had a dream that the cabin was scheduled to be in the wrong place. That weekend, without any resistance, Charles and Bill Turnbull and I redesigned that house so that Matti could build it the next day in the right place so that my wife Anna would never know.

In that house Charles designed and painted a two-story art piece of shelves — an exuberantly painted cabinet for baskets, pots, and kachinas which linked the two floors. It was a present for Anna and me; a first example, I imagine, of his postmodernist fantasies. That was thirty years ago, and it has illuminated our lives ever since. In my studio there, Charles urged me with one strong gesture to turn the mezzanine at right angles to the sea rather than parallel to it, as usual, making magic out of the ordinary.

I think here at Sea Ranch of our workshops together in which we lived out the early "agony and ecstasy" of community participation. I think of the personal attention Charles constantly gave to the houses and lives of his clients. He brought a sense of joyous fantasy and wonderful experiences to people; serving more as a healer than the usual staid architect.

CHAPTER SIXTEEN

Moore/Andersson

Moore/Andersson Architects in Austin, Texas, was Charles's last firm.

Moore's and Andersson's first collaboration was the Wonderwall for the New Orleans Fair, a spectacle that matched in spirit the one that Jean Labatut had created for the New York Fair in 1939.

In that Austin compound there were virtually no closed doors. Interns often would come in for coffee with Charles in the morning, everyone stored their lunches in his refrigerator, slept in his "opium den" when work extended late into the night (as it usually did), and often borrowed the keys to his Mustang convertible.

Moore came to Texas largely on the energy of the former dean, Hal Box, who had built up one of the most impressive architecture schools in the country. Moore was given his own graduate studio (in an historic Cass Gilbert campus building) where he was allowed to invent his own program, often collaborating with Wayne Attoe, Peter Zweig, Robert Mugerauer, Hal Box, Andrew Vernooy, and Simon Atkinson. He also had a generous allowance for field trips throughout Mexico and the southern regions of the United States. Stanley Hensley, who was in Moore's last graduate studio, remembers:

> Charles Moore lived as a liberal democrat in the best Athenian and Jeffersonian traditions. He taught architecture as a means to contribute to a well-designed environment, with positive effects on both the individual and society. Although he said, "I do not think buildings can produce a liberal democratic social order all by themselves," he knew that expressive buildings could make a realm to which people, "if they have any predispositions to have relations with each other" could make a contribution. And although he knew this couldn't always work, this belief sustained his work. He encouraged tolerance through his example. His values remained true, regardless of today's mean-spirited political climate or selfish design obsessions. He let the process lead, he listened to life, he nurtured people, and taught his students to see.
>
> In his last years when I was studying with him, he may have tottered, been slow on his feet, or misplaced his canes, but he continued to dwell in the public domain and sought for us to see its value. If the American city could not provide a public domain — a piazza — his own home would have one instead, with its endless stream of students, friends, visitors, and gatherings of the cognoscenti.
>
> Charles knew good design could be accomplished with a minimum of means

and was never impressed by architectural bravado. When I asked him why he chose fake plastic-laminate marble for his kitchen cabinets, he said drolly, "You didn't want me to use that stippled speckled stuff, did you?" He said that materials aren't very interesting in themselves — it's what you do with them. You would not find Charles blowing the budget on materials; instead he concentrated on complex and exciting spaces meant to contribute to a person's experience of architecture.

Upon arrival in Moore's postprofessional master's program, we were presented with our first design problem: to design a transportation system for "Desertafelix," a mythical community whose residents were all accomplished skateboarders! The problem was to design a skateboard course, suitably contoured, that would link all of the parts of the community. Not your typical graduate school project, it was meant to open our minds and release our imagination. Everyone had to rethink their basic assumptions.

When Charles slowed the frenetic pace of his students swarming over some obscure architectural delight, he often had a strong reason. On one of our early outings to a magnificent ruin in Gran Quarai, New Mexico, he took what seemed days to get to a very particular place within the ancient walls, having an assistant carry along and then precisely position a chair. (Those who weren't paying attention didn't notice this process.) As the rest of the group exhausted the site's possibilities and snapped another world-record photo shoot, Charles remained in the chair. Finally we gravitated back to his seat, where from exactly his point of view, the most remarkable and impressive view appeared — the cosmos opened up and revealed itself.

With a constant twinkle in his eyes, mischievous, self-deprecating, whether sitting in the pool, eating out, enjoying a movie, munching popcorn, or on one of our evening searches for the new and exotic in Austin, his bonding with students, professionals, and teachers revived and kept architecture alive. He knew everybody (especially everybody who mattered), and used these relationships to advocate simultaneously elitism and populism, high and low coexisting, giving all human life validation.

To extol these virtues did not require a disciplinarian, yet his architecture accomplished more with less. His famous Sea Ranch remains the perfect balance of appropriateness, where a stellar connection is maintained in a transient life. This creation and discovery of place preoccupied Moore's approach, enjoying it like a child — drawing that out of students remains his legacy. He represented our need for village, hearth, and center, to act locally and think globally, to keep the myth off the floor, to willfully cross the demarcation of public and private, to improve the livability of cities and houses, all to support the idea of the good life on earth.

∾

The work of Moore/Andersson's Austin office provided chances for making theater, of tinkering with the real, of drawing in the connections of places, and ultimately in the design of the Washington State History Museum, of drawing lessons from Louis Kahn and establishing bold, monumental forms, but tempering them with human-scaled habitable places. Arthur Andersson, in the next essay, recounts the evolution of his place making with Charles.

Episodes in life usually go far beyond, or at least sideways, from the intended goal. This was the case of working with Charles for fourteen years, and in some respects, the nature of his work as I came to know it focused not so much on addressing immediate architectural problems, but inventing a scenario in which to design. Charles delighted in architecture that was based on experience rather than on abstract ideas. He had an encyclopedic capacity to draw from architectural history, which he combined with an intuitive understanding of the cultures that make places rich.

The first built project we worked on together was the Louisiana World's Exposition in New Orleans. Though the Fair was open for six months between June and October 1984, the design and construction required four full years. The project architect was Perez Associates, and the Fair was designed under the supervision of Allen Eskew. Charles and Bill Turnbull were "masterplan consultants," and took the approach of coming into town every month or so for several days at a time to work (and eat) intensively, then embark to a distant destination allowing the New

Wonderwall, Charles Moore and William Turnbull, Jr., New Orleans World's Fair. Photo by Jane Lidz.

Wonderwall, Lighting by Richard Peters. Photo by Jane Lidz.

Orleans team to make the necessary models and drawings for the next session. Each time Charles would return from a trip, new influences came forth which inevitably impacted the scheme. For Charles (and he is not alone in this regard), the practice of architecture was a "Grand Tour," as with the architects of the eighteenth and nineteenth centuries, and his patience allowed him to sustain his energy and insight over literally hundreds of lengthy airline trips.

With Charles, creativity stemmed from the act of looking and interpreting. Clearly an imaginative designer, his real genius was as a critic and editor. Years of careful observing enabled him to see with heightened insight, and his exposure to both places and people brought an uncanny sense of reality to the small sketches that came from his pencil. Design was conversational, with multiple thoughts gen-erating for everyone around the table a kind of architectural grab bag. While there was an aura of seriousness in the room, Charles often admonished us not to hold precious the outcome of the day . . . it always could and would evolve into some-thing else.

Several influences affected our work in New Orleans. The traditions of Mardi Gras were the most important. Early on in the process, Charles rented a small apartment which he immediately festooned with posters of Mardi Gras floats, circa 1900. Subliminal inspiration perhaps, but those images kept reappearing on sketches for various pieces of the design. He certainly understood what potential gardens

World's Fair Centennial Pavilion Photographed from the "Kodak Spot." Photo by Alan Karchmer.

have, even for a six-month project such as this, and Bill Turnbull's horticultural expertise enabled their eventual inclusion in the project.

Movies played an important role, as did the imagery of various southern writers. Federico Fellini's *Satyricon,* with its flattened, silhouetted ships passing in the night, was the kind of ethereal imagery we wanted in the "Wonderwall," the main centerpiece of the Fair that would simultaneously be a dreamlike apparition of an architectural fantasyland. William Faulkner, Walker Percy, and especially John Kennedy Toole's recently published *A Confederacy of Dunces* set our moods into the complex, lugubrious Southern mode. Over plates of crawfish étouffée (that Charles had pledged to sample in every restaurant within a hundred-mile radius of New Orleans) influences slowly simmered.

Our job evolved into both the planning and designing of the public spaces for the Fair, as well as organizing the geometry for all of the exhibitors to build their individual (and very disparate) pavilions. This took a strategy of some delicacy, providing marketable space for the exhibitors while keeping our own "themed" world in the foreground. We looked at plans of Disneyland (perhaps the most successful place in the world at juggling several very different images at once), but were also intent on responding to New Orleans's unique spirit and climate. Water in the August heat was essential, as were architectural shading devices, such as canopies, porches, loggias and colonnades. The nearby French Quarter's buildings were designed long before air-conditioning, and I remember how I could easily walk from my apartment in the Quarter to the office on the other side of Canal Street during a rainstorm without getting drenched because the buildings all had colonnaded porches.

Our design for the Fair evolved into a necklace stretching over a half mile between two lagoons, bulging in places where we would build gardens, and narrow in the long Wonderwall street. The north lagoon, just inside the main gate to the Fair, was the place where the Wonderwall began. Both of the lagoons' edges were bounded by covered walkways. The first we derived from the Grand Empress's walk in Peking, a richly ornamented colonnade with benches, banners, and lights. The second, designed by Bill Turnbull and Leonard Salvato, was a "Cajun Walk," surrounded by exhibits of local character. To counter the large expanse of open water and to invent something that might serve as a lasting image of the Fair, we resurrected the 1884 World's Cotton Exposition (held a century before a few miles up St. Charles Avenue in what is now Audubon Park), a mammoth, glassy Victorian assemblage of seven pavilions. With the laws of perspective in mind, we spaced our specially sized pavilions over the five-hundred-foot length of the lagoon so that it could be photographed (with any ordinary camera) from a "Kodak Spot" to magically recreate that 1884 building elevation.

Like a kind of fanciful voyage, solutions for each space evolved from observation or experience. Charles often quoted Paul Klee's idea of "taking the line for a walk." Designing was much the same form of exercise, solving complex problems not head-on with a dogmatic set of rules, but rather a stream of design consciousness allowed to unfold. There were, of course, organizational devices such as the aedicula, Charles's penchant for layering spaces using thin walls and light, as well as Bill's ability to make poetry from the simple vocabulary of Louisiana vernacular. While we designed as a team, Charles had the capacity in what would normally be a very intense ego-laden situation to keep the tempo brisk yet light (most of the time) and was quietly respected for captaining the ship.

Not a financial success, the Fair proved to be fertile ground for an ephemeral architectural expression. The work from the World's Fair was in many ways a primer, an exercise in how far we could push the theatrics of building.

In 1985, Charles left Los Angeles and began teaching at the University of Texas. He wanted to set up an office to work on only a few exhibitions and small buildings, and asked me to move to Austin to head this with him. In circuslike fashion, the show moved on to Texas.

Our conversations about Austin evolved into a discussion of Taliesin West, Frank Lloyd Wright's atelier in the Arizona desert that combined working and living environments in an informal yet rigorous place. In the same spirit, we saw the Quarry Road Compound as an assemblage of central Texas farm buildings. (These kinds of fictional responses to design problems were typical of Charles, forever inventing a drama where none existed, representing an endearing ingenuity, not so much the great creator, but rather the philosophical rethinker.) Over many

Andersson Interior, Quarry Road, 1985. Photo by Timothy Hursley.

discussions, we mutually established two guidelines for the project. First was the geode, keeping the exterior of a palette and scale friendly to the neighborhood. Second was the "Lazy-O" gesture that would unify the buildings on the compound. A grand entrance tower was positioned to break through the crust of the geode and make a connection to the energetic and private courtyard — an interior, shared piazza of public spaces. The edge of this piazza became an ornamental armature as well as the organizing spatial gesture for the two houses. Charles decorated the wall in his with metaphorical suits of armor, while mine was influenced by Banaras, India, with its clifflike buildings steeply rising out of the Ganges River. Vertical towers housed the library and had at their tops photographic busts of the Founding Fathers of the Republic of Texas.

While this construction was going on the office consisted of Charles and me, and Steven Dvorak and Chris Wise, two recent architecture graduates whose talent and stamina were largely responsible for our early successes. Our first project to be built was a house in Dallas for Robert Hoffman, a passionate collector of modern art. At the same time, the Smithsonian Institution sponsored the "Festival of India" exhibition, an exercise that allowed a dozen "western" architects and artists to work for several weeks with craftspeople in India.

Most inspiring was a trip to Banaras, the ancient city on the Ganges and older than Agamemnon. This settlement, with its ghats, colors, and layered temples was full of tremendous richness, amazingly complex buildings that were based on surprisingly simple diagrams — concentric rectangles of stepped tanks or centrally planned, square temples. As with the New Orleans Wonderwall, these diagrams became a point of departure for us. We derived the Hoffman house scheme from the stepped bathing tanks, making layers of walls to accommodate the painting and sculpture collection. Within the house, spaces were articulated with a series of canopies over each of the main rooms that would deflect light to the paintings in subtle natural washes. Layered transitions made of little temples with fanciful domes and oversized pivoting doors made dramatic thresholds between the rooms, in keeping with Charles's then very evolved attitude that some of the greatest architecture has the characteristics of a geode. The outside of the house was a relatively quiet soft-brown brick, with a weathered copper roof, but inside was a courtyard planted with flowering Mexican plum trees around the source of water, a swimming pool.

Simultaneously we were serendipitously contacted by the Episcopal Diocese of North Dakota for a new cathedral to replace their century-old church that had burned to the ground months before. After receiving the project, we began working with the congregation to engage their collective spirit for the design of the new cathedral.

Our scheme for designing the building included a proposed workshop method which Charles had used several years before for St. Matthew's in California. With Jim Burns's help and humor, we listened and showed hundreds of images of churches, courtyards, gardens, and monuments, and talked at length about the image of the building from the outside, how it could represent the agricultural heritage of the northern plains. Gradually, we gained the confidence of the congregation, the dean, and the bishop.

The construction budget was minimal, and the parishioners' desire for austerity allowed the use of standard agricultural building materials. Exterior walls were simple wooden boards with battens at the joints; inside, prefabricated wooden scissors trusses spanned the nave, and divided the building into several bays, each defined with a ceiling canopy painted the rich crimson of the Episcopal flag. Walls on the inside were concrete block, stained in a warm cream to resemble limestone.

Despite the cataclysmic fire, several pews, the altar, lectern, baptismal font, and some panels of stained glass survived. As a symbol of the faith involved with raising a cathedral from the ashes, we integrated the

Festival of India Lamp, Designed by Moore and Andersson.

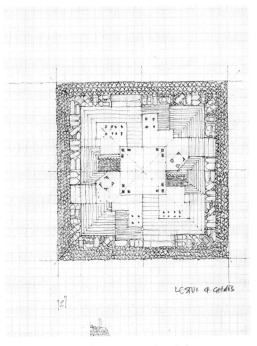

Indian Temple Plan, Drawing by Arthur Andersson.

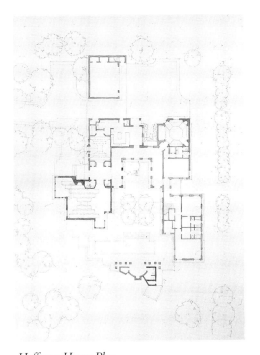

Hoffman House Plan.

Gethsemane Cathedral, Charles Moore and Arthur Andersson with Charles Southall, Mercedes de la Garza, 1994. Photo by Timothy Hursley.

pieces from the old church into the new. These pieces, their intimate scale contrasting the monumental scale of the structure, engaged the congregation and sharply contrasted the expansive landscape on the outside.

During the course of the three-year Gethsemane project, our office grew to include two more architects, Susan Benz and Charles Southall, as well as an office manager, Barbara Shepherd. The focus consisted simultaneously of a number of museum exhibitions and competitions. (How we managed to stay financially afloat, I still can't fully reconcile.) The first was a retrospective of Charles's work which was the opening design for Centerbrook's Williams College Museum of Art. More interesting was a toy show at the Hood Museum (which we did not, unfortunately, have the foresight to call Toyz 'n the Hood) featuring Charles's collection of folk art and Matthew Wysocki's toys. That show, I think, was the best work we were doing at the time, a richly layered dioramic world full of texture, light, hierarchy, and color.

Gethsemane Cathedral. Photo by Timothy Hursley.

Gethsemane Chapel. Photo by Timothy Hursley.

Our most important public competition at the time was for the Washington History Museum in Tacoma. Our fellow competitors were Michael Graves, Thomas Beebe, and Arthur Erickson. The future museum for the Historical Society was to be located on the main street of Tacoma, Pacific Avenue. The site is adjacent to perhaps the most noble building in the city, Union Station, built in 1911 by Reed and Stem. When it opened, the station was the end of the national rail in a city that was being planned by Frederick Law Olmsted. Unfortunately the city plan was not realized, but Pacific Avenue was a vestige of the original Olmsted scheme. Other influences included a row of substantial warehouses across the street and a breathtaking view of Mt. Rainier in the distance.

In looking at the context it became clear very early on that the stoic nobility of Union Station must prevail for the city's sake, while the identity of the new museum should also have a lasting image and presence. The scheme relied heavily on the Union Station building for its form, and in fact the order of the

Hood Museum Toy Show.

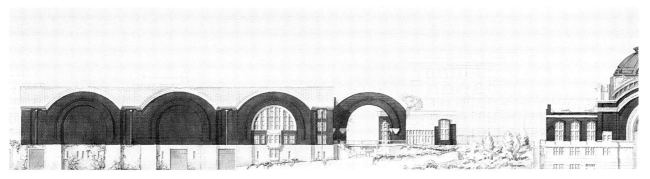

Washington State History Museum, Charles Moore and Arthur Andersson with Steven Dvorak, Susan Benz, Charles Southall, Gong Szeto, and Chris Wise.

Light That Plays, *Memory Palace, Model by Steven Dvorak, Gary Furman, and Arthur Andersson.*

plan evolved into a simple sequence of bays which were exactly the dimension of the bays supporting the station's dome.

The diagram, we thought, was strikingly beautiful as with Louis Kahn's Trenton Bath House. Though not a checkerboard, this linear set of spaces had a sublime relationship to the beautiful Beaux Arts Union Station. It also had, as in Kahn's buildings and in their Roman predecessors, a volume and a plan shape large enough to accommodate the oversized exhibition and make a dramatic lobby. This simple diagram became the starting point for further spatial complexities. Two elevator towers stood as sentinels inside the building to mark the entrance for the exhibits, while a sweeping stair redefined for our building a vestige of the circular plan of Union Station.

This perhaps was Charles's greatest legacy: while making a strong order, Charles's particular gift was not only to resolve, but to embellish.

Arthur Andersson and Moore.

G6. Zeus. life principle
Dionysos. dividing principle
Hades. death. life destroyed
this creates need for resurrection god
Osiris
Adonais
Resurrection of Lord

Yin & Yang not good or bad. but equals. like
male and female. which must be held in some
kind of equilibrium.
good. to hold opposites in harmony.

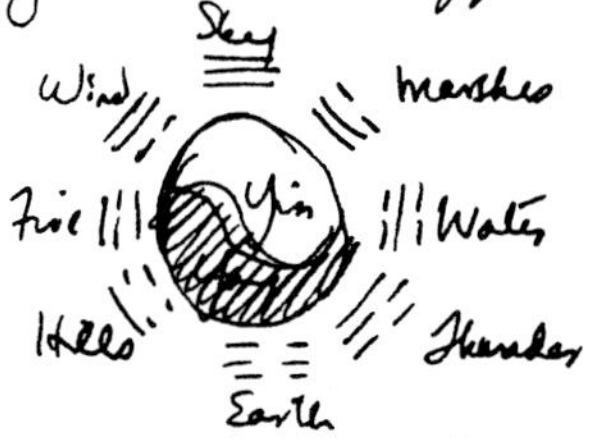

Symbolic method of conveying universe
No conception of sin.

3d unifies. political. social
Shang Ti: gives way to abstract Heaven.
ruler is son of Heaven
ritual regulator between heavens &
any disaster ∴ failure of ruler
nature of universe. & man. intermingled
Shang astrology becomes Chou astronomy
order of heaven to be observed on earth
religion thinks not of gods but of Tao
ruler existed only as long as he was Harmonies Regulator
Yin Yang. the powers of Harmony

4) Ancestor worship.
no longing for the father
but ancestor worship out of cult of dead
satisfied human relation between us here + those gone
makes death anthropomorphic gods unnecessary, if you have Tao
propitiation needed. and real devotion

Moore's Notes from George Rowley's Course at Princeton, 1956.

CHAPTER SEVENTEEN

A Fading Century

Moore semijokingly regarded 1957 as the most important year of the twentieth century because he believed it was the year time ended. "Time ended in 1957," he said, "because the Hall of the Future at Disneyland was closed."

Terezia Nemeth, a young architect, remembered the time she told Charles about a dream she had:

> I answered a knock at the door to Unit #9 at the Sea Ranch. A young man asked to see Charles Moore. A large crowd of people followed him inside. As he pointed to Charles he said in a very considered tone, "1957, the garden of earthly delights." Charles, in just as considered a tone answered, "All right. Now get out." When I recounted my dream at the dinner table the next night, there was laughter all around. Charles said matter-of-factly, "I always knew time was parallel around 1957," and continued to eat his penne al' arabiata.

Moore often spoke about the Chinese notion of yin-yang, the concept of balancing opposites — it was his way of looking at the twentieth century. In a century of unparalleled assertiveness, individuality, and progress, Moore called for a time of gentleness, collaboration, and nostalgia to balance the wheel.

Moore taught that time and place are intertwined; buildings of an age are records of lives and dreams. Charles saw this in Medinet Habu of 1200 B.C. He tried to understand the Palace of Agamemnon as if Clytemnestra and Aegisthus were there. He saw this in Hadrian's Villa of 125 B.C. and later in the builders of the soaring nave and pinnacles of Chartres. Again he saw the wonderful relevance of time and culture and aspirations in the work of Soane, Schinkel, and Jefferson. While architecture is to be experienced through your body — walking, touching, sitting, exploring, climbing — it also is to be experienced through the imagination, in the kind of leap into another dimension that allowed, for instance, Joaquín Rodrigo, blind since childhood, to compose vividly lyrical music about the town of Aranjuez, which he never saw.

Charles spent his last birthday, in 1993, weeks before his death, with students in Morélia, Mexico, for the Dia de los Muertos celebrations. They toured villages and markets throughout the day, where he bought another ceramic Last Supper to add to his collection, this one with twelve mermaid-disciples eating wedges of watermelon. At midnight they floated in

Lago de Pátzcuaro, Mexico.

boats to an island in the Lago de Pátzcuaro to visit its cemetery and listen to mariachi bands as the villagers adorned graves with carnations and candles. It was a lesson of place as experience.

James Volney Righter, a student in Moore's first-year class at Yale, recalled: "Charles once said that Jean Labatut's way to design was 'look, learn, forget, and create.' But Charles saw it differently. He pictured it more like 'image gathering, choreography, emphasis, and massage.' Rather than Labatut's 'creative forgetfulness' Charles saw it more as 'creative remembrances.'"

Moore knew it was important to capture his own time. He began studying when conformity and rigidity and sterility were supreme. "I had little patience," Moore wrote "with the people who were so intent on grandiosity, on megastructural bombast that they forgot what it's like to be in the places that they designed." With uncanny clarity, Moore knew where he was going as early as 1957 when he wrote in a book proposal:

> I have come to architectural history from the practice of architecture because of a conviction, in the face of increasingly technical emphases, that the most promising answers to the difficult problems of our visual environment lie in the chance to develop architecture as a humanist discipline, in which the right kind of use of the past can bring order and richness to our own approach to composition. I have taught architectural history and design, and have concentrated, in my graduate work, on the combination of history and composition. I am writing this book to make explicit the concept of architecture as a humanist discipline, dependent not only on intuition and techniques, but on a study of ourselves and the past.

Moore's humanistic contributions to architecture, teaching, and writing were recognized in 1991. When he was in Austin recovering from one of his especially draining travel escapades, he received a call from then AIA president Sylvester Damianos, telling him that he had just been awarded that year's Gold Medal — America's highest honor for architects. From a hospital window, Charles watched as Paul Cret's university tower on campus, lit only by strict decree, was illuminated in bright orange glory in celebration of the announcement.

Many architects who had meant so much throughout his life as historic mentors and colleagues had also received the medal: Frank Lloyd Wright, Le Corbusier, Alvar Aalto, Louis Kahn, Joseph Esherick, E. Fay Jones, Thomas Jefferson (awarded posthumously in 1993), and Cesar Pelli in 1995. When William Wurster won the medal in 1969, Charles wrote to him:

"Twenty-Five-Year-Olds," Photo by Alice Wingwall, Taken in Honor of the Sea Ranch Condominium's AIA Twenty-Five-Year Award.

I have just come in the great pile of papers on my desk on the September *AIA Journal* and have read your words on receiving the Gold Medal. I can't tell you how much they meant to me, partly for what they said, but mostly for the way they sounded, so very much like those Saturdays in the Ark years ago, when you came to write the endless promotion letters. Those were very important days for me, and I write to thank you for them, even more to offer my belated congratulations on the Gold Medal itself (which is wonderful — but you had it in my book years before).

Moore traveled at the head of a national delegation of family, friends, and colleagues to Washington, D.C., where Chief Justice William Rehnquist bestowed the medal. The citation is as follows:

The American Institute of Architects
is privileged to confer
The 1991 Gold Medal
on
Charles Willard Moore, FAIA

Architect, educator, and writer whose vivid imagination, spirited genius, and unselfish dedication to the profession have inspired countless students and fellow architects for more than four decades. Drawing from the wellspring of his fertile mind and inexhaustible energy, he has produced architecture of remarkable vitality and great beauty. Respectful of the past yet committed to the future, his buildings are exuberant celebrations of the spirit of their place, often colorful, sometimes fanciful, but always firmly rooted in a profound respect for nature, people, and the bond that unites them. Encouraging his students to express and explore all points of view, he introduced pluralism to architecture and invigorated the profession with new creative freedom.

≈

The following are remembrances of some of Charles's colleagues:

Charles seemed to design with no apparent effort, while being in complete control of his craft. He seemed to be able to structure his design process in such a way that by starting the ball rolling and giving it an occasional push (sometimes very occasionally), he would somehow get the ball to the other end, right where he wanted it, or at least for those of us on the outside, where we thought he wanted it.

One of his great abilities was to choose collaborators; all of them were perfectly selected. We first worked together for the 1976 Venice Biennale. We, along with Craig Hodgetts (all of us were teaching at UCLA), were invited to design a suburban house. Each of us was to do an entry, and it turned out that all three were totally different, designed in three totally different ways of working.

I like to plan my work closely, follow it through in every step, and finish ahead of schedule. So I started my project quite a bit early. Charles, however, started and then disappeared completely. He called his office a couple of times to check up on the progress. His house design was based on the mobile home idea, which he did very smoothly. I was very impressed by his performance.

Moore at his Gold Medal Celebration, 1992. Back Row, Left to Right: Jean Paul Carlhian, Former Gold Medalists Joseph Esherick and E. Fay Jones, Kent Bloomer, Nona Bloomer. Front Row: Gus Jones, Lisa Findley, Moore, Norma Esherick.

Another time that we worked alongside was the White River Park in Indiana. I was designing a celebratory tower, and Charles was working on a version of the Tivoli Gardens. Again Charles disappeared for a month, and left his young assistants to work from his sketches. When I arrived the day before the presentation, I thought Charles's scheme was awful, it looked completely unresolved. Charles then arrived, saw the model (probably for the first time) and felt the same about it. But he was completely unperturbed. He sent people out to buy gold and silver paper, which he cut like doilies with scissors, and layered it all over. He turned a dome upside down. He kept the basic functions, but changed the character completely, with total nonchalance. And it turned out wonderfully, a very Charles Moore scheme — it was like pulling a rabbit out of a hat.

Bunker Hill was another project, a very important one, that we worked on together, along with Legorreta, Gehry, Myers, Hardy, and Halprin. It was an incredibly good effort done with ease. It was fresh and important, unusually farseeing, and contained the germs of many future developments. Things were not simply thrown together, it was an agglomeration with order; there was an underlying structure that accommodated an incredible variety of shapes and forms. The scheme was decided against, however, and it was a great shame that it was never built. It was financial bureaucracy at its worst, in combination with the worst in city politics. (It was not a complete loss, however: for me, that project led to the World Financial Center commission.)

Charles was also a great teacher. I met him after his Yale period, and when I myself became Dean there I invited him to teach often. Once we made plans for him to come and teach for a week. (Plans had to be made a year in advance since his schedule was so tight.) His plan was to fly from Africa to New Haven, teach for the week, and then he had to fly to San Francisco and then to the Orient. However, as it came closer, he was delayed in Africa, and would only be able to be in New Haven for three days. I thought he would be completely exhausted and useless. But when he arrived, he worked with the students in the studio for a little while, and then suddenly he took all of them on a field trip to Boston!

The essential problem and process of architecture is observing and learning. And if one has good eyes, one can learn and refine one's architecture by knowing how to look, and what connections to make. When Charles came from the West Coast, he gave slide lectures, obviously just thrown together — the verticals and horizontals were mixed up, all were snapshots (mostly of funky buildings in California), some out of focus, and some overexposed. But somehow the poor slides made one concentrate on his observations. He showed how details and pieces contributed to the character of the places and how they solved problems. He could bring students into his mind. And students loved him.

I have the greatest admiration for Charles Moore. I never knew of any other architect whose intent matched so closely his abilities; his way of working was so completely part of his life.

Cesar Pelli

Charles was one of those rare individuals who could not be, although at times he would like to be, unnoticed. Almost always we relate him to architecture, but his presence and influence went much further than that — he was a true and honest humanist. My work with him was related to education, and almost immediately after meeting him some twenty years ago, a feeling of admiration, respect, and friendship grew with deep roots in my soul.

His influence always was founded — as everything he did — on ideas that were profound, humanitarian, and always positive. In each conversation, conference, or simply in his attitude, he left in me the desire to improve, to be more positive, and to be aware that there are causes worth fighting for. He could never say no to projects when he felt he had something to contribute.

It is to these qualities we add sensitivity, creative talent, and authentic free thoughts, and we can understand why Charles was an extraordinary architect and educator, who, having his concepts of design well-defined, respected and supported the good aspects of other theories and cultures.

Charles deeply loved Mexico, creating in us Mexicans the desire to know and love our country more and to be better Mexicans. I saw him transmit this feeling to architects and students from numerous other cultures as well.

Aware of his enormous talent and personality, he never attempted to impose his ideas. On the contrary, he managed to bring out the best in those around him. Even in his most successful moments he never took himself seriously. With humility and a sense of humor, he celebrated each success as just another event in his life.

That was Charles. An exceptional man, a great architect, and an unforgettable character who, with his conversations and actions, taught us to be better human beings and consequently better architects and above all to give the best within us.

Charles left deep and indelible footprints — for that we can say the most beautiful that can be said of another person.

Ricardo Legorreta

I first met Charles Moore in the late '50s when he and Donlyn Lyndon, then graduate students at Princeton, drove down to Philadelphia and included a visit to my office on their trip — I was then working in association with Cope and Lippincott. We had a nice talk, and they graciously invited me to lecture informally at Princeton — this was to be my first lecture at a university.

Later, in the mid '60s when I was teaching at Yale at the invitation of Charles, I remember having lunch with Charles at the old Duncan Hotel behind the Art & Architecture Building where he advised me what to see in Los Angeles as I was about to make my second visit there — Denise Scott Brown had invited me to teach and lecture at UCLA for a week. It was wonderful later to see Los Angeles through his simpatico eyes, as well as my own and Denise's — remember, Los Angeles in those days was a pariah to architects and planners who despised sprawl and the commercial vernacular. When Denise and I married the next year he lent us his Sea Ranch house for our honeymoon.

Charles could wonderfully acknowledge the joy of the everyday in his work and his writing which itself was elegant and clear and in glorious contrast to the architectural writing of today that glories in obscurity to appear profound.

Our work and Charles's paralleled and diverged in their evolutions over the years; both accommodate ornament and symbolism — but Charles's was consistently lyrical while ours can embrace dissonance as well as lyricism. We are sometimes consciously gauche — there can be a kind of tension between the generic ordinariness and the occasional fanfare of what we do — and I guess our kind of agony is what makes us mannerists. There was never any gaucheness in what Charles did, but his consistent lyricism was supremely poetic.

Robert Venturi

When I taught at Penn in the early 1960s it was the school and the planning school in the U. S. — it was the great place to be. Then, in about 1962, Bill Wheaton went from Penn to U. C. Berkeley, and the College of Environmental Design became our West Coast antipodes. Bill occasionally talked of Chuck Moore — "Chuck Moore," not "Charles Moore."

In 1965 Bill invited me to Berkeley, and I think that was when I first met Charles. Martin Meyerson was dean, William Wurster had recently retired, Bill was chair of planning, and Charles was chair of architecture. Charles welcomed me warmly as a colleague.

The tensions between planning and architecture at Penn intrigued me. Other architects felt the planners were churlish Philistines, but Bob and I found social planners and thinkers like Herbert Gans and Paul Davidoff challenging. Charles was equally receptive to the social planners and scientists at Berkeley, and "You Have to Pay for the Public Life" derived in part from the social planning debate there in the late fifties and early sixties. So, in this regard, Charles and we reverberated on the same wavelength.

Having read Charles on the public life, one of the first things I did when starting to teach at UCLA was to visit Disneyland with my students.

Eventually our work and Charles's diverged. Our *Learning from Las Vegas* drew us to symbols rather than forms as the locus for complexity in architecture, and from that evolved the notion of the decorated shed. I think Charles found this formulation too stark and disagreed with the direction our architecture took thereafter. There is an edge to what we do; the monumentality we seek is eroded by messy immediacies. Lou Kahn said of a building, "You hate it and you hate it and you hate it until you love it, because it's the way it has to be." Like Lou, we prefer our beauty agonized. Charles, I think, liked his unadulterated.

For all their differences, Charles's buildings and ours laugh through tears, and sometimes they laugh at themselves, though not at the client. And our heads, like his, are "swivel-tilted." Wherever he went, Charles looked intently at what he saw. He viewed the world, not with alarm or disdain, but with some sort of irony — mature, humorous, gentle, and slightly self-mocking.

Denise Scott Brown

Charles was very accessible to me; he was accepting and supportive and helpful, and easy to talk to. (I must have seemed like some weirdo to him, architecturally anyway, but he didn't treat me that way.) I remember him taking me to his stairway of an apartment, which had, in my memory, a living room, bedroom, kitchen, and library. And I remember leaving there and trying to draw it, and I couldn't.

We competed with each other; as I recall, he always won. (I think it was just one time though.) During the Beverly Hills City Hall Competition I knew I was finished when I saw Charles's white model. It was just the right scheme. In pondering it over the years, I realized, of course, that none of us liked the old City Hall building. Because we were too accepting of it as it was, we were afraid to touch it. Only Charles, because of his background, had the guts to take it, move it, and change it. With authority he took that arm and just reached it out parallel to Santa Monica Boulevard and embraced the courtyard and made an extraordinary space.

I saw those flashes of genius many times with him at the Chicago World's Fair, and in the most exciting voyeurism I watched him when he made Wonderwall in New Orleans. A bunch of us were brought there to meet with potential clients who were going to build the Fair. We sat for a few days and listened to them explaining the fair and most of us were horrified — it sounded like Disneyland — and how were we going to do that? We each had to get up and talk about it, and each one of us said that we couldn't make Disneyland in New Orleans. Then Charles got up and said just the opposite and captured the whole project! I was furious! The Wonderwall he concocted was truly, truly, a wonderwall, and surpassed everything that Disneyland had by a lot.

I always felt Charles was working on fast-forward. I always had the feeling that he was even ahead of himself and couldn't catch up. So I didn't know how all of those guys who worked with him could hang on to the sprint, to the ideas that were rolling out so fast and wonderfully.

Frank Gehry

I guess among all of the architects in these pages, I knew Charles the least. We never were friends, we were quite often enemies, but I realize now what his importance was. I am also one of the few architects of my generation to write here, and I can only tell you that the world changed in the sixties when Charles made those pronouncements. All I can tell you is reading those few words — those precise, those clear, those simple words — for me it was a Declaration of Independence, a Declaration of Freedom from the old binds of the International Style, the Bauhaus, and Walter Gropius.

To me Charles declared the new era in very simple and moving terms, and since then I have been touring and touring Disneyland and appreciate it more every single time. In fact, I get the words and experiences of Disneyland mixed up in my mind, but they're obviously his words, not the actual experience of walking down the streets that are especially potent. But the change of scale, the way you walk in among fire hydrants, the way you feel small and yet big at the same time, Charles understood all of that more instinctively than I, the driest academic, could ever have. And so I just want to thank Charles from the bottom of my heart for freeing us all, and making this cacophony that we all have now so very, very pleasant.

Philip Johnson

≈

The following is Moore's acceptance speech for the 1991 Gold Medal:

Thank you! My talk today is not as an architect's talk would have been some decades ago — it's not a manifesto which proposes a new order, or a new style, or a new anything to replace what we have with the opposite — we've been treated to too many manifestos in our century. I propose rather an arrangement like, I understand, Goldilocks had. She could note that something was too hot or too large or too hard and that something else was too cold or too small or too soft. Then she could discover a set of things in between that were just right. The underlying impulse which helps determine what is just right for architects was pointed out to me years ago by Donlyn Lyndon. He noted that every building is a repository of human energy. Buildings that have had enough human energy and care and love pay us back like the biblical bread cast upon the waters. If a building hasn't been adequately endowed with human care and energy it remains inert and we are unsatisfied.

What follows from that perception is the realization that no one, not even an architect, can do it alone. For a building to be adequately endowed with human energy many people — the architects, the builders, the bankers, and especially the inhabitants — have to invest their energies. This speaks urgently for collaboration, so that as many people as possible get involved with making a building and with caring for it. How to encourage that? My most frequent message to students is to relax enough to open themselves up to other people's visions and dreams as well as their own. What it means for buildings is a freedom of speech so that buildings can be special to their special places: winsome or wily or shy or dazzling or silly. Occasionally maybe even important. Without that freedom, we get buildings that seem to be aspiring to be branch savings and loans, touching nobody's soul.

What also follows is an inversion of that great Mies van der Rohe announcement my generation was brought up on — "I don't want to be interesting, I want to be good." Which is not to say that I am not advocating being good, but it is to say that I think it is an important part of the architect's role to try to be interesting, to enlist all those other people to care about their buildings.

Part of the urgency of relaxing is to ward off the petrifaction that comes from fear, especially the fear of slipping into schlock. Now I'm sure that schlock is not something that any of us seeks, but I'm also sure that too morbid a fear of falling into it restricts our energies in devastating ways. I do worry, on the other hand, about things getting too simple. I was in on the Wonderwall at the New Orleans World's Fair in 1984. This started as a sort of joke, to keep fairgoers' minds off a tangle of overhead wires that marched the length of the fairgrounds. After it was all constructed, it started to make more and more urban sense. Kent Bloomer and I found ourselves noting that what made the Wonderwall contribute to the fair fabric was a number of overlapping agendas — Bill Turnbull's and Leonard Salvato's and Arthur Andersson's and mine for the structure, plus Richard Peters's for the lighting, plus Tina Beebe's for the color, plus Luis Guevara's for the landscape, plus quite a few others. On the other hand there are simple ways into the complexity. My partners and I have found a great deal of help in the aedicula — the four postered pavilion that makes a special place for and lends dignity to human beings, and a sense of being at the appropriate scale. We've found help in the power of water to give a symbolic and expressive dimension to the places we make.

These handles — and each of us has his own handles — get their power from human memory, which has to lie at the base of all we do. Much earlier in this century I used to sit by the radio. I was lost in the wonders of Buck Rogers or Flash Gordon. Our eyes were on the future, where the world we knew had been blown away. The links that connected us to the civilization of the past had been snapped and replaced by the hi-tech wonder of Imperium. In the last fifty years one thing has become abundantly apparent. There is no future worth contemplating that doesn't build on the great storehouse of energy our history provides. In our time, memory has been in some way linked with self-indulgence and nostalgia, a concept apparently almost as shocking as schlock. That is not at all to say that we must search for nostalgia or base our lives on its little comforts. But we must not be so frightened of it that we are scared to make the rich connections that memory lets us make. "We have nothing to fear," as Franklin Roosevelt pointed out, "but fear itself."

In many ways, when Charles was awarded the Topaz Medallion in 1989, it represented an even greater honor, since it recognizes excellence in architectural teaching. Again, there were recipients linked to Moore's past: the first medallion was bestowed on Jean Labatut in 1976, and two Berkeley colleagues, Joseph Esherick and Spiro Kostof, received the award in 1982 and 1992, respectively.

Since Moore's prior commitments had him judging buildings for the Aga Khan International Islamic Awards in Turkey when the award was given, his acceptance speech was delivered by Kent Bloomer.

Thank you. I'm deeply honored and though these words are being delivered while I am five thousand miles away, I feel present in spirit to receive what is surely the most important honor that has ever been bestowed on me. This short address of acceptance is the opportunity to do two things: recognize the teachers and colleagues whom I have had the chance to learn from and to deliver again, much condensed, the messages I have phrased in so many ways over the last forty years.

The Topaz Medallion, I think the implication is, is being bestowed not just on me but on a group of great teachers who by their patience and care lit up my life.

Moore with Students.

Roger Bailey was the first one in Ann Arbor forty-five years ago. He opened up my eyes to a whole wonderful architectural spatial culture that I had only dimly seen before then. He was my understanding boss when he brought me to the University of Utah in 1950 with colleagues James Acland and Gordon Heck. We were part of a wonderfully fluid new school of architecture where the curriculum was revised almost every night and presented in its new form almost every following morning. Roger Bailey remained mentor and friend until his death a few years ago.

Then there was Jean Labatut at Princeton who received this Topaz Medallion and who conducted what was surely one of the most open-minded yet passionately disciplined schools of architecture that recent times have offered.

At Princeton too there was the excitement of working with Enrico Peressutti. He was the first of my teachers to have accomplished a body of distinct and distinguished work, and it was a revelation that his commitment to his own vision, even his style of doing buildings, did not cripple his capacity for thinking about the work of students who had other visions.

Lou Kahn came to Princeton too, and I attached myself to him as his Teaching Assistant. He was surely the most powerful influence of all, with his urgent sense of morality of what architects should do as we let a brick or a wall or a beam of sunshine be what it wants to be. The intensity of the search was dazzling. The need to get things right provided more than a goal, more of a kind of holy grail that stays in our minds even as we repeatedly fail to attain it.

As important as the teachers have of course been, it was the colleagues, the fellow students, partners, and coworkers with whom the transmitted ideas were transformed. I've had a great many who have been very important to me, since I can't hold an architectural thought for very long unless it is illuminated or intensified or torn apart and put back together in another way by someone else.

Indeed most of the thoughts about architecture that I have held in the last third of a century come directly from Don Lyndon. The early sixties when Don Lyndon, Bill Turnbull, Dick Whitaker, and I were working together in MLTW was one of the really fruitful periods in all our lives.

My colleagues in the Connecticut office, now called Centerbrook Architects, made life after MLTW exciting. And in Los Angeles, after that, Ron Filson, John Ruble, and Buzz Yudell have contributed greatly to the excitement of making buildings.

Then there are the colleagues in the schools with whom I shared the excitement of making courses and affecting curricula. One of the most vivid memories from Berkeley is of a course in Oriental Architecture with Don Lyndon, enhanced by special assignments like casting shadows into the courtyards of the Alhambra. At Yale, Kent Bloomer and I taught for nine years the first-year graduate studio where we sought to free students' minds and to help build in the students confidence that their own visions and memories were legitimate basis for an architecture. That led to a book, *Body, Memory, and Architecture*. At UCLA Bill Mitchell and I taught for several years a course in the history of gardens which produced a book, *The Poetics of Gardens*. And at the University of Texas, Wayne Attoe and Peter Zweig have been colleagues in a program where I finally have the chance to go with a dozen students to look at places in Texas and New Mexico and Mexico to improve the students' capacity and my own to look at things, as in practice we try to listen to people.

The looking and the listening are for me much of what architecture and the teaching of it are about. I was brought up in an era where architects of any importance were meant to be original, and I think the desperate search for originality and novelty against overwhelming odds has brought about much of the uncomfortable, macho exhibitionism of our cities. We are coming I think to have an architectural climate more congenial to new buildings, fitting and responding to what is there already. In that I rejoice.

In addition to the teachers, of course, there is the point of it all — the students. I'm proud that there are so many and that so many have done so well. Any list would be a mistake because it would leave out many important names so I'll just say a mass "thank you" for causing me to be (at least in spirit) here.

Secondly, this response gives me the opportunity to talk about the architectural principles I think are important. Lou Kahn was eloquent about the morality of buildings, about doing the correct thing with the structure and the skin and the geometry as well as the poetry of a building. I like to switch the focus slightly so that the morality of the building has to do with its effect on the human inhabitants, with making combinations of the familiar and the surprising that give the inhabitants of our structures the chance to feel that they're in the middle of their world. This requires opening up the possibility for buildings to speak and for us to insist upon a kind of edificial freedom of speech that doesn't try to fit differing people into the same mold. That leaves me claiming that buildings have to be interesting so that they attract people to be interested in them, since it is, I'm certain, easier to inhabit a place you're interested in than one which leaves you cold, however pure its principles. One observation is that people are more interested in buildings that they've had some say about. A growing part of our practice (though I haven't figured out really how to teach it in school), involves ways of enlisting participation in the design of buildings. It's easy enough with houses: you work directly with the clients. At the scale of a local park or a city hall or a church ways of involving the inhabitants with the design have to be more carefully and elaborately devised with workshops and groups, and at the scale of the city there's a chance to involve television and other media. What is characteristic of all of them is that they involve working together — architects and inhabitants depending on the architect's highly developed faculty for listening as well as the expected highly developed faculty for seeing.

All this is based on the one essential tenet: that the world already contains many successful and wonderful places, places that have come to mean something to the people who inhabit them or visit them. The architect with his new program does not have to invent a solution from scratch — an original solution. In fact, given the number of places already existing, odds are heavily against the possibility of inventing an original place. "Discovery," said Mies van der Rohe, "not invention." And I've come to think that opening up students' eyes and minds to the wonders that are already there is the best way, or at least the best way for me, to help architects in the future achieve the kind of responsive, energized, interesting buildings that we need, buildings able to combine into congenial cities where every inhabitant can feel that he's at the center of his world.

Piazza d'Italia with Night Lighting by Richard Peters. Photo by Norman McGrath.

CHAPTER EIGHTEEN

Principles and Enthusiasms

Moore's ability to engage people through architecture, in a kind of physical and emotional communication, formed the basis for his transfer of enthusiasm.

For one so gifted with memory, it was not surprising that memory would become one of the great sources for his creativity. To respect place, to revel in the fact that culture makes places on the globe unique, was learned very early on from travels guided by his mother, and in his lifetime of exploring.

In 1956, Moore designed one of his early independent buildings, a small office near Monterey, California, where in his Princeton project he first started thinking about "the relationship of the past to the present," and which was just miles away from his Pebble Beach house where Kathryn Moore spent the last years of her life. It was built of plate glass and wooden siding. He knew his aim, but didn't know exactly how to throw the ball. He wanted to achieve some of the spatial layering that made Katsura such a potent experience. He knew that raising the ceilings high would create for the inhabitant a sense of space, drama, and inhabitable grandiosity; windows above would cast light at raking angles into the space, and a patio and gardens would enhance a sense of connection to nature. But he didn't yet know how to express it all, how to transform it into architecture, beyond mere construction.

Forty years later, he designed, a little more than a mile away from that small office, an addition to the Monterey Peninsula Museum of Art. As hesitant and uncertain and searching as that little office building was, this new building is a wonderfully mature vision of humane architecture. It respects the historic building that it nearly doubles in size. It masterfully pulls

Kathryn Moore near Santa Fe.

Seaside Professional Building.

Monterey Peninsula Museum of Art, Charles Moore with Urban Innovations Group, 1994. Photo by Marco Zecchin.

visitors into a dance, leading them from the garden forecourt, through a small lobby, into a constricted passage, and then suddenly releases them into a spacious, dynamic gallery, flooded with soft natural light, leading to windows looking to the wooded hillside and in the distance, the water of Monterey Bay.

Some of Moore's richest work came near the end of his life, with many buildings and projects still in construction. They too are full of all of the ideas that he explored in his earlier work, combined always with his constant sense of experiment and the trying of new things.

Nativity Catholic Church of 1993, in Rancho Santa Fe, California, is another building that may be seen as one of his greatest, most mature works. A generous court, that will be shaded once its orchard of trees fill out, lies beneath a tower and wall, pierced by a layering gable. Visitors are drawn to the wide wooden portal and enter the church not directly on axis (as one might expect), but on the diagonal. A small vestibule with a font precedes the main sanctuary, a dazzlingly complex space rendered geodic by the play of light as it sifts through wooden ceiling baffles, shimmers down a star-encrusted bronze baldachino, and glints in rays from windows hidden in deep corners. Exquisitely crafted furniture, art, and details relate to the whole. It is at once grand and uplifting, but also intimately inhabitable.

At the Berkeley Haas School of Business, just behind the architecture school where Moore once taught, generous courts and staircases spill like a waterfall through the large

Nativity Catholic Church, Moore Ruble Yudell with Renzo Zechetto, 1993. Photo by Timothy Hursley.

complex. Arches frame views of the university tower, and winding steps encourage movement through the space, with places to sit and absorb the shifting perspectives. It is filled
with a series of surprising spatial experiences, as ingeniously devised as a Soane plan. The
building is at once a good neighbor to the small-scaled residences nearby, but it also communicates with heroic gestures to the more grandly scaled campus it is a member of.

   The simplicity of plan brings another type of experience, rooted in Kahn, that will make
Moore's and Andersson's Washington State History Museum a fitting partner and neighbor
to the historic Tacoma grand station, strong enough to embellish but deferential enough to
respect its authority.

   As time went on, Moore's buildings contained more and more of the magic of his "Fantasy Drawings," elaborate, whimsical, carefully executed ink-line drawings, sometimes high-
lighted with watercolor, that he made throughout his life. One realizes that the fantastic and
the real were not so dissimilar, if one is free enough and open enough to look and see. This
was especially true in Moore's last home in Austin, a one-of-a-kind marvel, a stunning
repository of a lifetime of collecting, where space and folk toys and light and color and tex-

Nativity Catholic Church. Photo by Timothy Hursley.

ture all fused into one vigorous, personal Palace of Memory. To have witnessed hundreds of visitors arriving at that place and being instantly uplifted as they passed through the door was a great experience and proof that people can be changed by architecture, if they are engaged willfully by makers of places.

Moore's legacy will be a continuing one, ensured by his central commitment to collaboration, his eagerness to transfer confidence to students, and his willingness to expand the creative process.

∾

The following are Moore's "Principles and Enthusiasms":

> So far, I have extolled the riches of the world around us, and that brings me to a platform, with just five principles that I think will not change, but kept afloat on shifting, personal swarms of enthusiasms, which I have no desire to impose on anyone else, but which give me pleasure, and the energy to keep on addressing these principles.

Moore's Drawing "The Spaniards Introduce Palm Trees to Santa Catalina Island."

PRINCIPLE ONE

The spaces we feel, the shapes we see, and the ways we move in buildings should assist the human memory in reconstructing connections through space and time. Half a century ago, those passages of the mind seemed oppressive, and full of cobwebs, and much effort went to cleaning them out and closing them up. It certainly must have seemed a useful effort to Le Corbusier and the others, more than adequately justified by their sense of the oppressive shadows of the past and their faith in the future which would sweep that past away. By now, we have frequently enough seen the past swept away to speak with sense as well as sentiment when we demand to maintain our connections, or reinvest them. Then those of us — and that's most of the world by now — who lead lives complicatedly divorced from a single place in which we can find roots have, through the channels of our minds and our memories, a built environment which helps reestablish those roots.

PRINCIPLE TWO

If buildings are to speak, they must have freedom of speech. It seems to me that one of the most serious dangers to architecture is that people may just lose interest in it; the number of things buildings have in this half-century been allowed to say has so diminished that there is little chance for surprise or wonder. If architecture is to survive in the human consciousness, then the things buildings can say, be they wistful or wise or powerful or gentle or heretical or silly, have to respond to the wide range of human feelings.

Principle Three

Buildings must be inhabitable, by the bodies and minds and memories of humankind. The urge to dwell, to inhabit and enhance and protect a piece of the world, to fashion an inside and distinguish it from the outside is one of the basic human drives, but it has by now been so often thwarted that the act now often requires help, and surrogates which can stand upright (like chimneys or columns) or grow and flourish (like plants) or move and dance (like light) can act as important allies of inhabitation.

Principle Four

For each of us to feel at the center of our universe, we need to measure and describe points in space as people used to do — in terms of ourselves, not of the precise but meaningless relations of, for instance, Cartesian coordinates or "rational" geometries. Soon after our birth we arrive at a sense of front and back, left and right, up, down, and center which are so strong that we can and do assign moral significance to them. Our architecture needs to remember them, too, so that we can feel with our whole bodies the significance of where we are, not just see it with our eyes or reason it out in our minds.

Principle Five

If we are to devote our lives to making buildings, we have to believe they are worth it, that they live, and speak (of themselves, and the people who made them and thus inhabit them), and can receive investments of energy and care from their makers and their inhabitants, and can store those investments, and return them augmented, bread cast on the water comes back club sandwiches.

Enthusiasms

My principles are general (though not eternal; they will change as our needs change) but enthusiasms are personal, shared, I hope, but not necessarily with everybody. I especially like farms, in California or Pennsylvania or Japan or Finland, or almost anywhere because they are rich in unguarded responses to particular problems or possibilities, from fitting a hillside to joining two odd pieces of wood, and can be at once grand and gentle. But I like temples and palaces too, and am not scornful of people who prefer palaces to barns. Perhaps the best bet of all is something like the Yoshijima house in Takayama in Japan, which is both.

I am excited by miniatures that distill connections into tiny compass. I collect toys and souvenirs and enjoy juxtaposing familiar things in surprising ways.

I have a long-standing enthusiasm for water, for its particularly potent magical quality to lead our toughest from wherever they are to all the water in the world. I

Rural Finland.

Yoshijima House.

Armoire Stuffed with Miniatures.

did my Ph.D. thesis on water in architecture and forty years later have written a book called *Water and Architecture*.

I think that fairy tales have a great deal to teach us architects. The way that the most magical adventures, even ones involving whole dynasties, end in time for tea (back to the theme of alternating the familiar and surprising) seems to me worth careful looking into.

I am especially interested in vernacular architecture. It is familiar to me, I enjoy it, and I believe it is proper for it to be the prime source for my own work. I think it is important to note that ours is not a peasant society; to see vernacular architecture as hooked to the land, free of exotic influences or of pretension, at some odds with an aristocratic "high" architecture is, in the United States, altogether to miss the point. I was brought up in Battle Creek, Michigan, near the house that my great-great-grandfather had built, four years after the first settlers had driven off two Indians to establish possession of the land. My great-great-grandfather was a farmer, with modest holdings, but his home was a beautiful Greek Revival house. When his son introduced that Latin ruse that opened the University of Michigan to coeducation it was not your standard peasant activity, but still modest, down-home vernacular.

There is one line in Henry James's *Aspern Papers:* "I delight in a palpable imageable visitable past, the nearer distances and clearer mysteries." I do, too, and I like playing the near against the more distant and exotic, though in some ways the recent past and nearby places turn out to be the most poignant of all. The enthusiasm is frequently put down as an unworthy one, limp, and nostalgic, but I'm on the edge of pressing for Nostalgia as a guiding Principle.

Another doctrine I have toyed with, so far with incomplete success, I am pleased to call the doctrine of Immaculate Collision. The idea is that if two or more plans or shapes or systems can crash into each other so as to achieve some serendipity, to gain energy from the collision, rather than to be maimed or destroyed by it, then a new device for designing would be at hand. I have been enthusiastic, given the typical situation on raw land where there is little basis about deciding about the shape of a new building (or worse, a group of buildings by several architects) about the possibility of inventing a past, a set of ephemeral footprints against which new buildings might collide. The possibilities remain untested.

My favorite images generally involve multiple layers of facade or interior. I am especially excited about syncopated, layered facades, and geodes, or Russian eggs, objects rough and simple on the outside, crystalline and complex and magic on the inside. The Alhambra, fortress on the outside, plaster fantasy within, is an admirable geode.

For years I have been told that there are "rational" architects (good) and "irrational" architects (including me, and bad). I have come to suspect that there are impostors in the House of Reason, that the opposite of "rational" is not "irrational" but "real," and that the logically deduced but altogether untested postulates of architects who claim sweet reason for the constructs of rules are the historical parallel of the group, who have logically derived from science from the Greeks, and having decided that a ball would fall five times as fast as one one-fifth its weight, ridiculed Galileo for climbing up the stairs and dropping the balls off the tower. This time there are no balls to drop; maybe instead there are postcards to send. It is altogether likely that inhabitants themselves can be trusted to know where the real places on the planet are, to go to them, from Disneyland to the Athenian Acropolis and to send postcards back when the places have spoken to them, and they perceived, with great good feeling, that they were *somewhere*.

Moore in 1992. Photo by Ruth Shapiro.

Index

Boldface indicates illustrations

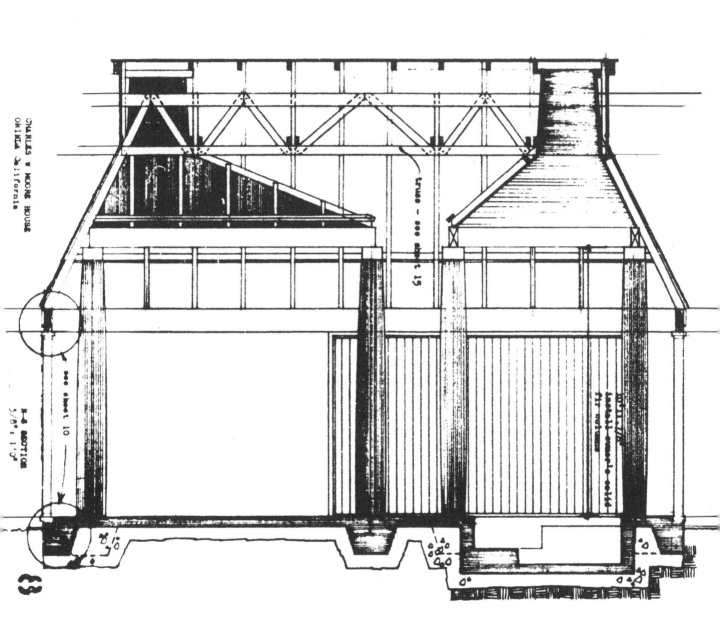

CHARLES W MOORE HOUSE
ORINDA California

true - see sheet 15

see sheet 10

A-A SECTION
3/8" 1'0"